How To Know

THE
BUTTERFLIES

Illustrated keys for determining to species all
butterflies found in North America, north of
Mexico, with notes on their distribution, habits,
and larval food, and suggestions for collecting
and studying them.

PAUL R. EHRLICH

Curator of Entomological Collections,
Natural History Museum
Stanford University

ANNE H. EHRLICH

With Sections Contributed by the Following Specialists:

D. L. BAUER	L. P. GREY
H. K. CLENCH	A. B. KLOTS
C. F. DOS PASSOS	W. S. McALPINE
J. C. DOWNEY	K. H. WILSON

WM. C. BROWN COMPANY PUBLISHERS
Dubuque, Iowa

Copyright © 1961 by
H. E. Jaques

Library of Congress Catalog Card Number: 61-2394

ISBN 0–697–04821–7 (Cloth)
ISBN 0–697–04820–9 (Paper)

THE PICTURED-KEY NATURE SERIES

How To Know The—

INTRODUCTION

It has become increasingly apparent to us over the last few years that there is a need for an inexpensive manual which will permit both the amateur butterfly collector and the professional entomologist to identify the species of North American butterflies.

Users of most previous works on our butterfly fauna have had to depend largely on comparison of specimens with figures for identification of species, and higher categories have been left largely undefined. In this book an attempt has been made to produce useful keys to all categories of North American butterflies from family to species. In addition, the family and subfamily keys are constructed to permit identification of any exotic butterfly to subfamily (you will note that, for this reason, a number of subfamilies not found in our area are included in the keys).

We have included all species that have been recorded from North America, north of Mexico, with the exception of a few almost certainly attributed to our fauna in error. Many of the stragglers and imports are of little biological significance, but it was felt that their inclusion would be a help to collectors who want specimens of all species that have been found north of the border.

Much of the content of this volume is based on previously published material. There is not room here to mention the hundreds of sources, but a particularly heavy debt is owed the works of F. M. Brown, R. L. Chermock, J. A. Comstock, W. D. Field, W. J. Holland, A. B. Klots, and S. H. Scudder.

The following persons have been most helpful in supplying us with specimens to figure, testing keys, checking manuscript, contributing information, etc: H. K. Clench (Carnegie Museum); J. A. Comstock (Del Mar, California); J. C. Downey (Southern Illinois University); H. S. Dybas, R. L. Wenzel, A. K. Wyatt (Chicago Natural History Museum); J. D. Eff (Boulder, Colorado); H. A. Freeman (Garland, Texas); A. B. Klots, F. H. Rindge (American Museum of Natural History); L. M. Martin (Los Angeles County Museum); R. H. T. Mattoni (University of California at Los Angeles); Noel McFarland (Apple Valley, California); G. W. Byers, C. D. Michener, K. H. Wilson (University of Kansas); C. S. Quelch (Transcona, Manitoba); C. L. Remington (Yale University); D. B. Stallings, J. R. Turner (Caldwell, Kansas).

Mr. C. F. dos Passos of the American Museum kindly lent us a draft copy of his new check list of North American butterflies, which has been an invaluable aid in preparing this book. Since we had only a preliminary copy of the list, and since it was not invariably followed, all responsibility for nomenclatorial errors must rest with us. Mr. dos Passos gave much of his valuable time in helping us with various matters pertaining to the book, and we are extremely grateful.

Listed below are people who have contributed signed sections to the book: D. L. Bauer, Bremerton, Washington (Melitaeiti); H. K. Clench, Carnegie Museum (Theclini, *Lycaena*, etc.); C. F. dos Passos, American Museum (*Oeneis, Polygonia*); J. C. Downey, Southern Illinois University (Plebejine generic key, *Plebejus, Philotes*); L. P. Grey, Lincoln, Maine (*Speyeria*); A. B. Klots, American Museum (*Colias, Boloria*); W. S. McAlpine, Milford, Michigan (*Calephelis*), and Kent H. Wilson, University of Kansas (Papilionidae). These people are the sole authors of their sections—our only contributions to them have been editorial and illustrative. It goes without saying that this book would not have been possible without the cooperation of these specialists.

A special debt is owed Professor H. E. Jaques, who has patiently answered our many questions and in numerous ways made our task less difficult.

This book was prepared while the senior author was on the staffs of the Chicago Academy of Sciences and of the University of Kansas.

Lawrence, Kansas

August, 1959

Anne H. Ehrlich

Paul R. Ehrlich

Butterflies are likely the most noticed as well as the most admired of insects. The average layman can probably recognize by name as many species of butterflies as of birds. Some common species are fairly well known, but to accurately name a sizeable collection of butterflies is a major undertaking. Doctor Ehrlich's book should now make that very much easier. For the first time practically every known species north of Mexico is keyed, pictured and described.

Mrs. Ehrlich has made a masterful contribution with the illustrations. Her artistry is superb and greatly increases the usefulness of the book.

INTRODUCING BUTTERFLIES

A butterfly is an insect belonging to one superfamily (Papilionoidea) of the great order Lepidoptera. The Lepidoptera differ from other insects in, among other things, having the wings covered with shingle-like flattened hairs, called scales. Like many other insects, Lepidoptera go through a complete metamorphosis. They have egg (ovum), caterpillar (larva), chrysalis (pupa), and adult (imago) stages. The mouthparts of the Lepidoptera, with minor exceptions, are modified into a tube through which liquid food is drawn by a bellowslike sucking pump.

Closely related to the butterflies are the skippers, which make up another lepidopteran superfamily, the Hesperioidea. The remainder of the Lepidoptera, some 80% of the approximately 125,000 species in the order, are a vast and varied assemblage known loosely as "moths." The characteristics which separate the butterflies from the skippers and moths are listed in the following table.

BUTTERFLIES (Papilionoidea)	SKIPPERS (Hesperioidea)	MOTHS (Rest of Lepidoptera)
1. Antennae swollen at end, but not recurved or hooked.	1. Antennae swollen at end and recurved or hooked.	1. Antennae varied in form, but rarely swollen at tip.
2. Body slender in proportion to wings.	2. Body broad in proportion to wings.	2. Body usually broad in proportion to wings.
3. Diurnal.	3. Diurnal.	3. Mostly nocturnal.
4. Wings not hooked together on underside by spine and clasp (frenulum and retinaculum).	4. Wings not hooked together on underside by spine and clasp (frenulum and retinaculum).	4. Wings are usually hooked together on underside by spine and clasp (frenulum and retinaculum).
5. Often brightly colored.	5. Mostly dull colored.	5. Mostly dull colored.
6. Pupa almost never enclosed in cocoon.	6. Pupa usually enclosed in a loose cocoon.	6. Pupa often in a cocoon.

7. Adults usually rest with wings held vertically over back.

7. Adults usually rest with wings held vertically over back.

7. Adults usually rest with wings held flat, not vertically over back.

BUTTERFLIES   SKIPPERS   MOTHS

TABLE OF CONTENTS

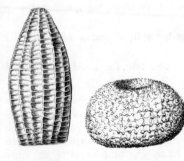

EGG. The female lays the eggs singly or in bunches on or near the food plant of the larva. The eggs present an extraordinary variety of form and sculpturing (Figs. 1, 2). Their thick protective shell or *chorion* is broken only by a single small opening, the *micropyle*, through which the sperm enters.

Fig. 1. Egg of *Anthocaris genutia* (after Scudder).

Fig. 2. Egg of *Satyrium acadica* (after Scudder).

LARVA. The structural features of a butterfly larva (caterpillar) are shown in figure 3. The larva is essentially a feeding machine. Most of the inside is occupied by the digestive tract, which processes the vast amount of food supplied by the powerful jaws.

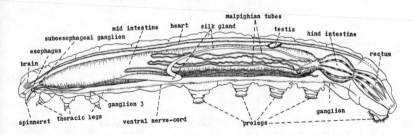

Fig. 3. Internal anatomy of male larva of *Danaus plexippus* (after Scudder).

The caterpillar is the chief growth stage of the butterfly. Since, as in all insects, its skeleton is on the outside (an *exoskeleton*), the only way it can grow is by periodically shedding its skin. This process is known as molting or *ecdysis*. Most larvae molt four or five times in the course of their growth. The periods between molts are called *instars;* a "first instar larva" is one which has hatched from the egg but not yet molted.

PUPA. The pupa is the stage in which the transformation from wormlike caterpillar to winged adult is accomplished. The majority of larval tissues are dissolved, and the structures of the adult are formed by proliferation of the cells of the *imaginal disks*. These disks are small areas of adult tissue which were differentiated in the embryo.

When the adult is fully formed, it bursts the old pupal skin and emerges.

ADULT. After emerging from the pupal skin, the adult laboriously spreads its wings by forcing fluid into them from its body cavity. When the wings have dried in an extended position, the insect is ready for flight.

The external structures of an adult butterfly (*Danaus plexippus* L.) are shown in figures 4-10.

The body is divided into three main sections; the *head, thorax,* and *abdomen.*

HEAD. The most striking features of the head capsule are the roughly hemispherical *compound eyes,* each of which occupies an entire side of the head. These eyes are made up of very numerous facets or *ommatidia.* Near the top of the head, between the eyes, are the bases of the jointed *antennae.* Each antenna consists of three parts: a basal ring (*scape*) which articulates with the head, a second smaller ring (*pedicel*), and the long, many segmented terminal part, the *flagellum.* The flagellum has a widened area at the distal end called the *club.*

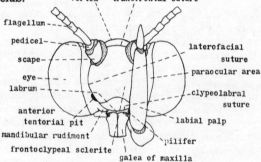

Fig. 4. Front view of head of *Danaus plexippus.*

The mouthparts are highly modified from the primitive chewing (mandibulate) type found in most insects. The *mandibles,* which are prominent in the caterpillar, are reduced to functionless nubs. The sucking tube or "tongue" (*proboscis*) is formed by the grooving together of the elongated, concave *galeae* of the *maxillae.* The remaining structures of the maxillae, including the maxillary palps, are greatly reduced. All that remains of the *labium* is a small plate, the *labial sclerite,* to which are attached the large, three-segmented *labial palps.* The reader who is unfamiliar with the structure of the more common type of chewing mouth parts found in insects is urged to consult a general book on insects (see LITERATURE) in order to appreciate the great degree of modification found in butterflies.

CERVIX. The head is connected to the first segment of the thorax by a membranous neck, the *cervix.* Imbedded in this membrane on

2

each side is a small sclerite shaped somewhat like a "T" lying on its side. These are known as the *cervical sclerites*; they act as levers in protracting the head.

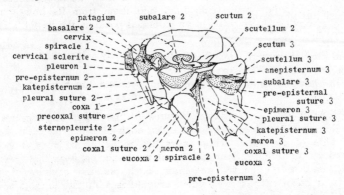

Fig. 5. Lateral view of thorax of *Danaus plexippus*.

THORAX. As in all insects, the thorax is divided into three segments, the pro-, meso- and metathoraces. Each segment is divided into three major sections, dorsal (*tergum*), ventral (*sternum*), and lateral (*pleuron*). All three segments bear legs, and the mesothorax and metathorax each carries a pair of wings. For this reason they are sometimes referred to jointly as the *pterothorax*. The prothorax, lacking wings, is much reduced. The form of the various thoracic sclerites and sutures, the degree of sclerotization of certain structures, and the general form of the thorax are important characters used in studying the classification and relationships of the butterflies. The names and positions of the most important structures can be seen in the figures.

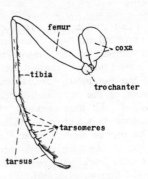

Fig. 6. Mesothoracic leg of *Danaus plexippus*.

LEGS. Each leg is made up of five basic segments: a proximal coxa followed by a small ball-like trochanter, a long, sturdy, undivided femur, a long, undivided, rather slender tibia, and a terminal tarsus which is usually divided into five subsegments or tarsomeres. Attached to

3

the last tarsomere are a pair of *tarsal claws*. Between these claws there is a fleshy pad, the *arolium*, and lateral to them are membranous lobes, the *pulvilli*. The arolium and pulvilli may be greatly reduced in size.

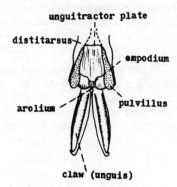

Fig. 7. Pterothoracic distitarsus of *Danaus plexippus*.

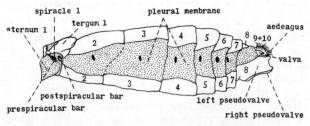

Fig. 8. Male abdomen of *Danaus plexippus*.

In some of the butterflies (all Nymphalidae; male Libytheidae and Lycaenidae) the prothoracic legs are noticeably smaller than those of the pterothorax, and may be atrophied. The extreme case of reduction occurs in certain tropical nymphalids of the subfamily Ithomiinae, in which the tibia and tarsus of the prothoracic leg are reduced to a small ball at the end of the femur.

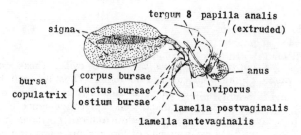

Fig. 9. Female genital structures of *Danaus plexippus*, end of abdomen shown by broken lines.

WINGS. The membranous wings are supported by a system of tubular struts, called *veins*. The wings are articulated with the thorax through a series of small plates, the *axillary sclerites*. The motion of the wings is supplied primarily by thoracic dorso-ventral muscles which flatten the thorax (and in so doing raise the wings), and longitudinal muscles which return it to its original shape (and lower the wings).

There are eight principal veins in each wing. They are (Fig. 10) the costa (C), subcosta (Sc), radius (R), media (M), cubitus (Cu), and 3 vannal veins (1V, 2V, 3V). The pattern of reduction and/or branching of these veins is of considerable assistance in identifying butterflies. A subscript number next to the code letter for a vein indicates a branch. Thus R_5 is the fifth branch of the radius. In the hind wing R_1 is invariably united with the subcosta ($Sc+R_1$), and the remainder of the radius is unbranched and called the radial sector (Rs).

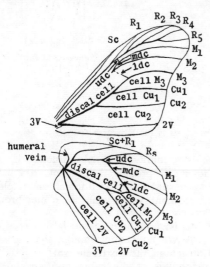

The discal cell in both wings is usually closed at the outer end by three cross veins, the upper discocellular (udc) between R_5 (Rs) and M_1, the middle discocellular (mdc) between M_1 and M_2, and the lower discocellular (ldc) between M_2 and M_3.

Fig. 10. Wing venation of *Danaus plexippus*; all veins and larger cells labelled.

The spaces between the veins are called *cells*. These generally take the name of the vein anterior to them. Thus the cell between vein M_3 and vein Cu_1 is referred to as cell M_3. In the keys a simple reference to "cell" indicates the discal cell. For convenience in descriptions certain areas of the wing and certain pattern positions are given names. These, as well as the names of the various veins and cells are shown in Figs. 10, 11. The reader is also advised to consult Figs. 22, 71, 133 and 134, which will give some idea of the diversity of venation pattern.

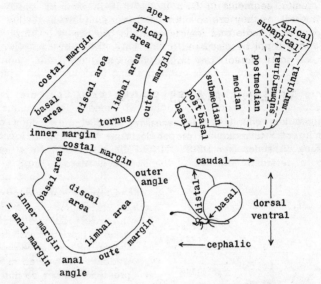

Fig. 11. Areas and margins of wings (left); pattern positions (upper right); directions (lower right).

ABDOMEN. The abdomen is a relatively simple structure in comparison with the thorax. The seven pregenital segments are in the form of rings with sclerotized terga and sterna, and membranous pleura (with the exception of the first segment, which also has a membranous sternum).

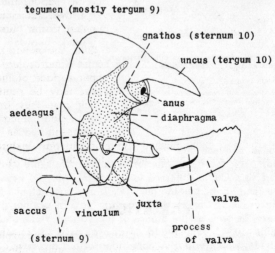

Fig. 12. Male genital structures of typical butterfly, lateral view, left valva removed (diagrammatic).

6

The genital segments (9-10 in males, 8-10 in females) are of particular interest, as they are so often used in identifying butterflies. The basic features of male and female genitalia are shown in Figs. 12, 13 and 9, and will not be discussed further here. The genitalia of various species (or parts thereof) are figured throughout the book.

⚿ TELLING MALES FROM FEMALES

In some key couplets it is necessary to distinguish males from females in order to make the proper decision. While this can always be done by dissection (see DISSECTING THE GENITALIA), it is usually possible to determine the sex of the specimen without going to this trouble.

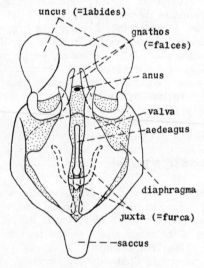

uncus (=labides)

gnathos (=falces)

anus

valva

aedeagus

diaphragma

juxta (=furca)

saccus

Fig. 13. Male genital structures of lycaenid butterfly, ventral view (diagrammatic).

Examine the ventral side of the end of the abdomen. In males you will often be able to see the valvae, or the tip of the aedeagus protruding. The valvae may be pressed together, so that you will be able to see the line of their joining as a *longitudinal* slit.

Females usually have a terminal rosette of scales around the papillae anales, and a subterminal, *transverse*, oval slit marking the opening to the bursa.

Often males will have sex-scales (androconia) on the upper surface of the wings. These may be scattered (in which case they are of no help in determining the sex) or concentrated in patches. Sex patches are best distinguished by their different texture. They appear rougher, coarser or more "mealy" than the smoothly shingled scales of the rest of the wing.

VARIATION

There are a number of kinds of variation which may explain why your specimen keys out to a species, but looks quite different from the individual figured.

SEXUAL VARIATION. In some species the males and females are superficially quite different. Many male lycaenids are brightly colored on the dorsal surface, while the females are quite drab. Note the striking differences between male *Papilio glaucus* (see Fig. 46) and the dark form of the female (see Fig. 47).

GEOGRAPHICAL VARIATION. Specimens from different parts of a species' range are often very divergent in appearance. For instance, *Erebia rossii* specimens from the northern Arctic (Boothia Peninsula area) are almost or completely immaculate above. Specimens from Churchill, Manitoba, have numerous bright ocelli on the dorsal surface.

INDIVIDUAL VARIATION. No two butterfly specimens are identical. Occasionally mutations or exposure to very unusual environmental conditions cause individuals to deviate greatly from the average appearance of the population to which they belong. These specimens are known as "aberrations." Once, on the radiator of their car, the authors found a specimen of *Colias philodice* which was completely dark on both surfaces of the wings, with the exception of some small yellow streaks below. We have seen literally tens of thousands of individuals of this species before and since, but never another specimen even remotely approaching this condition.

CLASSIFICATION

Each species or kind of butterfly has a three-part scientific name. The first part is the generic name; it is *always* capitalized. The second part is the specific name; it is *never* capitalized. Added to the generic and specific names is the name of the person responsible for first describing the species. Thus "*Battus philenor* Linnaeus" refers to the species of *Battus* that was named "*philenor*" by Linnaeus. The generic and specific names are, by custom, italicized—that of the author is not.

Entire books have been written on the subject "what is a species?" It is a very complex problem; one well beyond the scope of this book. A brief and very inadequate definition might be: A species consists of all individuals which are capable of interbreeding with reasonable success if they have the opportunity in nature. For practical purposes we will consider species to mean "distinct kinds." By the way, the singular of *species* is *species*. The word "specie" means "hard money" and has no biological meaning. The plural of *genus* is *genera*.

The various species of butterflies are grouped into subgenera, genera, subtribes, tribes, subfamilies and families within the superfamily Papilionoidea. Each of these groupings has a name with a characteristic ending, as you can see in the classification of a butterfly given below.

Kingdom: Animalia (all animals).

Subkingdom: Metazoa (multicellular animals).

Branch: Enterozoa (having a digestive cavity or tract).

Section: Eucoelomata (with a true coelom or body cavity—includes echinoderms, mollusks, annelids, arthropods, chordates, etc.).

Phylum: Arthropoda (having jointed legs, exoskeleton, etc.—includes crustaceans, insects, myriapods, arachnids, etc.).

Class: Insecta (body divided into head, thorax and abdomen—includes all true insects).

Order: Lepidoptera (having two pairs of membranous wings covered with flattened hairs called scales, sucking mouth parts, etc.).

Suborder: Frenatae or Heteroneura (venation and shape of FW and HW very different, frenulum present or secondarily lost).

Superfamily: Papilionoida (true butterflies).

Family: Lycaenidae (blues, metalmarks, etc.)

Subfamily: Lycaeninae (blues, coppers, hairstreaks, harvesters, etc.).

Tribe: Theclini (hairstreaks).

Subtribe: Strymoniti (*Strymon* and relatives).

Genus: *Callophrys* Billberg.

Subgenus: *Mitoura* Scudder.

Species: *Callophrys siva* Edwards.

Members of the same genus presumably are more closely related evolutionarily (e.g., have diverged less from each other) than members of different genera, and so on up the hierarchy. The only reasonably objective method of measuring this divergence is to compare as many characters as possible to gain an estimate of overall similarity. Since this requires that a great many species be compared simultaneously (if our study is to have significance), the best techniques involve the use of a digital computer.

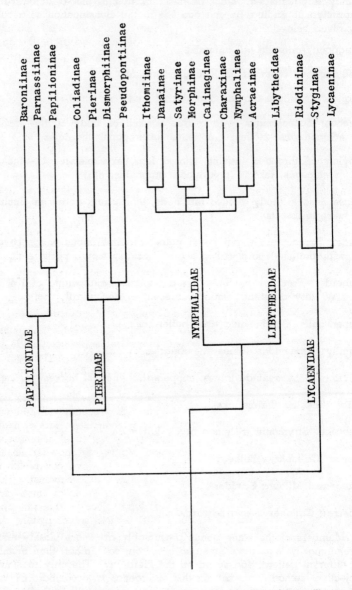

Fig. 14. Relationships of the families and subfamilies of butterflies.

Figure 14 is a diagram giving an estimate of the evolutionary relationships of the families and subfamilies of butterflies. The vertical scale might be described as "evolutionary distance," being evolutionary rate multiplied by time. It is impossible to separate the latter quantities without fossil evidence. The horizontal arrangement of groups and spacings of lines are determined by convenience.

EQUIPMENT

In order to start a butterfly collection, one needs a minimum of six items of equipment. Of these, four may be made by the collector; the other two must be purchased (see list of dealers on p. 15).

1. NET. The author has always preferred a net of simple design (Fig. 15) with a 34" wooden handle (¾" dowl) and a hoop of heavy wire with a diameter of 15". The net bag is made of silk or nylon bobbinet, is about 30" deep, and rather sharply tapered. The sleeve for the hoop is made of unbleached muslin. Be sure to have a net designed so that the bag can be replaced, and carry at least one spare bag with you. Preferences in net color, hoop diameter, handle length, and general design vary from collector to collector. With a little experience you will soon be altering your net to suit yourself.

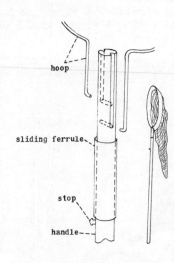

Fig. 15. A simple net design.

2. KILLING BOTTLE. The standard killing bottle is the cyanide jar. This is best purchased, as cyanide is an *extremely deadly poison*, and therefore dangerous to handle. However, should you wish to make your own jars, the procedure is quite simple. Use wide-mouthed jars of heavy glass. Place a ½" layer of potassium cyanide lumps (not powder) in the bottom of the jar and cover with an inch of fine, dry sawdust. Then pour in a ½" layer of thick plaster of Paris. Leave the jar open until the plaster is completely dry. Be sure to work in a well-ventilated place and take care that every bit of cyanide is accounted for. Cyanide is readily soluable in water, and it is wise to give all tools as well as the working surface a thorough washing when the job is done. *Take no chances with cyanide—your first accident is likely to be your last.*

All cyanide jars, whether home-made or purchased, should be bound with adhesive tape from the bottom to the level of the plaster.

This will prevent an injection of cyanide via a shard of glass should the jar be accidentally broken. Cyanide jars will usually retain their potency for a few years—weak ones may often be revitalized by adding a few drops of water. Judge the potency by the length of time required to kill an insect—*do not sniff the jar*. The fumes are quite deadly if inhaled in any quantity.

Be sure that all of your jars are labelled "CYANIDE—DEADLY POISON" and are stored out of reach of small children.

A relatively safe killing jar for use by children can be made by placing cotton or chopped-up rubber bands under a piece of blotting paper in the bottom of a wide-mouthed jar. Carbon tetrachloride is added to this through a hole in the blotting paper with an eye dropper. This sort of jar must be charged frequently and is less satisfactory than a cyanide jar as it often leaves specimens stiff and difficult to mount.

3. FORCEPS. These are essential for handling specimens without damaging the wings. I personally prefer a pair which curves to a fine point. Other collectors like stamp tongs.

4. INSECT PINS. These must be purchased. Size #3 will do for all but the smallest butterflies, for which #2 and #1 pins should be used.

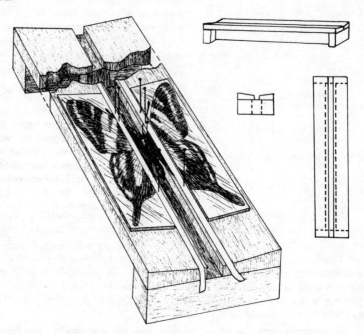

Fig. 16. Spreading board, with properly spread butterfly.

5. SPREADING BOARDS. There are many designs for these, a simple one is shown in Fig. 16. The center strip should be made of balsa and the side strips of a soft wood such as pine. The slight slope of the side pieces will compensate for any tendency of the wings to droop after removal of the specimen from the board. A small variety of sizes of spreading boards will be needed for handling different sizes of butterflies.

6. STORAGE BOXES. These range from cigar boxes with two layers of corrugated paper glued into the bottom to finely made glass-topped drawers which fit into handsome cabinets. There are, in the long run, only two major requirements for a satisfactory box. It must be sufficiently tight to keep out any insect pests which might eat your specimens, and it must have a pinning bottom which will hold a pin firmly without corroding it.

Although for temporary storage cigar boxes will do, for permanent use you will want a wooden box with a lid which fits down tightly over a rounded flange, making a pest-proof seal. The pinning bottom can be made of composition "wall board" or balsa wood, but neither is as satisfactory as entomological cork (which can be obtained from dealers). Various cork substitutes may, in time, corrode the points of your pins.

If you are handy with tools, satisfactory boxes are no problem to build. If not, they can be obtained quite reasonably from dealers, especially if you do not require a highly polished finish and shiny brass fittings!

Aside from the "essential 6" you will find other items of equipment most useful.

If you do not mount your specimens as soon as you bring them in from the field, you should store them in paper envelopes on which you write the complete data (p. 17). Glassine envelopes (without glue on the flaps) are excellent, or you can fold your own triangles as shown in Fig. 17. This type of storage is known to lepidopterists as "papering."

In order to mount dry, papered specimens it is necessary to relax them. This is simply done in any tight container. Place newspapers or sand in the bottom and wet thoroughly. Throw in a handful of paradichlorobenzine (to discourage mold) and then put in the specimens on top of a piece of screen or any other device to keep them from contact with the wet substrate. Wrapping the top of the container in cloth will prevent condensed water from dripping on the specimens.

A NOTEBOOK should be used to record your field observations. The loose-leaf kind is the best. Take only blank sheets with you into

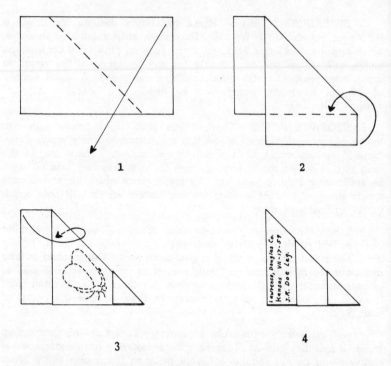

Fig. 17. "Papering" a butterfly.

the field, to avoid the possibility of losing all of your notes should the book be lost or destroyed.

A COLLECTING BAG, such as a surplus musette bag, is almost indispensable for carrying your paraphernalia.

A set of MICRODISSECTING TOOLS will be needed if you wish to study the genitalia or other anatomical features of butterflies. The most useful will be a pair of watchmaker's forceps (sizes 4-7). I prefer to use a curved and straight pair simultaneously for most dissection, carefully pulling apart the structures. Also very handy are tiny needles (minuten nadeln—available from dealers). The blunt ends of these can be forced into match sticks, which make good handles. A couple of clipped water-color brushes (for removing scales), a pair of fine embroidery scissors, and an eye dropper or two drawn out to a fine point, complete the set.

A HAND LENS (8-12x doublet magnifier) will help in examining structures which are a little too small to study with the naked eye. Try out a number and select one which gives a good flat field with no blurring at the edges.

DEALERS

The following are some of the dealers from whom you can purchase various items of equipment.

Bio Metal Associates, Box 346, Beverly Hills, California.

Carolina Biological Supply Company, Elon College, North Carolina.

General Biological Supply House, 8200 South Hoyne Ave., Chicago 20, Illinois.

Robert G. Wind, 702 Ocean View Ave., Monterey, California.

Ward's Natural Science Establishment, Rochester, New York.

COLLECTING

There are no magic rules for becoming a successful collector, but a few brief hints may start you on your way. As in many other things, experience is the best teacher.

1. Butterflies are rarely caught in a mad chase (cartoons not withstanding). Slow stalking and a quick sweep of the net is almost always more successful.

WRONG

RIGHT

2. Hold your net handle with one hand, and the end of the net bag with the other. The net will then always be open when the time to swing comes. Each swing should end with a twist of the wrist which flips the end of the net bag over the hoop and traps the specimen.

3. Avoid clapping the net over a specimen resting near the ground. It is much easier to sweep it in as it rises.

4. Rather than trying to maneuver a specimen into the cyanide jar while it is madly beating itself to pieces in the net, try "pinching." When the butterfly has its wings folded over its back, give it a sharp pinch on *the thorax* with your thumb and forefinger. A little practice (and some sticky fingers!) will show you how much pressure is "just enough" to stun the specimen without smashing it.

5. Do not put more than a few specimens in a jar. A crowded jar carried in the field will result in battered specimens covered with their neighbor's scales. Empty your jars frequently into a stationary "stock bottle," and paper your specimens as soon as possible.

6. Collect in as many different habitats as you can, and try different seasons of the year. The species in a marsh will be quite different from those on a dry hillside, and these in turn will not be the same ones found visiting flowers in a woodland glade. Equally, the species present in a locality in April will be mostly different from those found in the same place in August. If you live near mountains, be sure to try collecting at all altitudes.

Many flowers attract butterflies, and provide excellent collecting. However, some of our species rarely visit flowers and must be hunted down elsewhere. *Callophrys hesseli* is a denizen of white cedar swamps, where virtually no other butterflies are found. For this reason it went undiscovered through years of heavy collecting in its immediate vicinity at Lakehurst, New Jersey. One year the species was especially abundant and specimens were discovered on flowers outside of the swamps. In normal years it is not unusual to spend hours wading through the cold, knee-deep swamp water to be rewarded by the capture of only one or two specimens!

SPREADING

The technique for spreading specimens is simple, but requires practice. A properly spread specimen is shown in Fig. 16.

Thrust the pin through the center of the mesothorax vertical to the long axis of the body. Move the specimen up the pin until the top of the thorax is slightly less than ½" from the top of the pin.

Work from the center of your spreading boards towards the ends. Place two strips of paper about ¼" wide on each side of the center groove, holding them with pins at their center end. Then push the pin with the butterfly vertically into the center of the soft balsa center strip about one inch from the center of the board (use a board with a groove as nearly the width of the butterfly as possible) until the wings are level with the side strips. Push another pin into the center strip so that it touches the base of the abdomen at the left-hand side, to prevent the body from pivoting when you move the left-hand wings. Take the left-hand strip of paper and move it over the left-hand wings and antenna. While holding the former down with the paper strip, move the FW forward until its inner margin forms a right angle with the body. This is easily done by inserting a fine insect pin behind the strong radial vein. When the wing is in position, push the pin gently into the board. In a like manner move the HW into the position shown in the figure.

When the wings are properly positioned, pull the paper strip tight and pin it in place with pins right in front of the FW and behind the HW. Then remove the other pins from the wings and cover them with a small rectangle of glass (microscope slides do nicely). In a similar manner spread the right-hand wings.

The next specimen is placed on the board right behind the first, and so on until the entire side is filled. Then turn the board around and start all over again.

Leave the specimens on the boards until thoroughly dry (the abdomen should not wiggle when nudged). Relaxed specimens of small species may dry overnight if the humidity is low; large fresh specimens take much longer.

Be sure to keep your data with your specimens. We letter each end of our boards and then spindle the empty envelope or slip of paper bearing the data after placing on it a code number indicating what specimen it belongs to (e.g. "B3" is the third specimen from the center on side B of board A-B). Permanent labels are then made while the specimens are on the board.

Store your drying specimens out of reach of rodents or insects which might eat them.

LABELLING

A specimen without adequate data is worthless for anything but practice dissection. The absolute minimum information which should be attached to each specimen is: 1. the exact locality; 2. the altitude (if the specimen is taken in mountainous country); 3. the date of collection; and 4. the collector's name. In addition a brief description of the habitat should be included on the label whenever possible. If the specimen has been reared this should be stated (e.g. "ex larva, on *Nolina microcarpa*. Emgd. VI-29-59").

When recording a locality in the United States the county should be included. Always give a reference to the nearest large city or landmark (e.g. "5 mi. SW of Kansas City"). Anyone who has tried to locate "Bear Creek, Montana" or "Big Mountain, Pennsylvania" will understand why this is important. An example of good data might read "La Cueva Canyon, 6800', W. slope of Sandia Mts., Bernallilo Co., New Mexico, V-15-59, Noel McFarland leg., visiting *Nolina microcarpa*." Note that the date is given with the month in Roman numerals, and that "leg." is used for "collected by" (an abbreviation of the Latin). If you are collecting in little known or poorly settled areas such as the Arctic it is very valuable to include latitude and longitude on your labels.

You will find topographic maps a great help in determining latitude and longitude and also altitudes (write to U.S. Geological Survey, Washington 25, D.C.). A war surplus or commercial altimeter is invaluable. Be sure to calibrate it frequently at places of known elevation so as to correct for variations in atmospheric pressure.

On spread specimens, the labels are placed on the pin below the butterfly. Write neatly on little rectangles of high-grade paper, using a crow-quill pen and India ink. Use two or three labels on a small bug, rather than one large one which sticks out in all directions.

One final caution—never use field numbers on specimens as the only record of the data. The book in which the data are recorded invariably gets separated from the specimen, leaving the latter worthless.

PESTPROOFING

Dermestid beetles and other pests will happily eat your dried butterflies if given the opportunity. Therefore you should always keep some paradichlorobenzine (PDB) in the container with your specimens to repell and kill these insects. In boxes with pinned specimens it is convenient to put the PDB nuggets in a small cloth bag, and pin the latter to the bottom of the box.

Some people prefer flake naphthalene ("moth crystals") as their anti-pest weapon. It has the advantage of evaporating more slowly than PDB; thus it remains longer as an effective repellant. However, PDB will kill most pests rather rapidly, while naphthalene will merely repell them or kill them very slowly.

PRESERVATION IN FLUID

In many ways a butterfly specimen preserved in fluid is more valuable than one dried. The entire anatomy is then available for study.

ADULTS should be placed in Kahle's fluid (15 parts 95% commercial ethyl alcohol, 30 parts distilled water; 6 parts formalin; 1 part glacial acetic acid) for 24-72 hours and then transferred to 80% alcohol for storage. For temporary storage the specimen may be run through the fluids in a triangular envelope with the corners stapled and the data written in soft pencil on the flap. For permanent storage the specimens are placed in vials with labels written in India ink. Our collection is kept in shell vials (without a lip). In each is a series of specimens from the same locality (often different species) and a label bearing the data. The shell vials are filled with alcohol, plugged with cotton, and inverted in a large jar which is also filled with alcohol. Such double jar storage makes the level of alcohol very easy to maintain, since it is only necessary to add to the large jar. We maintain a card file which lists the species in each vial.

EGGS should be placed directly into Pempel's fluid (same as Kahle's except there are four parts of glacial acetic acid). They may be left there, or transferred to 80% alcohol to which a little glycerine has been added.

LARVAE should be killed by dropping into water that has been brought to a boil and removed from the fire long enough to stop bubbling. When the water is cool, remove the larvae and drop into Pempel's fluid. They can be left in this or transferred to 80% alcohol to which a few drops of glycerine have been added.

EGG SHELLS, CAST LARVAL SKINS, AND PUPAL CASES should be preserved in 80% alcohol.

NOTE—in an emergency 80% alcohol can be used instead of Kahle's or Pempel's fluid. The preservation will be somewhat inferior, but most specimens will be usable.

STUDYING WING VENATION

At many places in the keys you will find it necessary to consult the pattern of the wing venation. Simple examination of the under surface (where the veins are most prominent) will suffice in most cases. If difficulty is encountered, as it may be in the crowded area of the radial branches, it often helps to wet the area with a few drops of 95% alcohol. This will evaporate rapidly and leave the specimen undamaged.

For detailed study the wings may be broken off, wetted with alcohol, and bleached in diluted *Clorox* (a 5.25% by weight solution of sodium hypochlorite—best diluted about 1:1 with water). Take care not to bleach too long, or the entire wing may be dissolved! The bleached wings may then be mounted on cards with drops of glue, or bound between pieces of glass.

GENITALIC DISSECTIONS

Many places in the keys to follow you will find references to the male genitalia, and, in a few places, the female genitalia. In the butterflies the form of the sclerotized parts of the male sexual apparatus (the "external genitalia" or just "genitalia") is often uniform within a given species or genus, and quite different from those of related forms. Therefore examination of these structures will often be an invaluable aid in properly identifying your specimens.

You will need a binocular (stereoscopic) dissecting microscope or (for the largest species) a good dissecting lens. Since even second hand dissecting scopes are quite expensive, I suggest that you ask your local high school's biology teacher to permit you to use one of his instruments.

The male genitalia are easily dissected. The abdomen is broken off the specimen and wetted with 95% ethyl alcohol. It is then dropped into a 10% solution of potassium hydroxide (KOH) until the viscera are semi-liquid. Overnight will do for average material, but large specimens may take much longer. Be careful not to leave the specimen in the KOH too long or even the heavily sclerotized parts will be destroyed.

Remove the abdomen to a dish of water and swirl it around to wash out the excess KOH. (Handle KOH with great care at all times. It is extremely corrosive—getting it in your eyes may result in blindness, and it will badly burn the skin if not washed off immediately.) Then place the abdomen in a shallow dish of water under the dissecting scope. You will note that the image is upright and not reversed, permitting easy manipulation. Usually 6-15 magnifications are convenient for dissecting. Using a curved forceps or other blunt tool, squeeze the abdominal contents out of the hole at the anterior end. While this is being done the heavily sclerotized (dark) genitalia will probably be extruded from the posterior end. If they are not, they may be teased out with fine needles or watchmaker's forceps (see EQUIPMENT). Using these tools, the membrane connecting the vinculum (see Fig. 12) with the eighth abdominal segment is severed. The pelt of the abdomen and the genitalia are then cleaned with streams of water from a fine eye dropper, fine forceps, and brushes (be sure to remove all the scales from the abdomen).

The cleaned abdomen and genitalia should be carefully cross-labeled with the remainder of the specimen and then stored in vials of 80% ethyl alcohol to which a few drops of glycerine have been added. Perhaps your dentist will save his old procaine tubes for you —washed out they make fine vials.

Complicated as it may sound, the entire process outlined above (exclusive of the KOH soaking) should, with a little practice, take less than 5 minutes.

Dissection of the female genitalia is similar, but more tedious. Care must be taken not to tear the bursa (see Fig. 9), so that the abdominal contents must be removed more gently. You may find it helpful to pull them out through a long slit in the pleural membrane (see Fig. 8). I personally prefer to completely sever the membrane connecting abdominal segments 6 and 7 or 7 and 8 (being very careful not to cut too deeply and damage the bursa) and pull the abdomen apart, leaving the lamellae ante- and postvaginalis and the bursa attached to the posterior segments. These are then thoroughly cleaned and stored in the same manner as the male genitalia.

There is no best method of dealing with the female genitalia; techniques should be altered to expose the characters in the group worked with.

STUDYING THE ENTIRE SKELETAL MORPHOLOGY

The procedures for studying the entire skeletal anatomy are not unlike those used in the genitalic work. The wings are removed and stored in a glassine envelope along with the data labels. The wings and body are then cross-labelled with the same number. The entire body is then given the treatment described for the abdomen alone in the previous section. Care should be taken when brushing off the scales, especially in the region of the cervix and legs, or you will have loose patagia, tegulae, and tarsi floating around. The thoracic viscera are best removed by breaking the meso-metathoracic membrane ventrally and sucking the soft parts out with an eye-dropper. The abdominal viscera may be taken out in the same manner through a slit in the connective membrane between two of the middle segments (3-5). In order to view the tentorium, one eye may be removed and the head contents flushed out. Most of the internal structures can be seen through the semi-transparent integument, but if you have a number of specimens you should cut some apart to expose the apodemal structures. The only internal structure used in the keys is the form of the lamella of the mesodiscrimen (see Figs. 19, 20). This is easily seen by slitting the pleuron of the mesothorax and carefully folding back the lower portion. Once you are familiar with this structure, you will, in most specimens, be able to discern its shape without dissecting the thoracic wall (it will not be visible through the wall in heavily sclerotized species).

STUDYING THE VISCERAL ANATOMY

Specimens for the study of the soft (visceral) anatomy should be placed alive (preferably) or freshly killed in Kahle's fluid (see PRESERVATION IN FLUID). After a day in this, they should be transferred to 80% alcohol for storage. If it is at all possible you should do your first dissections on freshly killed, unpreserved specimens, as these are by far the easiest to work with.

Techniques of dissection vary with the size of the specimen, the system to be studied, and individual preferences. Start with a big species (such as a *Papilio* or *Danaus*) and slice a specimen longitudinally with a razor into bilaterally symmetrical halves. With the aid of Fig. 18, most of the major systems can be recognized. The silvery tracheae (respiratory tubes) can be readily located at the spiracles and traced. The delicate loop of the heart through the longitudinal wing muscles can be seen by carefully picking away the overlying muscle fibers.

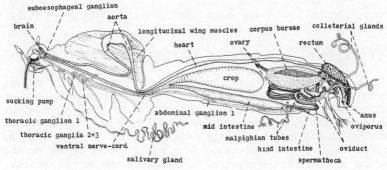

Fig. 18. Internal anatomy of adult ♀ *Danaus plexippus*, tracheae, most of malpighian tubes, and left ovary removed (modified from Scudder).

In general, dissections should be done under a binocular dissecting microscope. Use a shallow dish with a paraffin bottom. Various parts can then be held out of the way with insect pins.

The comparative visceral morphology of the butterflies is largely *terra incognita*—new discoveries await you at every turn.

STUDYING BUTTERFLIES SCIENTIFICALLY

Collectors often ask "can I make scientific contributions by studying butterflies?" The answer is emphatically "yes." The relatively untrained worker can contribute in many ways:

COLLECTING. He can collect long series of carefully labelled specimens and make them available to scientists through loans and by depositing duplicates in major museums. Material properly preserved in fluid is especially valuable.

REARING. He can add to our knowledge of butterfly life cycles and genetics. Whenever a species is raised, specimens of the eggs, all larval stages, and pupae should be carefully preserved. If the parents are known, they should be clearly cross-labelled with the offspring. Any parasites attacking the butterfly should also be saved (mount flies and larger wasps on insect pins, place smaller wasps in 80% alcohol). Through the Lepidopterists' Society you can learn where to send these parasites to have them identified. If you are not sure of the identity of the larval food plant, be sure to press some specimens (leaves, flowers and fruits if possible—if too large, take notes on size, bark color and consistency, etc.) so that they can be identified. The botanists at your state university will probably be glad to help you out.

OBSERVATION. Just watching butterflies and taking copious notes on what they do is sure to turn up interesting things. Migrations, regular daily movements, "mud puddle aggregations," mating habits, predators, flight dates, habitat preferences, flower preferences, carrion visiting, in fact just about anything a butterfly does is of interest. Important new observations can be published in suitable journals (see LITERATURE).

A WORD OF CAUTION. Untrained and unguided amateurs have published a great deal on individual and geographic variation in butterflies. Proper prosecution of such studies demands training in population genetics, biometrics, evolutionary theory, and the like. It is therefore not surprising that 95% of this material is scientifically useless! By all means, before you publish anything submit it to a trained entomologist for criticism. A professional scientist will rarely publish until he has exposed his work to the criticism of his colleagues. Better to make mistakes in front of your friends than in front of the world!

HOW TO USE THE KEYS

If you do not have any idea of the group to which a specimen belongs, you should first run it through the key to families of butterflies. Starting with the first couplet (numbers 1a and 1b), decide which of the two opposing statements best describes the specimen. Then go to the couplet indicated by the number at the end of the correct statement. Continue this process until there is a family name at the end of the statement (you will note that if your specimen belonged to the Lycaenidae it would be identified by the first couplet). Having identified your specimen to family, turn to the page indicated after the family name for the keys to the group within the family. Continue through the keys until you reach a species name. Then check your specimen against the figure for that species to be sure that you have identified it properly. *Do not expect any specimen to agree exactly with the butterfly pictured.* All species are variable to one degree or another. Make certain that your specimen comes from a locality within or near the range given in the short species write-up. It is quite possible that you will find specimens from outside of this range, as many butterflies have poorly known distributions, and others are often blown or wander far from their normal haunts. However, if you have taken a butterfly in your back yard in Philadelphia and you key it out as *Philotes speciosa* (which flies in the Mohave Desert of California) or *Erebia fasciata* (a denizen of the Far Arctic), you have almost certainly made an error.

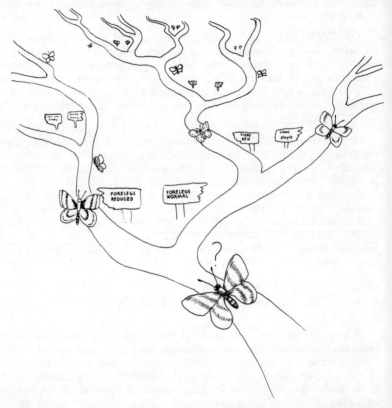

When a certain familiarity with the various groups of butterflies is attained, you will find it unnecessary to use the higher group keys for most specimens. Indeed, in a very short time you should have little difficulty in identifying the majority of species to genus "at first sight."

A word of advice. If you are unable to decide which half of a couplet is correct, take the specimen through both indicated sections of the key. Very often one path will lead to an absurd choice or identification. You will doubtless run into occasional specimens which you cannot identify with assurance. Label these with the best possible identification (e.g. "*Erebia* species," "*Philotes,* near *enoptes,*" "*Anthocaris cethura*??," etc.), and at the first opportunity take them to a museum or send them to an expert to have the identification checked. *Never* put a positive identification on a specimen unless you are sure it is properly determined. Virtually all great collections are full of labels such as those above—only beginners insist on absolute pigeonholing of every specimen.

All technical terms are defined. Check the INDEX AND PICTURED-GLOSSARY. You will either find the definition there, or find a reference to the page on which the term is defined. A list of abbreviations used in the keys is given on p. 28.

While you will be able to identify a great many species merely by comparing specimens with the pictures, you will have a great deal more success (and learn a lot more) if you become sufficiently familiar with butterfly structures to use all of the keys. The wing venation, especially, should be learned thoroughly. Every opportunity should be taken to familiarize yourself with the general integumental anatomy, and the genitalia (see sections on WING VENATION, GENITALIC DISSECTIONS, and STUDYING THE ENTIRE SKELETAL MORPHOLOGY).

FAUNAL REGIONS AND LIFE ZONES

FAUNAL REGIONS

In the comments on distribution which follow, you will find references to the major zoogeographic areas of the world (faunal regions). These are:

1. NEARCTIC: taking in all of North America north of tropical Mexico.

2. NEOTROPICAL: all of tropical America south to Cape Horn.

3. PALAEARCTIC: the temperate and arctic Eurasian land mass (north of the Himalayas) and North Africa north of the Sahara Desert.

4. ETHIOPIAN: Africa south of the Sahara.

5. INDO-AUSTRALIAN: the tropical outliers of Eurasia plus Australia.

The NEARCTIC and PALAEARCTIC regions are often combined as the HOLARCTIC REGION.

LIFE ZONES

The Nearctic Region has been divided into life zones based originally on temperature zones, but generally recognized by characteristic plant and animal inhabitants. Although unsatisfactory from many points of view (especially that of modern botanists, who prefer to deal with vegetation types) these zones are often useful in describing distributions. A life zone map can be found in *Systematic Zoology*, vol. 1, no. 1, pp. 24-25, 1952. The discussion of the zones below is necessarily brief and incomplete.

1. ARCTIC-ALPINE: the treeless areas of the Far North and the tops of high mountains. Plants: lichens, grasses, sedges, dwarf willows, various Ericaceae. Animals: ptarmigan, muskoxen, arctic fox, *Aedes* mosquitoes, *Erebia fasciata, Oeneis melissa, Boloria chariclea, Colias nastes.*

2. HUDSONIAN: this is the ecotone or "tension zone" between the treeless areas and the Canadian Zone coniferous forests. Plants: stunted spruce-fir complex. Animals: pika, Harris sparrow, *Papilio machaon*, *Parnassius eversmanni*, *Erebia disa*, *Colias meadii*.

3. CANADIAN: this is the zone of the climax coniferous forests of the North (taiga) and subalpine coniferous forests of the southern mountains . Plants: in Northeast, spruce, fir; white, Norway, and jack pines. In places replaced by beech, yellow birch, and sugar maple deciduous forest. Secondary growth often *Populus tremuloides*. In western mountains characterized by Douglas fir, yellow pine, white fir, Colorado and Engelmann spruces, and (at lower edge) lodgepole pine. Animals: lynx, snowshoe hare, moose, *Colias interior*, *Anthocaris sara*, *Erebia epipsodea*, *Speyeria atlantis*, *Boloria titania*.

4. TRANSITION: this is the border between the "boreal" (Arctic-Canadian) and Austral Zones. Its flora and fauna are characteristically a mixture of elements from the adjacent zones. In the West, sometimes with willows and cottonwood prominent. Animals: red-backed junco, western tanager, *Pieris virginiensis*, *Chlosyne harrisii*, *Satyrium edwardsii*, *Limenitis weidemeyeri*, *Lycaena helloides*, *Plebejus acmon*.

5. AUSTRAL or SONORAN: this zone is called the *Austral* or *Carolinian* in the more humid East, and *Sonoran* in the relatively dry West. Both are divided into upper and lower sections.

UPPER AUSTRAL: occupying most of the north central states from eastern Nebraska and Kansas east to the Appalachian Piedmont and the northeastern coastal plain. Broken by Transition and Canadian Zone areas in the Appalachian Mountains. Plants: oak, hickory, beech, yellow birch, red maples, osage orange, etc. Animals: black rat snake, timber rattlesnake, *Anthocaris genutia*, *Speyeria diana*, *Speyeria idalia*, *Euptychia cymela*.

LOWER AUSTRAL (AUSTRORIPARIAN): this is the zone of the southeastern coastal plain, the Gulf Coast, and northern peninsular Florida. Plants: longleaf, loblolly and slash pines (*Pinus palustris*, *taeda* and *caribaea*), live oak, bald cypress, tupelo, red gum. Animals: cane-brake rattlesnake, cotton mouse, *Papilio palamedes*, *Euptychia hermes*, *Atlides halesus*, *Calycopis cecrops*, *Eurema daira*.

UPPER SONORAN: this is the dominant life-zone of the Great Basin and other non-montane areas north of southern California, Arizona, and New Mexico, and southwestern Texas (it penetrates as far north as southeastern Washington and parts of southern Montana). Plants: piñon pine, junipers, scrub oak, live oak, shadscale. Animals: rock squirrel, piñon jay, *Speyeria coronis*, *Apodemia mormo*, *Callophrys siva*, *Callophrys mcfarlandi*.

LOWER SONORAN: this is the hot desert life zone. Plants: greasewood, saltbush, creosote bush, yucca, cacti. Animals: black-throated desert sparrow, road runner, kangaroo rat, sidewinder, *Philotes speciosa*, *Philotes mohave*, *Plebejus emigdionis*, *Anthocaris cethura*.

6. SUBTROPICAL: our subtropical areas are restricted to southern Florida and extreme southern Texas. Plants: wild tamarind (*Lysiloma*), magnolias, strangler fig (*Ficus aurea*), gumbo limbo (*Bursera*), vines, and epiphytes such as bromeliads (pineapple family). Animals: black-whiskered vireo, *Papilio aristodemus*, *Heliconius charitonius*, *Marpesia petreus*, *Eunica tatila*, *Eumaeus atala*.

LITERATURE

BOOKS. A number of books which you will find useful are listed below. Do not ignore those which deal with insects in general—a broad knowledge of entomology will add much to your understanding of butterflies.

Chu, H. F., 1949, *How to Know the Immature Insects*. By far the handiest book for identifying larvae, nymphs, and pupae.

Comstock, J. A., 1927, *Butterflies of California*. Handsomely illustrated in color; rich in figures of early stages. Although some parts are out of date, and there is too much emphasis on aberrations, this book is highly recommended to the western collector.

Comstock, J. H., 1927, *An Introduction to Entomology*. A good general text with emphasis on life histories, etc.

Ford, E. B., 1945, *Butterflies*. Deals with evolution, genetics, distribution, dispersal, protective devices, etc. in butterflies. Should be read by everyone with an interest in Lepidoptera.

Ford, E. B., 1955, *Moths*. Much the same plan as the preceding, but using moths as the subject matter. Excellent.

Holland, W. J., 1932, *Butterfly Book, Revised Edition*. Almost all North American butterflies are figured in the fine colored plates. In many ways out of date, but still a "must" for the serious collector.

Imms, A. D., 1957, *A General Textbook of Entomology, Revised Edition*. Highly technical, authoritative, and somewhat difficult. A good source book.

Jaques, H. E., 1947, *How to Know the Insects*. Our handiest manual for identifying families of adult insects.

Klots, A. B., 1951, *Field Guide to the Butterflies*. A superb little book dealing with our eastern species. Well-done colored plates. This book should be on every collector's shelf.

Ross, H. H., 1956, *A Textbook of Entomology, Revised Edition*. Clearly written and well-balanced. A good book for the individual who wants some general knowledge of insects without going into detail.

Periodical. If you have a serious interest in butterflies, you should join the Lepidopterists' Society. With membership you will receive the *Journal of the Lepidopterists' Society* and the *News of the Lepidopter-*

ists' Society, which contain articles written for both the professional and the amateur. Perhaps most important, you will receive a membership list which gives the names, addresses, and interests of people in the United States and some 40 other countries who are engaged in collecting and/or studying butterflies and moths. Many of these people will be willing to exchange specimens and information with you, and help you to identify specimens. Annual meetings are held in the United States, at which you can meet other people with your interests. The membership fee in this non-profit organization is, at present, $5.00 a year. If interested write to: Lepidopterists' Society. c/o Osborn Zoological Laboratory, Yale University, New Haven 11, Connecticut.

FIGURES

Each figure of an adult butterfly has been drawn from an actual specimen or, in a very few cases, from photographs of actual specimens. You will note that in the caption after the name of the species there is a D or a V indicating whether the dorsal or ventral surface is shown. The size of the specimens may be easily judged by the scale lines drawn next to them. *In all cases these scale lines represent one-half inch.*

ABBREVIATIONS AND CONVENTIONS

Cell = discal cell. All other cells always designated by reference to the preceding vein (e.g., "cell Cu_1").

D = dorsal (upper) surface of the wings.

DFW = dorsal surface of the forewing.

DHW = dorsal surface of the hindwing.

FW = forewing.

HW = hindwing.

LFW = length of the forewing, from the base of the subcostal vein to the apex (Fig. ...).

V = ventral (lower) surface of the wings.

VFW = ventral surface of the forewing.

VHW = ventral surface of the hindwing.

i-xii = January-December (approximate flight dates given with Roman numerals indicating the months).

> = greater than (e.g., "LFW > 25 mm." means that the length of the forewing is greater than 25 millimeters).

< = less than.

♂ = male.

♀ = female.

KEY TO THE FAMILIES OF BUTTERFLIES

Superfamily PAPILIONOIDEA

Butterflies

SUPERFICIAL KEY TO THE FAMILIES OF PAPILIONOIDEA (FOR NORTH AMERICAN SPECIMENS ONLY).

1a Palpi as long or longer than thorax............Libytheidae p. 174
1b Palpi much shorter than thorax................................2

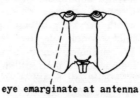

2a Eyes at least slightly emarginate at antennae (Fig. 18A); width of face between eyes much less than length ....Lycaenidae p. 175

eye emarginate at antenna

Fig. 18A. Front view of head of *Lycaena helloides*.

2b Eyes not emarginate at antennae; width of face between eyes as great as length..3
3a Prothoracic legs much less than one-half the size of pterothoracic legs..Nymphalidae p. 81
3b Prothoracic legs about same size as pterothoracic legs.........4
4a Prothoracic legs bearing tibial epiphyses (see Fig. 21); HW with vein 3V absent; tarsal claws not bifid...............Papilionidae p. 30
4b Prothoracic legs lacking tibial epiphyses; HW with vein 3V present; tarsal claws bifid..................................Pieridae p. 51

STRUCTURAL KEY TO THE FAMILIES OF PAPILIONOIDEA (VALID IR-RESPECTIVE OF GEOGRAPHICAL AREA).

1a Lamella of mesodiscrimen continuous with furca, dorsum of lamella essentially straight (Fig. 19); eyes not emarginate at antennae; patagia either sclerotized or unsclerotized...2

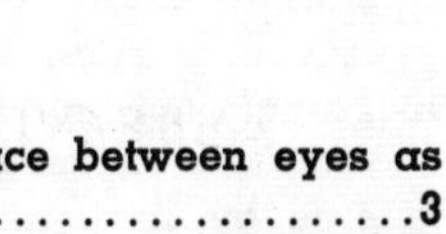

lamella   furca

Fig. 19. Lamella of the mesodiscrimen of *Danaus plexippus*, lateral v i e w (semidiagramma- tic).

furca

lamella

Fig. 20. Lamella of the mesodiscrimen of *Lycaena helloides*, lateral view (semidiagrammatic).

1b. Lamella of mesodiscrimen not continuous with furca, curving downward to base of furca (Fig. 20); eyes usually emarginate at antennae; patagia unsclerotized......
......................Lycaenidae p. 175

2a Cervical sclerites not joined beneath cervix; protibial epiphyses absent; HW with two distinct vannal veins....................3
2b Cervical sclerites joined or nearly joined by a sclerotic band beneath cervix; protibial epiphyses present; HW with only one distinct vannal vein (two in *Baronia*)..............Papilionidae p. 30
3a Prespiracular bar at base of abdomen well-developed; prothoracic legs smaller than pterothoracic legs (only slightly in females of Libytheidae); tarsal claws very rarely strongly bifid............4
3b Prespiracular bar at base of abdomen reduced or absent; prothoracic legs fully developed (as large as pterothoracic legs); tarsal Claws always strongly bifid.......................Pieridae p. 51
4a Patagia prominent, rounded, sclerotized structures; metanotum not entirely below mesoscutellum, only partially covered by it.......
....Nymphalidae p. 81
4b Patagia not prominent or rounded, bearing only small lateral sclerotizations; metanotum essentially entirely below mesoscutellum, covered by it....................................Libytheidae p. 174

Family PAPILIONIDAE
SWALLOWTAILS AND PARNASSIANS
by Kent H. Wilson

The species of papilionids range in size from medium (Parnassiinae) to large (Papilioninae); the largest North American butterfly and also the largest in the world are members of this family. The Papilionidae are separated from their closest relatives, the Pieridae, and the other three families of butterflies by having: 1) tibial epiphyses on the prothoracic legs (Fig. 21), 2) the cervical sclerites united beneath the cervix,

coxa

epiphysis

Fig. 21. Prothoracic leg of *Papilio machaon*.

and 3) only one vannal vein in the HW (except in *Baronia*). (Some riodinines also have only one vannal vein).

Most of the some 530 species of this cosmopolitan group are found in the tropics. Many of these are brilliantly marked, some displaying metallic structural colors. The North American forms tend to be yellow or white with black markings; in many cases there are light blue areas and/or a red anal spot on the HW.

The larvae possess an *osmaterium* (Fig. 21A), a forked organ which is extruded when they are disturbed, and which emits a pungent odor. This structure is found only in the papilionids, where it is universal. The diversely marked larvae (see Figs. 23, 30, 35, 40) are either smooth, possess fleshy processes on each segment, or are covered with short hairs.

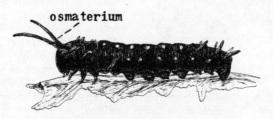

Fig. 21A. Larva of *Battus philenor* (after Scudder).

The pupae (see Figs. 31, 36, 41) are either attached to some object by means of crochets on the caudal end (which are enmeshed in a silken network) and a silken girdle which supports the mid section (Papilioninae) or they are found among the debris on the surface of the ground (Parnassiinae).

KEY TO THE SUBFAMILIES OF PAPILIONIDAE.

1a FW with cu-v crossvein (Fig. 22); worldwide.....Papilioninae p. 34

1b FW without cu-v crossvein....2

2a HW with one vannal vein; Northern Hemisphere................ ....Parnassiinae p. 31

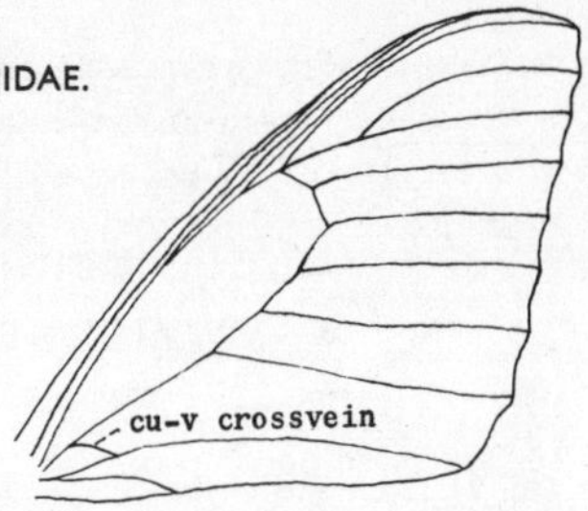

Fig. 22. FW venation of *Papilio machaon*.

2b HW with two vannal veins; one species, *Baronia brevicornis* Salvin, from the Rio Balsas Basin of southwestern Mexico.....Baroniinae

SUPERFICIAL KEY TO THE NORTH AMERICAN PAPILIONINAE.

1a Tail-less; white or yellowish with dark bands....Parnassiinae p. 31

1b Tailed or, if tail-less, not white or yellowish.....Papilioninae p. 34

Subfamily PARNASSIINAE

This subfamily is limited to the Northern Hemisphere. It consists of two tribes, Zerynthiini and Parnassiini, but in North America is represented by only a single genus, *Parnassius*. Of the many species in this genus, only three are found in our region.

Genus PARNASSIUS Latreille

These are medium-sized white or yellowish butterflies with dark bands and, in some cases, black and/or red spots. The abdomens of the males are hairy, while those of the females are naked dorsally or have at most only scattered hairs. All females possess a sphragus (Figs. 24-26) after copulation. This whitish structure is attached to the ventral caudal portion of the abdomen of the female by the male. The larvae (Fig. 23) are covered with a fine black or dark brown down. Each segment has a similar set of slightly raised areas which are orange or yellow. The pupae are found in debris on the ground. This moth-like condition may well be an adaptation to the harsh climate in which these butterflies live.

Fig. 23. Larva of *Parnassius*.

KEY TO THE SPECIES OF *PARNASSIUS*.

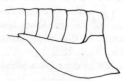

Fig. 24. Sphragus of *Parnassius eversmanni*.

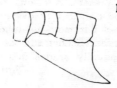

Fig. 25. Sphragus of *Parnassius clodius*.

1a Antennae b l a c k; DFW spots in middle and at distal end of cell approximately as dark as the other dark markings on the wings; these spots at least twice as long as broad; sphragus without keel on ventral surface (Figs. 24, 25)....2

Fig. 26. Sphragus of *Parnassius phoebus*.

1b Antennae white with black rings (club black); DFW spots in middle and at distal end of cell *much* darker than other markings on wings, these spots slightly longer than broad; sphragus with strong keel on cephalic ventral surface (Fig. 26)..............................4

2a Ground color yellow (males) or yellowish white (females). Fig. 27...........
......*Parnassius eversmanni* Menetries

Range: mountainous eastern Asia and
the mountains of the Yukon River drainage
in North America.

Food plant: *Corydalis gigantea* (Fumari-
aceae).

Fig. 27. *Parnassius eversmanni* ♂ D. Mt. McKinley
National Park, Alaska.

2b Ground color white (newly emerged individuals may have a slight
yellow cast; ventral body hairs may be yellowish)..............3

3a FW with three distinct bands approximately parallel to the outer
margin in the distal portion of the wing (beyond the cell), *and* HW
with red spot distal to cell connected to anal red bar by dark scales;
HW with black suffusion of anal margin sharply separated from
white in, above and beyond the cell; females...................
................*Parnassius eversmanni* Menetries. See couplet 2a.

3b FW with third innermost band not present (except as a segment
distal to cell), or, if present, HW with red spot distal to cell not
connected to anal red bar; if dark overscaling is great enough the
red spot and anal red bar may be united as in 4a, but then the
distal bands of FW are indistinct and the margin of the anal black
suffusion on HW gradually grades into white. Fig. 28...........
.....................................*Parnassius clodius* **Menetries**

Range: mountainous and some coastal
areas of California, far western rim of
Nevada, north to southern Alaska and
eastward across Idaho to western mountains of Montana and Wyoming.

Food plants: *Viola*, *Sedum* (stonecrop),
Vaccinium?, *Rubus?*. This is the only
species of *Parnassius* which is limited
to North America.

Fig. 28. *Parnassius clodius* ♂
D. Molalla River, Oregon.

4a Palps with cream colored long hairs on ventral surface (a few black in some specimens); DFW with red spot(s) just beyond cell almost always present in females, sometimes present in males. Fig. 29.............................*Parnassius phoebus* Fabricius

Range: widely distributed in Europe, Asia, and western North America; Alaska south of the Arctic Circle, south to the mountains of New Mexico, Utah and California.

Food plants: *Sedum stenopetalum* and *Sempervivum* (Crassulaceae) and *Saxifraga*. American *phoebus* is widely known in our literature as *P. smintheus* Doubleday and Hewitson.

Fig. 29. *Parnassius phoebus* ♂ D. Monarch Mountain, Colorado.

4b Palps mainly with black long hairs on ventral surface; DFW lacks red spots beyond the cell...........*Parnassius nomion* Waldheim
Range: a Palaearctic species reported from North America, but almost certainly erroneously due to misidentification or (more likely) dealer mislabelling.

Subfamily PAPILIONINAE

This worldwide subfamily is the largest of the three in the family, containing about 480 species. At one time almost all of these species were placed in the one large genus *Papilio*. By comparing the magnitude of the differences found among members of this "genus" with that found within other families of butterflies, it was discovered that more diversification exists among various "Papilios" than within some of the families of nymphalid butterflies. Accordingly the old genus *Papilio* has been divided into several tribes and genera, and the nymphalid "families" have been placed as subfamilies under the Nymphalidae. All four genera into which "Papilio" has been broken are represented in North America (*Parides* only by a straggler).

KEY TO THE GENERA OF PAPILIONINAE.
1a D with only submarginal spots present (may have a few spots on costal edge of FW near distal end of cell); dark areas have a metallic gun-blue or blue-green luster (may be faint in females)......
...*Battus* p. 35

1b Not as above—either lacks submarginal spots or has them accompanied by other markings.....................................2

2a VHW with red spot on middle part of costal margin or red stripe from costal edge to anal spot; HW with long, thin tail (6 to 8 times as long as wide); general pattern dark stripes on white or greenish white background..........................*Graphium* p. 37

2b VHW with no red spot on costal margin, or red stripe (anal spot may be present); if VHW has orange spot on distal part of costal margin, ground color is not white; tailed or tail-less, if present tails 3 to 5 times as long as wide..................................3

3a Males: DFW with green patch in discal area; HW has anal area covered with silky hairs; females: DFW with creamy-white patch crossing cell almost at distal end and continuing below cell to vein M₃; both sexes lack submarginal spots and have a large red patch on DHW which is represented on VHW as a single pink patch cut by black veins; a single straggler in our area........*Parides* p. 38

3b FW without green patch; HW without silky hairs in anal area; if submarginal spots lacking and red area on HW is present, the red area on VHW is broken into separate spots (in some cases two rows of spots, the outer pink and the inner purplish red)....*Papilio* p. 38

Genus BATTUS Scopoli

This genus is restricted to the Western Hemisphere. Of the 14 species it contains, only three are found in our area. In most cases the food plant is *Aristolochia*. All of the larvae bear fleshy tubercles and are dark brown or black. (Fig. 30). The pupae (Fig. 31) are convex on the dorsal surface and are laterally expanded.

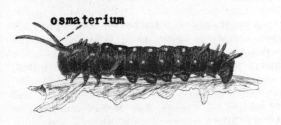

Fig. 30. Larva of *Battus philenor* (after Scudder).

Fig. 31. Pupa of
Battus philenor
(after Scudder).

KEY TO THE SPECIES OF *BATTUS*.

1a Tailed; D submarginal spots all white..........................2

**1b Tail-less; DFW submarginal spots yellow; DHW submarginal spots light yellow-green (if submarginal spots on both FW and HW are light yellow, see *Papilio astyalus*). Fig. 32.......................
....*Battus polydamas* Linnaeus**

Range: Georgia, Florida, and the Gulf States southward to northern Argentina. Food plant: various species of *Aristolochia*.

Fig. 32. *Battus polyda-mas* ♂ V. No data.

2a VHW submarginal spots brick red and distally lined with silver, the spots in cells M$_2$ and M$_3$ contiguous; D submarginal spots of FW whitish, of HW light blue. Fig. 33......*Battus devilliers* Godart

Range: Cuba, doubtfully recorded from Florida. Food plant: *Aristolochia trilobata*.

Fig. 33. *Battus devil-liers* ♀ V. Cuba.

**2b VHW submarginal spots dull orange or dull red-orange and marked with white anteriorly and/or posteriorly, the spots in cells M$_2$ and M$_3$ not contiguous; D submarginal spots all whitish. Fig. 34......
.................*Battus philenor* Linnaeus. Pipe Vine Swallowtail.**

Range: New England west to Nebraska, south to Florida, Texas and Costa Rica, and westward through New Mexico and Arizona to California. Food plant: various species of *Aristolochia*, also *Asarum* and *Polygonum*. This species is said to be distasteful to predators and thus to serve as a model for various dark mimicking species and forms found in the eastern United States. These include *Papilio troilus*, *Papilio glaucus* (dark form of female), *Papilio polyxenes* (female), *Speyeria diana* (female) and *Limenitis astyanax*.

Fig. 34. *Battus phile-nor* ♂ V. Otterville, Missouri.

Genus GRAPHIUM Scopoli

This worldwide genus is limited in large part to the tropics; of the 130 species, one is found in North America and ten in the Palearctic region. The larvae (Fig. 35) are smooth, without processes or hairs. The pupae (Fig. 36) have a prominent dorsal process.

Fig. 35. Larva of *Graphium marcellus* (after Scudder).

Fig. 36. Pupa of *Graphium marcellus* (after Scudder).

KEY TO THE SPECIES OF *GRAPHIUM*.

**1a VHW with red band from costal to anal margin; VHW with two light and two dark stripes which cross cell not equal in width or parallel, the outermost stripe (dark) crossing partly within the cell and partly distal to the cell end. Fig. 37.........................
...............*Graphium marcellus* Cramer. Zebra Swallowtail.**

Range: Florida to Texas, northward to Canada (rare in northern part of range). One record from Vancouver Island, almost certainly an imported specimen. Food plant: *Asimina* (paw-paw), rarely Ericaceae and Lauraceae.

Fig. 37. *Graphium marcellus* ♂ V. Lawrence, Kansas.

1b VHW with red spot of costal margin not connected to anal red spot; VHW with two light and two dark stripes which cross cell approximately same width and parallel, the outermost stripe (dark) crossing entirely within cell (reaching distad just to cell end). Fig. 38..................................*Graphium celadon* Lucas.

Range: Cuba. Doubtfully recorded from Florida, probably due to dealer mislabelling.

Fig. 38. *Graphium celadon* ♀ V. Antilles.

Genus PARIDES Hübner

The 88 species in this genus are found mainly in the Neotropical and Indo-Australian regions. The larvae are usually dark with paired

light colored tubercles on each segment. The pupae are similar to those of *Battus* and *Papilio*. A single species, *Parides arcas* Cramer (Fig. 39) is known from our area.

Range: Colombia and the Guianas north to Mexico, and, as a rare straggler, to Texas (one record and one unauthenticated report in *National Geographic Magazine*).

Fig. 39. *Parides arcas* ♂ D. No data.

Genus PAPILIO Linnaeus

Most of the some 200 species are tropical. The Nearctic species are usually black and yellow with a red-orange anal spot. The postmedian area of the HW may have a series of blue spots or areas; these

are most pronounced in females. The only
papilionid species that are of economic importance in our area belong to this genus,
feeding on parsley, *Citrus*, and a few other
crops. The larvae (Fig. 40) are smooth and
hairless. The pupae (Fig. 41) are nearly
cylindrical and have no large lateral projections as are found in *Battus*.

Fig. 40. Larva of *Papilio cresphontes* (after Scudder).

Fig. 41. Pupa of *Pa-
pilio glaucus*.

KEY TO THE SPECIES OF *PAPILIO*.

1a Wings divided by longitudinal black or black-brown stripes on a
yellow or white background (except for dark brown females of *P.
glaucus* [See Fig. 47] which show traces of stripes on V and lack
orange costal spot on HW of *P. troilus*, which they otherwise resemble) 2
1b Wings not divided by longitudinal dark stripes.................7
2a FW cell crossed by three dark bands, not including dark marking
at base of wing (outer band at least contiguous with cell end)....
....Glaucus group 3
2b FW cell crossed by two dark bands, not including dark marking
at base of wing. Troilus group (in part). Fig. 42................
......................................*Papilio pilumnus* Boisduval.

Range: Southern Arizona, Mexico, to Guatemala. Food plant: "laurel."

Fig. 42. *Papilio pilumnus*
♂ V. Victoria, Mexico.

3a HW with more than one tail. Fig. 43.... *Papilio multicaudata Kirby.*

Range: British Columbia to California, eastward to west Texas, Colorado, western Nebraska and Montana, and south into Mexico. Food plants: *Prunus*, *Ligustrum* (privet), *Fraxinus* (ash), *Ptelea* (hop-tree), *Amelanchier* (shadberry), etc.

Fig. 43. *Papilio multicaudata* ♂ V. Chimney Gulch, Colorado.

3b HW with one tail..4

4a Ground color white or nearly white. Fig. 44...................
.......................................*Papilio eurymedon Lucas.*

Range: British Columbia to California, eastward to Colorado. Food plants: *Ceanothus* (mountain laurel, New Jersey tea, snow brush, etc.), *Rhamnus* (buckthorn), *Prunus, Crataegus* (hawthorn), *Ribes* (currant), *Alnus* (alder), etc.

Fig. 44. *Papilio eurymedon* ♂ V. Napa County, California.

4b Ground color yellow or orange-yellow..........................5

5a VHW with all marginal spots having at least some orange; DHW with first marginal spot (in cell $Sc+R_1$) with at least a trace of orange 6

5b Marginal spots without orange. Fig. 45.........................
................Papilio rutulus Lucas. Western Tiger Swallowtail.

Range: British Columbia to California and
Arizona, eastward to New Mexico and Colorado. Food plants: *Salix* (willows), *Populus*
(aspen, cottonwood), *Platanus* (sycamore), *Al-*
nus (alder), *Prunus*, *Liriodendron* (tulip-tree),
Persea (red bay), etc.

Fig. 45. *Papilio rutulus* ♂
V. Denver, Colorado.

6a FW with second black band from end of cell rarely found in cell
Cu₂; HW with submarginal spot in cell Sc+R₁ always present;
VHW with distal side of light spot in end of cell not straight but
3-sided and spot not twice as long as wide. Figs. 46, 47.........
..............Papilio glaucus Linnaeus. Eastern Tiger Swallowtail.

Range: Florida to the Hudsonian Zone of Canada, west
to Texas, easternmost Colo-
rada, Montana, Alberta and
Alaska. Food plants: *Prunus*
(wild cherry), *Betula* (birch),
Sorbus (mountain-ash), *Popu-*
lus (poplar), *Liriodendron* (tu-
lip tree), *Fraxinus* (ash), *Salix*
(willow), *Tilia* (basswood),
etc.

Fig. 46. *Papilio glaucus* ♂
V. Barberton, Ohio.

Fig. 47. *Papilio glaucus* ♀
(dark form) D. Lawrence,
Kansas.

6b FW with second black band from end of cell continuing into cell
CU₂; HW with submarginal spot in cell Sc+R₁ absent or barely
visible; VHW with distal side of light spot in end of cell essentially
straight and spot at least twice as long as wide...............
.....................Papilio eurymedon Lucas. See couplet 4a.

7a Submarginal spots lacking; HW with postmedian red spots. Anchisiades group. Fig. 48.................*Papilio anchisiades* Esper.

Range: southern Brazil to Mexico and southern Texas. Food plant: *Citrus*.

Fig. 48. *Papilio anchisiades*
♂ D. No data.

7b Submarginal spots present; HW without postmedian red spots....8

8a VFW without light yellow bar at end of cell...................19

8b VFW with light yellow bar at end of cell.......Machaon group 9
(Note: the status of the various "species" in the Machaon group has long been in doubt. It is expected that genetic work now in progress will solve many of the problems. Rather than make arbitrary decisions, the most prominent named forms are keyed out below without regard for their possible specific affinities.)

9a VHW with three submarginal spots anterior to tail containing some orange (if slight, found in middle of spot)....................10

9b VHW with no orange in the three submarginal spots anterior to the tail (in a few cases a very small amount along basal edge of spot).13

10a DHW with cell all yellow except for small amount of black at base; HW anal spot with round black center. Fig. 49.................
....*Papilio zelicaon* Lucas.

Range: British Columbia and Alberta south to California, Arizona and New Mexico. Food plants: various Umbelliferae including *Pimpinella, Daucus, Petroselinum, Foeniculum* and *Carum*.

Fig. 49. *Papilio zelicaon* ♂ D. Wallowa Lake, Oregon.

10b DHW cell all black, or only distal tip yellow; HW anal spot variable 11

11a DFW with postmedian spots longer than those on DHW (compare spot in cell Cu₁ of DFW with spot in cell CU₁ of DHW); DFW with yellow bar at end of cell; DHW usually without small yellow spot at end of cell; females similar to males......................12

11b DFW with postmedian spots shorter than those on DHW (compare spot in cell Cu₁ of DFW with spot in cell Cu₁ of DHW); DFW usually without yellow bar at end of cell; DHW usually with small yellow spot at end of cell; females usually lack most of the postmedian yellow spots, especially those caudal to Cu₁ of DFW, and have the blue on DHW greatly increased. Fig. 50................
................*Papilio polyxenes* Fabricius. Black Swallowtail.

Range: southern Canada to northern South America; in North America generally east of the Rock Mountains. This is the only Machaon group swallowtail found in the eastern United States. Food plants: a great variety of Umbelliferae.

Fig. 50. *Papilio polyxenes* ♂ V. Streator, Illinois.

12a VHW with submarginal spots anterior to tail strongly orange; eastern Canada. Fig. 51................*Papilio brevicauda* Saunders.

Range: lower St. Lawrence area, Maritime Provinces, Newfoundland and southern Labrador. Food plant: *Ligusticum scothicum* (Scotch lovage), perhaps *Coelopleurum.*

Fig. 51. *Papilio brevicauda* ♀ D. Doyles Station, Newfoundland.

12b VHW with submarginal spots anterior to tail with orange scaling very faint or only present as a few scattered scales in the center and at the basal edge of spots; Riding Mountains of Manitoba....
....*Papilio kahli* Chermock.
This population may be related to *P. brevicauda* or *P. polyxenes.* Food plant: *Pastinaca sativa.*

13a Palpus black; light markings yellowish white (very pale); tails often very short, but 3 to 5 times as long as wide in specimens from southern California, Arizona and vicinity; D light band may be greatly reduced or absent in specimens from Arizona and western Colorado, or greatly expanded in southern California desert populations. Fig. 52...............*Papilio indra* Reakirt.

Range: Washington to southern California, eastward to Wyoming, Colorado, and Arizona. Food plant: *Velaea parishii, Artemisia dracunculoides, Cymopterus panamintensis.*

Fig. 52. *Papilio indra*
♂D. No data.

13b Palpus not black; light markings light yellow.................14

14a DHW cell entirely black or with only distal portion yellow; postmedian yellow bands of both wings approximately the same width 15

14b DHW cell yellow, with just a small amount of black at the base; postmedian yellow band of HW greatly expanded, especially into basal area 16

15a VHW with all postmedian spots having at least some orange; DHW with black center of anal spot connected to black anal margin. Fig. 53............................*Papilio bairdii* Edwards.

Range: Arizona, southern California, New Mexico, Utah, and Colorado. Food plant: *Artemisia species.*

Fig. 53. *Papilio bairdii*
♂ V. Arizona.

15b VHW with orange in postmedian spots restricted to those in cells
M₂ and M₃; DHW with black center of anal spot either connected
to black anal margin or "free." Fig. 54.....*Papilio nitra* Edwards.

Range: Montana and Alberta. A few *P. kahli*
will key out here; these may be separated by
locality (see couplet 12b.).

Fig. 54. *Papilio nitra*
♂ D. Judith Moun-
tains, Montana.

16a Distal margins of dark basal areas of DFW and DHW contiguous
(in spread specimens), making an oblique line towards the body.
DHW postmedian blue spots usually limited to cells M₃, Cu₁ and
Cu₂. DHW black postmedian band almost as wide as yellow
median band. DFW yellow bar at distal end of cell very narrow,
about 1 mm. wide. Fig. 55............*Papilio rudkini* Comstock.

Range: southern California and western Arizona.
Food plant: *Thamnosma montana* (turpentine
broom).

Fig. 55. *Papilio
rudkini* ♂ D.
Ibanpah Moun-
tains, California.

16b Distal margin of dark basal area of DFW very distad (in spread
specimens) of the dark basal area of DHW; DFW dark area covers
almost half of inner margin, while DHW dark area covers only
basal one-eight of costal margin. DHW postmedian blue spots
usually found in all postmedian cells, may be lacking in cell
Sc-R₁. DHW black postmedian band about 1/3 as wide as yellow
median band. DFW yellow bar at distal end of cell narrow, about
2 mm. wide...17

17a DHW with black center of anal spot connected to black anal margin, or almost connected to margin..........................18

17b DHW with black center of anal spot not connected to black anal
margin ("free")..........*Papilio zelicaon* Lucas. See couplet 10a.

18a DHW with black of anal spot not clubbed, distal to red; tails 2 to 3 times as long as wide. Fig. 56.....*Papilio machaon* Linnaeus.

Range: widespread in Palaearctic region; Alaska and Yukon southeastward to Alberta, eastward to southern Hudson Bay, James Bay, and parts of more southern Manitoba and Ontario. Found primarily in Hudsonian and Canadian Zones. Food plants: various Umbelliferae, also reported on *Artemisia arctica*.

Fig. 56. *Papilio machaon* ♂ D. Eagle Summit, Alaska.

18b DHW with black anal spot having a slight swollen club at end away from anal margin, usually with some orange-red distal to spot, tails about 4 times as long as wide. Fig. 57.............
......................................*Papilio oregonius* Edwards.

Range: Oregon, Washington, and southern British Columbia to Idaho, Montana, Wyoming, southern Nebraska, and Colorado, generally in dry areas. Food plant: *Artemisia dracunculoides*.

Fig. 57. *Papilio oregonius* ♂ DHW. Brewster, Washington.

19a Underside of abdomen yellow (or if black, with yellow markings in pleural areas, especially near spiracles); usually with a diagonal row of yellow spots crossing both wings from apex to anal margin, but some females almost solid black.............*Thoas* group 20

19b Underside of abdomen with black and yellow stripes (or if black, with a row of yellow spots on the dorso-lateral areas of tergites); wings without a diagonal row of spots.......................
......................................*Troilus* group (in part) 28

46

20a DFW without marginal or submarginal spots; a wide, solid, yellow band crosses both wings; DFW with one yellow bar near distal end of cell. Fig. 58...........*Papilio andraemon* Hübner

Range: Greater Antilles and Bahamas, some *dubious* Florida records. Food plant: *Citrus* species and *Ruta graveolens*.

Fig. 58. *Papilio andraemon* ♂ D. No data.

20b DFW with marginal and/or submarginal spots; DFW usually with a diagonal row of yellow spots; some females almost solid black 21

21a D with a diagonal row of yellow spots from apex of FW to anal margin of HW...22

21b D without diagonal row of yellow spots......................26

22a VHW with red or orange basad of each light blue spot in median area. Tails all black, or only vein with light scales............23

22b VHW with red or orange basad of only two light blue spots in median area, those in cells M_2 and M_3. Tails usually with light centers 25

23a VHW with red-brown irregular band between distal end of cell and blue postmedian band (may be absent or limited to area just distal to cell); VHW with lighter areas cream yellow, sometimes with some orange or brownish overscaling; DFW with postmedian spot in cell R_5 in the form of a double-headed comma. Fig. 59........*Papilio aristodemus* Esper.

Range: Florida Keys, Cuba, Hispañiola, Puerto Rico. Food plant: *Amyris elemifera* (torchwood).

Fig. 59. *Papilio aristodemus* ♂ V. No data.

23b VHW with red postmedian band basally edged with orange (may or may not form a continuous band); VHW with lighter areas whitish cream yellow; DFW with postmedian spot in cell R_5 not in the form of a double-headed comma (may have dark center)..24

24a Male DFW with small spot in postmedian position of cell above lower edge; DFW with diagonal band broader than black postmedian area. Fig. 60..................*Papilio astyalus* Godart.

Fig. 60. *Papilio astyalus* ♂ DFW. Victoria, Mexico.

Range: southern Texas to South America. Food plant: *Citrus*. This species used to be known as *P. lycophron* Hübner. There is striking sexual dimorphism. The females

Fig. 61. *Papilio astyalus* ♀ DHW. No data.

(Fig. 61) either have a tail similar to that of the males, or a slight elongation at each vein giving the HW a scalloped edge. They have several rows of colored spots on the HW (whitish-yellow, orange and green or light blue).

24b Male DFW cell without spots; DFW with diagonal band approximately as broad as black postmedian area, or narrower. Figs. 62, 63.............................*Papilio ornythion* Boisduval.

Fig. 62. *Papilio ornythion* ♂ DFW, Mexico.

Range: southern Texas to South America. Food plant: *Citrus*. Females either similar to males except colors duller, or the light markings may be very faint.

Fig. 63. *Papilio ornythion* ♂ VHW, Mexico.

25a DFW with postmedian spot in cell M₂ longer than spot in cell M₃; DFW usually with only three submarginal spots (outside of diagonal band); DFW with postmedian spots in cells M₃ and Cu₁ roughly spheroid (usually); on spread specimens the diagonal band is much narrower on inner margin of DFW than on costal margin of DHW. Fig. 64....*Papilio cresphontes* Cramer. Giant Swallowtail.

Range: Canada to Costa Rica, rare in northern areas. Food plants: *Citrus*, *Dictamnus* (gas plant), *Zanthoxylum* (prickly ash), *Ptelea* (hop tree).

This is our largest butterfly species.

Fig. 64. *Papilio cresphontes* ♀ V. Overland, Missouri.

25b DFW with postmedian spot in cell M₂ approximately equal to spot in cell M₃; DFW usually with four submarginal spots (outside of diagonal band); DFW with postmedian spots in cells M₃ and Cu₁ usually nearly rectangular; on spread specimens the diagonal band is not much narrower on inner margin of DFW than on costal margin of DHW. Fig. 65......... ....*Papilio thoas* Linnaeus.

Range: southern Texas to Argentina, also reported from Florida. Food plant: *Citrus*.

Fig. 65. *Papilio thoas* ♂ V. Mexico.

26a Tail-less; female. (See Fig. 61)..........*Papilio astyalus* Godart. See couplet 24a.

26b Tailed **27**

27a DHW with submarginal spots distinct; DHW may have a row of small orange spots in between the veins in the postmedian area (beyond the cell); female..............*Papilio astyalus* Godart. See couplet 24a.

27b DHW with submarginal spots indistinct, heavily overcast with brown; female. Fig. 66..........*Papilio ornythion* Boisduval. See couplet 24b.

Fig. 66. *Papilio ornythion* ♀ DHW. Victoria, Mexico.

28a D spots yellow; DFW with yellow bar in cell; DHW crossed by a yellow band; DHW with no red-orange spot in postmedian area of costal margin. Fig. 67..............*Papilio palamedes* Drury.

Range: Pennsylvania and New Jersey (rare) south on coastal plain to Florida; Gulf States west to east Texas; Mississippi Valley (recorded as far north as Missouri, but very rare in this area); Nuevo Leon, Mexico. Food plants: *Magnolia, Persea* (red bay), *Sassafras*.

Fig. 67. *Papilio palamedes* ♂ V. Florida.

28b D spots cream colored, bluish, and light green; DFW without bar in cell; DHW not crossed by yellow band; DHW with red-orange spot in postmedian area of costal margin. Fig. 68..............
................*Papilio troilus* Linnaeus. Spicebush Swallowtail.

Range: Eastern United States and southern Canada west to eastern Texas, eastern Kansas, Manitoba. Food plants: *Benzoin* (spicebush), *Sassafras, Magnolia* (sweet bay), *Zanthoxylum* (prickly ash), etc.

Fig. 68. *Papilio troilus* ♂ V. Otterville, Missouri.

Family PIERIDAE
Whites and Sulphurs

This is a family of generally small to medium-sized butterflies closely related to the Papilionidae. The prothoracic legs are fully developed in both sexes, but lack the tibial epiphysis characteristic of the papilionids. The tarsal claws are bifid. This is the only butterfly family in which the prespiracular bar at the base of the abdomen is absent.

The larvae (Fig. 69) are slender, smooth, cylindrical, and usually green with longitudinal stripes. Osmateria and fleshy filaments are lacking. The crochets on the prolegs are arranged in a single row.

Fig. 69. Larva of *Phoebis sennae* (after Scudder).

The pupae (Fig. 70) are girdled, as in the Papilionidae, and often have the wing cases greatly developed forming a prominent arched keel. There is a single conical projection on the head (except in *Nathalis*), which is often very long.

The adults are mostly orange, yellow or white, with dark marginal markings. Many species are fond of congregating in "mud puddle aggregations." Others, such as *Phoebis sennae* and *Ascia monuste* are strong migrants. The family is cosmopolitan.

Fig. 70. Pupa of *Phoebis sennae* (after Scudder).

KEY TO THE SUBFAMILIES OF THE PIERIDAE.

1a FW with M_2 arising from end of discal cell; HW with $Sc+R_1$ not secondarily fused with Rs; HW with M_2 arising from discal cell...2

1b FW with M_2 stalked with R_{3+4+5}; HW with $Sc+R_1$ secondarily fused with Rs before middle of wing; HW with M_2 stalked with M_1; one species from West Equatorial Africa.....Pseudopontiinae

2a FW with 3 to 5 radials present, at least one arising from the cell; FW with cubitus appearing trifid (Fig. 71).....3

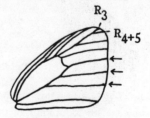

Fig. 71. Venation of *Ascia* (arrows indicate branches of "trifid cubitus").

2b FW with 5 radials present, all stalked; FW with cubitus appearing quadrifid (Fig. 72) ....Dismorphiinae p. 52

Fig. 72. Venation of *Dismorphia* (arrows indicate branches of "quadrifid cubitus").

3a Patagia unsclerotized; HW with humeral vein usually long; male genitalia with tegumen longer than uncus; ground color usually white...Pierinae p. 70

3b Patagia sclerotized; HW with humeral vein usually greatly reduced or absent; male genitalia with tegumen usually considerably shorter than uncus; ground color yellow, orange or white..Coliadinae p. 52

Subfamily DISMORPHIINAE

One representative of this subfamily has been recorded vaguely from the United States. The group is primarily Neotropical, but there is one small Palaearctic genus.

Genus ENANTIA Hübner

One species, *E. melite* Johansson (Figs. 73, 74), which is common in Mexico may occasionally stray across our southern border.

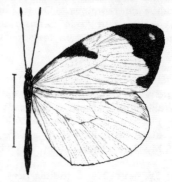

Fig. 73. *Enantia melite* ♂ D. No data.

Fig. 74. *Enantia melite* ♀ D. No data.

Subfamily COLIADINAE
The Sulphurs

This is a cosmopolitan subfamily, reaching its greatest variety in the tropics. The foodplants of the larvae are generally legumes. Most species are predominantly yellow, orange and white, with dark gray or black markings (often restricted largely to the marginal areas of the wings). In many species there is pronounced sexual dimorphism, with the ground color of the males yellow, and that of the females white.

KEY TO THE GENERA OF COLIADINAE.

1a FW with radius 3-branched; pupa with no frontal projection. . . .
. . . . *Nathalis* p. 53

1b FW with radius 4-branched; pupa with distinct frontal projection. . 2

2a Pretarsus with well-developed arolium and pulvillus; FW with R_2 arising from discal cell 3

2b Pretarsus with arolium and pulvillus absent; FW with R_2 often stalked on $R_3 + R_{4+5}$ . . . . *Colias* p. 53

3a LFW not over 28 mm. 4

3b LFW over 30 mm. 5

4a HW with udc longer than mdc; HW with outer margin rounded. . .
. . . . *Kricogonia* p. 63

4b HW with udc shorter than mdc, or HW angulate or with a sharp tail between M_3 and Cu_1 . . . . *Eurema* p. 63

5a HW with a sharp tail at end of M_3; FW with apex strongly acute. .
. . . . *Anteos* p. 67

5b HW without sharp tail at end of M_3; FW with apex not strongly acute. . . . . *Phoebis* p. 68

Genus NATHALIS Boisduval

This American genus of three species contains the smallest North American pierid. Only one species, *N. iole* Boisduval (Fig. 75) occurs in our area. Range: entire southern United States from California to Florida, north to the Great Lakes. Not found on the Atlantic coastal plain north of Georgia. Food plants: various marigolds (*Dyssodia, Bidens, Tagetes*), chickweed (*Stellaria*), sneezeweed (*Helenium*), storksbill (*Erodium*).

Fig. 75. *Nathalis iole* ♂ V. Oak Creek Canyon, Arizona.

Genus COLIAS Fabricius
Sulphurs and Dog Faces
by Alexander B. Klots

This is a very widespread genus, chiefly of the Northern Hemisphere, but with a group of species in South America. Some species occur only in the far arctic, others southward only in mountainous regions. The males are mostly yellow, orange or greenish with dark borders. In most of the species there are two genetically controlled forms of females, one essentially concolorous with the males, the other with the ground color white. The dark marginal borders of females are usually much narrower than those of the males, penetrated by spots of ground color, or absent.

There is considerable confusion about the status of many of the so-called "species." Some of these have not yet evolved clear-cut characteristics by means of which they can be differentiated from each other, and instead are characterized by overlapping combinations of minor and variable features. As a result it is frequently impossible to name individual specimens or even small series. Very likely some of what we now call "species" are really complexes of populations which might themselves qualify as "species" in the genetic sense. The problem is made much more difficult by great amounts of local, seasonal and individual variation, and by the occurence of considerable hybridization between "species" (e.g., *C. eurytheme* and *C. philodice*).

Three chief types of food plant preference are found, some complexes feeding on legumes (Fabaceae), others on willows (*Salix*), and still others on blueberry, bilberry or huckleberry *(Vaccinium);* but of course one cannot tell what was the food plant of an unknown flown specimen!

The following key uses chiefly characters common to both sexes, but in general males are more easily identified than females, the latter being best determined by association (date, environment and habits) with males. At best there will always, especially in the Northwest, be a considerable residue of unidentifiable specimens.

KEY TO THE SPECIES OF *COLIAS.*

1a FW apex more or less rounded, never falcate; males with inner margin of DFW border evenly curved—subgenus *Colias*........2

1b FW apex falcate; males (and some females) with inner margin of DFW border sharply sculptured forming the outline of a dog's face (the spot at the end of the discal cell being the eye)—subgenus **Zerene** 20

2a Male (and non-white female) D ground color yellow (may be pale) 3

2b Male (and non-white female) D ground color not yellow........14

3a DFW male almost always with light spots in dark border; VHW with dark rim of discal spot more or less smeared distally; subarctic and arctic. Fig. 76....................
............*Colias nastes* Boisduval.
See couplet 15b.

Fig. 76. *Colias nastes* ♂ D. Churchill, Manitoba.

3b DFW male without light spots in dark border; **VHW** with dark margin of discal spot seldom smeared distally.................4

4a V heavily clouded with dark scales, especially on **HW** and apical part of **FW**...5

4b V with little if any clouding of dark scales on **HW** and apical part of **FW**...11

5a VHW discal spot not ringed with pink or red...................6

5b VHW discal spot ringed with pink or red......................7

6a Male DHW with yellow ground color paler basally, flushed with orange-yellow distally along inner edge of marginal border. Fig. 77.....................................*Colias alexandra* Edwards.

Range: western North America, southern British Columbia and Manitoba south to California (rare), Arizona and New Mexico, Nebraska and Black Hills of South Dakota. Primarily in open areas in lower Canadian and Transition zones. Food plants: various legumes, including *Astragalus* (locoweeds), *Medicago* (alfalfa), etc. Includes both yellow, orange and intermediate populations, one of which has long been considered a separate species, *C. christina* Edwards. (see couplets 13a and 19a).

Fig. 77. *Colias alexandra* ♂ D. Banff, Alberta.

6b Male DHW not flushed with orange-yellow distally, yellow ground color paler only at extreme base and anal margin, if at all. Fig. 78.....................................*Colias palaeno* Linnaeus.

Range: Behring Sea east to southern Baffin Island and Labrador, south to northern Alberta and Manitoba (Churchill). Many European specimens have been sold, erroneously labelled "Labrador." Food plants: *Vaccinium* (bilberry), etc. Some far northern specimens show an indistinct darker rim around the VHW discal spot which might cause confusion in couplet 5.

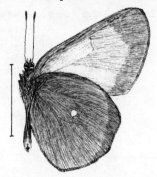

Fig. 78. *Colias palaeno* ♂ V. Labrador.

7a V with at least some dark submarginal spots, usually 3 on FW and 4 or 5 on HW **8**

7b V with no submarginal dark spots or with slight traces of one or two **10**

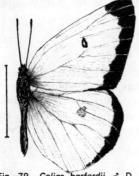

8a D warm, somewhat orange yellow, with very little dark dusting at bases of wings; California only. Fig. 79.. ....Colias harfordii Henry Edwards. See couplet 12a.

Fig. 79. *Colias harfordii* ♂ D. Pasadena, California.

8b D colder, more lemon-yellow (some specimens show discal orange flushes or patches); considerable dark dusting at bases of wings...9

9a VHW discal spot well-silvered, typically surrounded by two concentric, thin, pink or red rings more or less distinct from each other, and seldomed broadened, diffuse or elongated parallel to the basaldistal axis of the wing; discal spot usually with a small, well-defined, often ringed satellite spot. Fig. 80........................ ....Colias philodice Godart. Clouded Sulphur.

Fig. 80. *Colias philodice* ♀ D. Montreal, Quebec.

Range: Alaska west to Newfoundland in the subarctic, south throughout the United States (rare and spasmodic in the southern parts of its range). A population is also found in Guatemala. Food plants: preferably *Trifolium* (clovers), also *Medicago* (alfalfa), *Astragalus* (locoweeds) and other legumes. This species at present hybidizes to a considerable extent with C. eurytheme Boisduval, which has recently extended its range far northward. The hybrids have been shown to be less viable than the parental types, and it is presumed that natural selection will gradually remove from both species the tendency to hybridize.

9b VHW discal spot often pearly but seldom well-silvered, usually single, surrounded by a solid, pink or red border that is usually wide and more or less diffuse and often somewhat elongated parallel to the basal-distal axis of the wing. Fig. 81..
Colias occidentalis Scudder.

Range: Pacific Northwest, British Columbia to northern California. Food plants: probably legumes (Fabaceae).

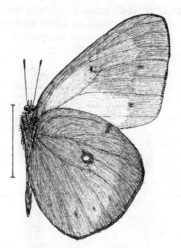

Fig. 81. *Colias occidentalis* ♂ V. Humboldt Co., California.

10a LFW 19-26 mm.; D usually with extensive dark basal dusting, especially in anal area of HW; VHW discal spot often small, circular, with inconspicuous pearly center; VFW often with heavy discal dark clouding (almost always present in specimens from Alberta and British Columbia to western Wyoming). Fig. 82...........
.......................*Colias pelidne* Boisduval and Leconte.

Range: Labrador; northern British Columbia south in Rocky Mountains to Utah and northern New Mexico.

Food plants: *Salix* (willow), perhaps also *Vaccinium* (blueberry). Included here is *C. scudderii* Reakirt which may, however, be a distinct species or conspecific with *C. gigantea* Strecker.

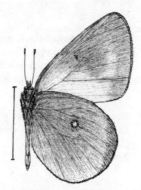

Fig. 82. *Colias pelidne* ♂ V. Ptarmigan Mountain, Alberta.

10b LFW 24-31 mm.; D usually with little dark basal dusting, especially in anal area of HW; VHW discal spot usually large and prominent with conspicuous pearly center; VFW never with heavy discal dark clouding. Fig. 83 .... *Colias gigantea* Strecker.

Range: subarctic Alaska to Manitoba (Churchill) south through Alberta to western Wyoming; British Columbia and Oregon. Southward in bogs. Food plant: *Salix* (willow), at Churchill *S. reticulata*.

Fig. 83. *Colias gigantea* ♂ D.
Riding Mountains, Manitoba.

11a V with at least some dark submarginal spots, usually 3 on FW and 4 or 5 on HW 12

11b V with no submarginal dark spots, or with slight traces of one or two 13

12a D warm, somewhat orange yellow, with very little dark dusting at bases of wings. (See Fig. 79.) ... *Colias harfordii* Henry Edwards. Range: central and southern California, chiefly in mountain meadows. Food plant: *Astragalus* (rattleweed).

12b D colder, more lemon yellow (some specimens show discal orange flushes or patches); considerable dark dusting at bases of wings. (See Fig. 80) .... *Colias philodice* Godart. See couplet 9a.

13a Male DHW with yellow ground color paler basally, flushed with more orange yellow distally along inner edge of marginal border; fringes not broadly and wholly pink. (See Fig. 77.) .... *Colias alexandra* Edwards. See couplet 6a.

58

13b Male DHW not distally flushed with orange-yellow, paler yellow only at extreme base, if at all; fringes broadly, often (especially V) wholly pink. Fig. 84................*Colias interior* **Scudder**

Range: British Columbia to Quebec and Newfoundland, south to Oregon, northern Idaho, Montana, Michigan, New York and New England in Canadian Zone; also, in isolated colonies, south in the mountains to Virginia. Food plant: *Vaccinium* (blueberry).

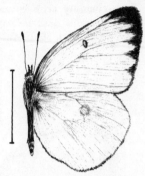

Fig. 84. *Colias interior* ♀ D. Peremouche, New Brunswick.

14a D dark green or greenish yellow...........................15
14b D orange or yellow with prominent orange areas.............16
15a D very dark, dull green; male DFW without light spots in dark border; DHW with prominent whitish discal spot; VHW with no prominent pink or reddish brown around discal spot; Sierra Nevada of California only. Fig. 85................*Colias behrii* **Edwards.**

Range: alpine meadows of Sierra Nevada of California. Food plants: *Vaccinium caespitosum* (dwarf bilberry) and *Gentiana newberryi.*

Fig. 85. *Colias behrii* ♂ D. Yosemite National Park, California.

15b D light green, gray-green to greenish-yellow; male DFW usually with light spots in dark border; DHW with light discal spot rarely prominent; VHW with prominent pink, red or reddish brown ring around discal spot, often smeared and elongated distally; an extremely variable arctic and subarctic species. (See Fig. 76.)......
....*Colias nastes* **Boisduval**
Range: circumpolar; American Arctic, going north to southern islands of the Arctic Archipelago and south in the Alpine Zone to southern British Columbia and Alberta, flying over dry tundra ridges. Food plants: *Astragalus alpinus, Hedysarum* sp., and other Fabaceae.

16a VHW discal spot well-silvered, typically surrounded by two concentric, thin, pink or red rings more or less distinct from each other, and seldom broadened, diffuse or elongated parallel to the wing axis; usually with a small, well-defined satellite spot; V almost always with dark submarginal spots, usually 3 on FW and 4 or 5 on HW. Fig. 86....*Colias eurytheme* Boisduval. Alfalfa Butterfly.

Range: southern Canada, entire United States and northern Mexico. Rare in northern and extreme southern parts of range; usually abundant elsewhere. Food plants: *Medicago sativa* (alfalfa) on which it is an economic pest, less frequently other legumes. Hybridizes with *C. philodice* (see couplet 9a).

Fig. 86. *Colias eurytheme* ♂ V. Lawrence, Kansas.

16b VHW discal spot seldom strongly silvered, typically surrounded by a single, pink or red, often more or less smeared or diffuse, ring; often without a well-defined white-centered satellite spot; V with only a few and faint submarginal dark spots, if any......17

17a Male D ground color a uniform, deep orange with little or no yellow; female with DHW very heavily dark-clouded with contrasty yellow or orange discal spot...............................18

17b Not so marked...19

18a Male DHW with sex patch at base of costal margin (in spread specimens often hidden under base of FW); Alpine Zone, Rocky Mountains. Fig. 87......................*Colias meadii* Edwards.

Range: Hudsonian and Alpine Zones of Rocky Mountains, Alberta to Colorado. Food plants: *Astragalus* and other alpine Fabaceae.

Fig. 87. *Colias meadii* ♂ D. Hall Valley, Colorado.

18b Male DHW without sex patch at base of costal margin; principally arctic. Fig. 88..............................*Colias hecla* Lefebre.

Range: circumpolar, American Arctic from northern limit of land (Greenland, Ellesmere Island) southward to Labrador, Churchill, Manitoba, and (an isolated colony) Rocky Mountain piedmont west of Red Deer, Alberta (3-4000 feet). Food plant: *Astragalus alpinus* and perhaps arctic willow (*Salix*).

Fig. 88. *Colias hecla* ♂ D. Disco Island, Greenland.

19a Male with D dark border extremely irregular basally or very narrow (less than one-sixth LFW at widest); VHW with discal spot heavily dark rimmed and considerably lengthened parallel to basal-distal axis of wing; arctic. Fig. 89.. .....*Colias boothii* Curtis.

Range: far arctic America. Recent evidence almost certainly disproves the formerly accepted theory that *boothii* specimens are hybrids between *C. hecla* and *C. nastes*.

Fig. 89. *Colias boothii* ♂ D. Southampton Island, Northwest Territories.

19b Male with D dark border regular basally and at its widest at least one-sixth of LFW; VHW with discal spot narrowly rimmed with light pink, inconspicuous and never lengthened parallel to basal-distal axis of wing; southern Canada southward............... ....*Colias alexandra* Edwards. See couplet 6a.

20a DHW usually without dark margining in both sexes; DFW of female normally nearly immaculate except for discal spot (rarely with gray or brownish limbal clouding); male DFW with "eye" of dog face often contiguous or nearly contiguous with dark border. Fig. 90..............................*Colias eurydice* Boisduval.

Range: California south into Mexico, rarely straying eastward. Food plant: *Amorpha californica* (false indigo or lead plant).

Fig. 90. *Colias eurydice* ♂ D. California.

20b DHW with dark margining in both sexes; DFW of female with wide dark border similar to that of male; male DFW with "eye" of dog face always well-separated from dark border. Fig. 91....
....*Colias cesonia* Stoll.

Range: New York, Wisconsin, Minnesota and Nebraska (rare) south to Central America. Quite common in southern United States. Food plants: *Amorpha* (false indigo) *Parosela* and *Trifolium* (clover).

Fig. 91. *Colias cesonia* ♀ D. Lakeland, Florida.

Genus KRICOGONIA Reakirt

There are two species in the genus *Kricogonia*, *cabrerai* Ramsden and *castalia* Fabricius (Fig. 92). The latter ranges from South America to southern Florida (infrequent) and Texas (where it is common). It strays northward to Colorado, Kansas, Nebraska, Illinois, etc. *Cabrerai* has not been recorded from our area, although it is found in Cuba. Our form of *castalia* has long gone under the name of *lyside* Godart.

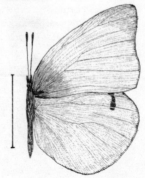

Fig. 92. *Kricogonia castalia* ♂
D. Laredo, Mexico.

Genus EUREMA Hübner
The Small Sulphurs

A very diverse, tropical group of small yellow, orange or white butterflies with dark bordered wings. The various species of *Eurema* are often difficult to determine correctly. Extreme sexual dimorphism and distinctive-looking seasonal forms add to the difficulties of making a workable key.

KEY TO THE SPECIES OF *EUREMA*.

1a HW with outer margin tailed or angulate......................2

1b HW with outer margin rounded...............................5

2a D ground color orange. Fig. 93........*Eurema proterpia* Fabricius.

Range: southern Texas west to southern Arizona, south to Colombia, Venezuela and Peru. The spring form has been considered a separate species, *E. gundlachia* Poey.

Fig. 93. *Eurema proterpia* ♂
D. South America.

2b D ground color not orange....................................3

3a D ground color yellow..4

3b D ground color white (some yellow in anterior part of HW). Fig. 94..................................*Eurema mexicana* Boisduval.

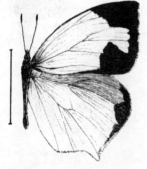

Range: South and Central America, Arizona, New Mexico, Texas, straying northward to Colorado, Wyoming, Nebraska and even Ontario. Food plants: *Cassia* (senna) in tropics, perhaps *Astragalus* in Colorado.

Fig. 94. *Eurema mexicana* ♂ D. Colorado.

4a Male DHW with border even, not sharply produced basad toward end of cell; female lacking dark border on HW. Fig. 95.........
....*Eurema salome* Felder.

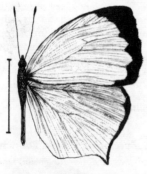

Range: Colombia, Venezuela, north to southern Arizona.

Fig. 95. *Eurema salome* ♂ D. New Mexico (?).

4b Male DHW with border sharply produced basad to end of cell; female with small dark border at apex of HW. Fig. 96...........
..................................*Eurema boisduvaliana* Felder.

Range: Central America, Cuba, southern Florida (v-vi) and perhaps southern Texas.

Fig. 96. *Eurema boisduvaliana* ♂ D. Jalisco, Mexico.

5a DFW with orange ground color. Fig. 97....*Eurema nicippe* Cramer.

Range: Brazil to New England, common in southern, rare in northern United States. Food plants: *Cassia* (senna) and white clover (in laboratory).

Fig. 97. *Eurema nicippe* ♂ D. Douglas County, Kansas.

5b DFW with ground color not orange...........................6

6a DFW of males (and some females) with black or dark gray bar just above and parallel to the inner margin (females which lack bar are best determined by comparison of V with males taken at same time and place). Fig. 98.........*Eurema daira* Latreille.

Range: Uruguay to southeastern United States and Texas. Food plants: various legumes. The pale summer form of this species has long been known as *E. jucunda* Boisduval and Leconte. A form occasionally taken in Florida which has a white HW is known as *E. palmira* Poey. It is also apparently conspecific with *daira*.

Fig. 98. *Eurema daira* ♂D. Greenville, South Carolina.

6b DFW without dark bar just above and parallel to the inner margin 7

7a D ground color white..8

7b D ground color not white...9

8a DFW with dark line at end of cell (sometimes faint in females). Fig. 99.......................*Eurema lisa* Boisduval and Leconte.

Range: Central America to New England, west to Rocky Mountains. Common in most of range, rare at northern and western fringe. Food plants: a wide variety of legumes.

Fig. 99. *Eurema lisa* ♂ D. Donna, Texas.

8b DFW with no markings at end of cell. Fig. 100................
...................................*Eurema messalina* Fabricius.

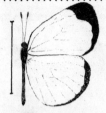

Range: Cuba, Jamaica, Bahamas. United
States records are of doubtful authenticity.
Food plants: *Desmodium* spp. (tick trefoil,
tick clover, beggar's ticks).

Fig. 100. *Eurema mes-
salina* ♂ D. No
data.

9a DFW with a dark mark at end of cell..........................10
9b DFW without a dark mark at end of cell.......................11
**10a HW with mdc straight, nearly continuous in a straight line with
M₂; HW border widest at ends of veins M₂ and M₃; females**....
.......................*Eurema nicippe* Cramer. See couplet 5a.
**10b HW with mdc decidedly curved, forming an angle of about 30°
with M₂; HW border widest at end of vein M₁**...............
............*Eurema lisa* Boisduval and Leconte. See couplet 8a.
11a D ground color pure yellow (no orange suffusion). Fig. 101.....
....*Eurema nise* Cramer.

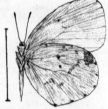

Range: tropical America north to southern
Florida and Texas. Food plant: *Mimosa pu-
dica* (sensitive plant).

Fig. 101. *Eurema nise*
♂ V. Donna, Texas.

11b D ground color yellow suffused with orange. Fig. 102.........
....*Eurema dina* Poey.

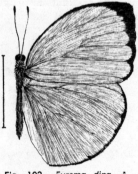

Range: a tropical species, doubtfully
recorded from the southern border of
the United States (Texas, Arizona). Food
plant: *Picramnia pentandra*.

Fig. 102. *Eurema dina* ♂
D. No data.

Genus ANTEOS Hübner
The Mammoth Sulphurs

Our two largest species of pierids belong to this genus.

KEY TO THE SPECIES OF ANTEOS.

1a Male D ground color yellow; female DHW with an orange-yellow
   spot. Fig. 103......................*Anteos maerula* Fabricius.

Range: tropics north to southern
Texas, Florida (occasional), rarely
strays northward (has been recorded
from Nebraska).

Fig. 103. *Anteos maerula* ♂
D. No data.

1b Male D ground color white; female DHW without an orange spot.
   Fig. 104...............................*Anteos clorinde* Godart

Range: southern Texas, Arizona,
southward to South America. Several
stragglers have been taken in Kansas.
Food plant: *Cassia spectabilis.*

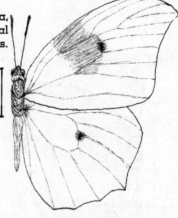

Fig. 104. *Anteos clorinde*
♂ D. No data.

67

Genus PHOEBIS Hübner
The Giant Sulphurs

These are large, fast flying butterflies, with a tendency towards migration. The females generally have more dark markings above than the males.

KEY TO THE SPECIES OF *PHOEBIS*.

1a HW with anal angle forming a short tail. Fig. 105.......
...*Phoebis neocypris* Hübner.

Range: a tropical species, recorded from southern Texas.

Fig. 105. *Phoebis neocypris* ♂ D. Mexico.

1b HW with rounded anal angle.................................2

2a DFW male yellow, with orange bar crossing cell; DHW both sexes yellow basally, orange distally. Fig. 106............
......*Phoebis philea* Linnaeus.

Range: Argentina north to southern Texas, Gulf Coast, Florida, straying farther north (Nebraska). Food plant: *Cassia* (senna).

Fig. 106. *Phoebis philea* ♂ D. Harris County, Texas.

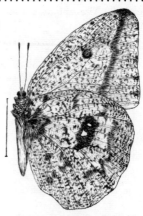

4a VFW with postmedian line nearly straight. Fig. 107.....
...*Phoebis agarithe* Boisduval.

Range: Central America to Gulf States and southeastern Arizona, straying northward (Nebraska).

Fig. 107. *Phoebis agarithe* ♀ V. Burnet County, Texas.

4b VFW with postmedian line zig-zag (irregular)...................
.....................................*Phoebis argante* Fabricius
Range: a tropical species common in Mexico, but only doubtfully occurring in the United States.
5a D male with basal two-thirds of wings yellow, outer third covered with dull "mealy" scales which are somewhat lighter (sometimes almost white); female VFW and VHW with spots at end of cell not prominent, distinctly duplex, or heavily silvered; female V with dark striations usually few and obscure. Fig. 108...............
....*Phoebis statira* Cramer.

Range: American tropics, Florida, southern Texas, rarely straying northward (Colorado). This species belongs to the subgenus *Aphrissa* Butler, which has been given generic stature by some authors.

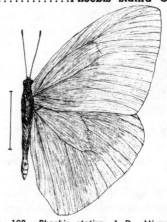

Fig. 108. *Phoebis statira* ♂ D. Miami, Florida.

69

5b D male not so marked; female VFW and VHW with spots at end of cell prominent, distinctly duplex, and heavily silvered; female V with a large number of prominent dark striations. Fig. 109......
....*Phoebis sennae* Linnaeus.

Range: Patagonia to New England, Wisconsin, California. Common in southern United States. Food plants: several species of *Cassia* (senna), other legumes. This species frequently migrates in huge swarms. In the literature it is often referred to as. *P. eubule* Linnaeus.

Fig. 109. *Phoebis sennae* ♀ V. Riverside, California.

Subfamily PIERINAE
The Whites and Orange Tips

This is a cosmopolitan subfamily, which has its greatest development in the tropics. The food plants are mostly crucifers; a number of pierines are pests on cultivated species. The ground color of the majority of our species is white. Sexual dimorphism generally is not as striking as in the Coliadinae.

KEY TO THE GENERA OF PIERINAE.

1a Male genitalia with valva bearing a well-developed process on its inner face (Fig. 110)—tribe Euchloini......2

Fig. 110. Euchloini. Inner face of right valca.

1b Male genitalia with valva unarmed—tribe Pierini...............3

2a DFW male usually with an orange patch at apex; male genitalia with dorsal margin of valva evenly curved, bearing no structures
....*Anthocaris* p. 71

2b DFW male never with an orange patch at apex; male genitalia with dorsal margin of valva bearing a strong pointed flap or tooth near the middle....................................*Euchloe* p. 74

3a FW with R_3 and R_{4+5} very long-stalked, the veins themselves very short (Fig. 110A) 4

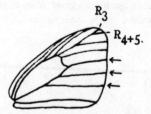

Fig. 110A. Venation of *Ascia* (arrows indicate branches of "trifid cubitus").

3b FW with R_3 and R_{4+5} shorter-stalked, the veins themselves relatively long (Fig. 111) 5

4a FW with 1dc straight or nearly straight . . . . *Pieris* p. 76

4b FW with 1dc curved or angled to at least 160° (Fig. 110A) . . . . *Ascia* p. 78

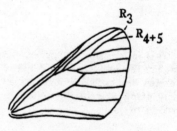

Fig. 111. *Neophasia.*

5a HW with humeral vein bent sharply distad from near its base . . . . *Appias* p. 80

5b HW with humeral vein straight . . . . *Neophasia* p. 80

Genus ANTHOCARIS Boisduval
Orange Tips

These are small, weak-flying butterflies, which are usually on the wing early in the spring.

KEY TO THE SPECIES OF *ANTHOCARIS.*

1a DFW with a distinct dark bar at end of cell which reaches or nearly reaches the costa; FW apex rounded or falcate—subgenus *Anthocaris* 2

1b DFW with a spot (sometimes somewhat elongate) at end of cell, well separated from the costa; FW apex falcate—subgenus *Falcapica* 4

2a Wings strongly suffused with yellow on both surfaces; DFW with dark border of apex rather broad, penetrating well into orange area (orange marking going basad of dark bar at end of cell); Arizona and eastern California. Fig. 112...............................
Anthocaris cethura Felder and Felder.

See couplet 3a.

Fig. 112. *Anthocaris cethura* ♂ V. Tucson, Arizona.

2b Wings usually with white ground color, if suffused with yellow this often restricted to D; DFW with dark border of apex rather narrow, orange marking not going basad of dark bar at end of cell 3

3a VHW suffused with greenish yellow; DFW with apical spot yellow-orange; VHW with mottling tending to fuse into bands. Fig. 113. ....*Anthocaris cethura* Felder and Felder.

Range: Arizona and California (ii-iv). A desert species. Food plants: wild mustards. Specimens from Arizona and eastern California are quite distinctive (see couplet 2a) and have been considered a separate species, *A. pima* Edwards. However, the two forms intergrade completely and are best considered conspecific.

Fig. 113. *Anthocaris cethura* ♂ V. Phelan, California.

3b VHW not suffused with greenish yellow; DFW with apical spot usually orange-red (rarely yellow-orange); VHW with very fine mottling which shows little or no tendency to fuse into bands. Fig. 114.................................Anthocaris sara Boisduval.

Range: Western States from Wyoming, Colorado and New Mexico to the Coast (late v—early vii). Food plant: *Arabis* and other crucifers.

Fig. 114. *Anthocaris sara* ♂
V. Oakland, California.

4a DFW male with orange apex (female white); VHW finely mottled with yellow and brown; east of the Rocky Mountains only. Fig. 115.................................Anthocaris genutia Fabricius.

Range: southern New England to Texas. Very local, in deciduous woods (iii-iv). Food plants: *Sisymbrium* (hedge mustard), *Arabis* (rock cress), *Cardamine* (bitter cress), *Barbarea* (winter cress), and other members of the mustard family.

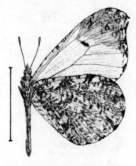

Fig. 115. *Anthocaris genutia*
♂ V. Lawrence, Kansas.

4b DFW both sexes lacking orange; VHW heavily dusted with brown scales; west of Rocky Mountains only. Fig. 116..................
..*Anthocaris lanceolata* Boisduval.

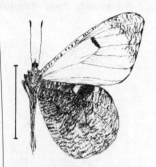

Range: Sierra Nevada (iii-v). Food plants: *Arabis* (rock cress) and other mustards. *Anthocaris dammersi* Comstock is apparently an aberration of this species in which the DFW apex is marked with orange, or a hybrid between this species and *A. sara* Boisduval.

Fig. 116. *Anthocaris lanceolata* ♂ V. California.

Genus EUCHLOE Hübner
Marbles

The species of *Euchloe* are rather closely related to those of *Anthocaris*. They uniformly lack orange tips on the FW. Three species are found in North America, some 10 others in the Old World.

KEY TO THE SPECIES OF *EUCHLOE*.

1a VHW with green marbling in three rather distinct bands, not invading anal angle; DFW with apex barely marked with gray. Fig. 117................................*Euchloe olympia* Edwards.

Range: West Virginia and Pennsylvania to Minnesota and Colorado and south to Texas (iv-v). Food plants: *Sisymbrium* (hedge mustard) and other crucifers.

Fig. 117. *Euchloe olympia* ♂ V. Lawrence, Kansas.

1b VHW with green marbling not in three bands, invading anal angle; DFW with apex well-marked with gray...........................2

2a DFW with bar at end of cell narrow (often more than twice as long as wide); D ground color white to creamy white; VHW with green marbling often penetrated by ground color. Fig. 118............
......................................*Euchloe ausonides* Boisduval.

Range: Manitoba, western Nebraska, Colorado, Arizona, and California north to Alaska (vi-ix). Food plants: *Arabis* (rock cress) and other crucifers.

Fig. 118. *Euchloe ausonides* ♂
D. Las Vegas, New Mexico.

2b DFW with bar at end of cell wide (about twice as long as wide); D ground color pure white; VHW with green marbling solid. Fig. 119.....................*Euchloe creusa* Doubleday and Hewitson.

Range: Colorado (v) north to Alberta and west to California (ii, in deserts) and British Columbia. This species is only doubtfully distinct from *E. ausonides*.

Fig. 119. *Euchloe creusa* ♀ D. Nevada.

Genus PIERIS Schrank
Cabbage Butterflies

This is a cosmopolitan genus. Several species are pests on cultivated crucifers.

KEY TO THE SPECIES OF *PIERIS*.

1a VHW unmarked; DFW with dark gray apex and one (male) or two
(female) dark gray postmedian spots; DHW with a single dark
gray spot on costal margin (dark markings are occasionally absent,
causing possible confusion with *P. napi*, but the brownish scaling
which so often outlines the VHW veins of *napi* is never present).
Fig. 120 ....*Pieris rapae* Linnaeus.
The European Cabbage Butterfly.

Range: found everywhere in North
America south of the Arctic. This
butterfly was accidentally introduced
from Europe in the middle of the
last century. It is of great economic
importance, being a serious pest on
cultivated Cruciferae.

Fig. 120. *Pieris rapae* ♂ V. Lawrence, Kansas.

1b Not so marked. 2
2a DFW never with a bar at end of cell; D often immaculate or nearly
so 3
2b DFW always with a bar at end of cell; D always marked.......4
3a VFW apex and VHW tinted with yellow; V with veins usually distinctly outlined with dark scales; wings opaque. Fig. 121........
....*Pieris napi* Linnaeus.

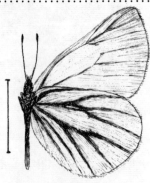

Range: circumpolar, ranging
southward to northern California,
Colorado and New York. Food
plants: various crucifers.

Fig. 121. *Pieris napi* ♂ V. Andes, New York.

3b V without yellow tinting; V with veins diffusely outlined with dark scales; wings semi-translucent. Fig. 122.........................
....*Pieris virginiensis* **Edwards.**

Range: Ontario, New England, south to Virginia in the Transition Zone (v). In the past this delicate species has been widely confused with *P. napi.* Food plant: *Dentaria* (toothwort).

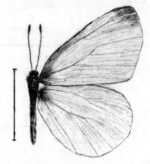

Fig. 122. *Pieris virginiensis* ♂
D. No data.

4a DFW with bar at end of cell nearly square, almost always centered with white; VHW with green markings which are clearly divided into basal and marginal elements by a white area. Fig. 123......
....*Pieris beckerii* **Edwards.**

Range: eastern slope of Sierras to western slope of Rockies. Food plants: *Isomeris arborea* (burro fat), *Stanleya pinnata,* other capers and crucifers.

Fig. 123. *Pieris beckerii* ♀ V.
Washoe County, Nevada.

4b DFW with bar at end of cell oblong, rarely centered with white beyond a trace; VHW with green, brown or gray markings (or immaculate—some male *protodice*) which are not clearly divided into basal and marginal elements..............................5

5a DFW with bar at end of cell narrow (more than twice as long as broad); all markings very crisply outlined, sharply contrasting with ground color; VHW with veins outlined in blackish brown; small (LFW usually < 23 mm.). Fig. 124......*Pieris sisymbrii* Boisduval.

Range: eastern slope of Rocky Mountains to California. Food plants: various cruciferae.

Fig. 124. *Pieris sisymbrii* ♂
V. Lake Tahoe, California.

5b DFW with bar at end of cell broad (no more than twice as long as wide); markings rather diffuse, not strongly contrasting with ground color; VHW with veins outlined in greenish or light brown; large (LFW usually > 23 mm.). Figs. 125, 126................
....*Pieris protodice* Linnaeus.

Range: entire United States and parts of southern Canada. Food plants: a very wide variety of crucifers, cultivated and wild.

Fig. 125. *Pieris protodice* ♂
D. Brownsville, Texas.

Fig. 126. *Pieris protodice* ♀
V. Rocky Mountain National Park, Colorado.

Genus ASCIA Linnaeus

This genus of four species is restricted to the Americas. Two species occur in our area.

KEY TO THE SPECIES OF *ASCIA*.

1a Male 2

1b Female **3**

2a D entirely white except for small black spot at end of FW cell; club of antenna ending gradually basally; D with prominent chalk white sex scaling along veins; LFW usually > 36 mm. Fig. 127........*Ascia josephina* Latreille. See couplet 3a.

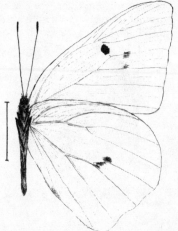

Fig. 127. *Ascia josephina* ♂ V. Texas.

2b D with dark serrate border or this border present in at least the apical portion of FW; black spot at end of FW cell absent; club of antenna ending abruptly basally; sex scaling absent; LFW usually < 36 mm..........*Ascia monuste* Linnaeus. See couplet 3b.

3a D ground color yellowish brown; DFW with large round spot at end of cell; club of antenna ending gradually basally; LFW usually > 36 mm.........................*Ascia josephina* Latreille. Range: southern Texas, straying northward to Kansas.

3b D ground color white, yellowish white, or brownish gray; DFW with dark bar at end of cell; club of antenna ending abruptly basally; LFW usually < 36 mm. Fig. 128......*Ascia monuste* Linnaeus.

Range: Gulf Coast, straying northward. In this very variable species, dark females indicate a migratory form. Food plants: cabbage, turnip, *Polanisia*, (clammy-weed), *Cleome*, and other crucifers and capers.

Fig. 128. *Ascia monuste* ♀ D. Miami, Florida.

Genus APPIAS Hübner

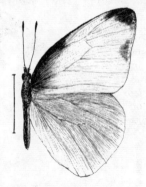

One species is found in North America, *Appias drusilla* Cramer (Fig. 129). Range: Florida and Texas, straying northward (Kansas, Nebraska, New York, etc.). Food plant: *Capparis* (caper). There is a characteristic pearly luster at the base of the wings which will separate this species from similar specimens of *Ascia monuste*.

Fig. 129. *Appias drusilla* ♀ D. Miami, Florida.

Genus NEOPHASIA Behr
Pine Whites

There are only two species in this interesting genus. The larvae show an approach to the extreme gregarious habits of the closely related Mexican pierid *Eucheira socialis* Westwood, whose larvae live together and pupate together in a web, going out to feed at night in a procession.

KEY TO THE SPECIES OF *NEOPHASIA*.

1a DFW cell completely filled with black. Fig. 130..................
....*Neophasia terlooti* Behr.

Range: northern Mexico, Arizona (x), California (?). Food plants: various conifers, including *Pinus ponderosa*. The ground color of male *terlooti* is white, that of females orange-red (some reportedly white).

Fig. 130. *Neophasia terlooti* ♂ D. Cochise County, Arizona.

1b DFW cell not completely filled with black. Fig. 131.............
.........................*Neophasia menapia* Felder and Felder.

Range: Rocky Mountains to Pacific Coast from Mexico to southern Canada, in pine forests. Food plants: various conifers, including *Pinus ponderosa* (ponderosa pine), *P. contorta* (lodge-pole pine), and *Abies balsamea* (balsam fir). This species is occasionally destructive. The ground color in both sexes is white.

Fig. 131. *Neophasia menapia* ♂ D. Scotts Mills, Oregon.

Family NYMPHALIDAE
Brush-footed Butterflies

This cosmopolitan group is the largest butterfly family. The adults are characterized by the great reduction of the prothoracic legs in both sexes (thus the common name "brush-footed" or "four-footed" butterflies). The larvae are very varied (see comment under subfamilies), and the pupae are usually suspended by the cremaster alone (a few satyrines pupate on the ground).

The species range from very small to very large, but most are in the larger half of the size spectrum.

KEY TO THE SUBFAMILIES OF NYMPHALIDAE.

1a Mesothoracic anepisternum absent as a distinct sclerite (Fig. 131A)
...2

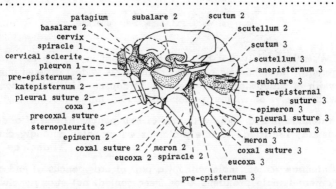

Fig. 131A. Lateral view of thorax of *Danaus plexippus*.

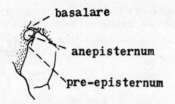

basalare

anepisternum

pre-episternum

Fig. 132. Front portion of mesothoracic pleuron of *Cercyonis*.

1b Mesothoracic anepisternum
present as a distinct sclerite
(Fig. 132)..................5

2a FW with vein 3V free at base (2V apparently bifid at base—Fig.
132A); mesothoracic pre-episternum at its widest much less than
one half width of katepisternum (Fig. 131A); mesomeron with prominent caudal bulge (Fig. 131A)....................................3

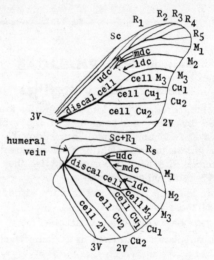

Fig. 132A. Wing venation of *Danaus plexippus*; all veins and larger cells labelled.

2b FW with vein 3V not free at base (except in a very few tropical
genera); mesothoracic pre-episternum at its widest at least one half
width of katepisternum (except in *Pardopsis*—African); mesomeron
with (rarely) or without prominent caudal bulge.................4

3a Antennae naked; male with pair of hair pencils at end of abdomen
(usually retracted); female protarsus 4-segmented, strongly clubbed
....Danainae p. 84

3b Antennae scaled; male without a pair of hair pencils at end of abdomen; female protarsus 4- or 5-segmented, not strongly clubbed;
no species in our area...............................Ithomiinae

4a HW cell closed by a well-developed tubular vein (ldc); tarsal claws usually toothed or asymmetrical, especially in males (normal in *Pardopsis*); gnathos absent or at most vestigial (*Pardopsis*); no species in our area....................................**Acraeinae**

4b HW cell not closed by tubular vein (ldc) vestigial or absent— Fig. 133—except in *Heliconius, Euides*); tarsal claws simple, symmetrical; gnathos usually well-developed ....
..........**Nymphalinae p. 106**

Fig. 133. Venation of HW of *Microtia.*

5a FW with veins not swollen at base; mesothoracic pre-episternum well-developed, varying in size; pre-episternal suture usually well-developed; HW cell often not closed by a tubular vein..........6

5b FW usually with at least one vein swollen at base (Fig. 134); mesothoracic pre - episternum usually greatly reduced or separated from katepisternum by a very weak pre-episternal suture; HW cell always closed by a tubular vein...........
...............**Satyrinae p. 86**

Fig. 134. Venation of FW of *Coenonympha.*

6a Parapatagia with at least a trace of sclerotization (Fig. 135); HW cell not closed by a tubular vein...............**Charaxinae p. 172**

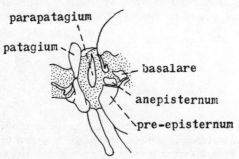

Fig. 135. Cervix, prothorax and cephalic portion of mesothorax of *Anaea andria.*

6b Parapatagia without any trace of sclerotization; HW cell sometimes closed by a tubular vein; no species in our area................7

7a FW with vein 3V free at base; female protarsus with small but perfect tarsal claws....................................**Calinaginae**

7b FW with vein 3V not free at base; female protarsus without claws
....**Morphinae**

Subfamily DANAINAE

A great many species of this family are reported to be distasteful to predators, presumably because of the acrid juices of the larval food (Asclepiadaceae and Solanaceae, the milkweed and nightshade families). Some butterflies of other groups seem to share this protection by closely mimicking danaines. The members of this subfamily are the only butterflies in our fauna with unscaled antennae. The larvae (Fig. 136) are brightly colored, hairless, and have a few well-developed fleshy filaments on the mesothorax (and sometimes on other segments). The pupae are rounded (Fig. 137).

Fig. 136. Larva of *Danaus plex-ippus* (after Scudder).

Fig. 137. Pupa of *Da-naus plexippus* (after Scudder).

KEY TO THE GENERA OF DANAINAE.

1a FW more than twice as long as broad.............*Lycorella* p. 84

1b FW not more than twice as long as broad...........*Danaus* p. 85

Genus LYCORELLA Hemming

One common tropical species, *Lycorella ceres* Cramer (Fig. 138), strays on rare occasions into southern Florida and southern Texas. Food plant: *Ficus* (fig).

Fig. 138. *Lycorella ceres* ♂ D. No data.

Genus DANAUS Hübner
Monarchs and Queens
Three species of this wide ranging genus are found in our area.
KEY TO THE SPECIES OF *DANAUS*.

1a DFW with inner margin bordered with black. Fig. 139...........
.......................*Danaus plexippus* Linnaeus. The Monarch.

Range: All of North America, south of the subarctic. Food plant: *Asclepias* (milkweed), rarely on *Apocynum* (dogbane) or *Acerates* (green milkweed). This species is mimicked by the nymphaline *Limenitis archippus*. The Monarch is, perhaps, our most familiar butterfly. It migrates southward every fall, not surviving the winter in our more northern areas. In the spring the progeny of the fall migrants move north, perhaps accompanied by a few of the original travelers.

Fig. 139. *Danaus plexippus* ♂ D. Lawrence, Kansas.

1b DFW with inner margin not bordered with black...............2
2a VHW with uniform ground color; VHW with veins black, with white borders along entire length. Fig. 140...........................
..........................*Danaus gilippus* Cramer. The Queen.

Range: Brazil to Florida and Gulf Coast, west to California and north to Kansas (rare) and Nebraska (stray). Food plants: *Asclepias, Nerium, Funastrum, Vincetoxicum, Philibertia, Stapelia* (all milkweeds). This species is also mimicked by geographic forms of *Limenitis archippus*.

Fig. 140. *Danaus gilippus* ♂ D. California.

2b VHW with ground color lighter limbally than basally; **HW** with veins black, with white borders only along a short segment about midway between end of cell and outer margin. Fig. 141. ..*Danaus eresimus* Cramer.

Range: southern Texas (common) and Florida (rare).

Fig. 141. *Danous eresimus* ♂ D. Florida.

Subfamily SATYRINAE
Satyrs, Wood Nymphs, Meadow Browns, etc.

This subfamily is the second largest in the Nymphalidae. Our species have a brown ground color, are usually marked with a few ocelli (D often being almost immaculate), have the cell closed on both wings, and usually have the FW veins strongly swollen at the base. These characters, along with their typical weak, bouncing flight, will permit the satyrs to be readily recognized.

The smooth larvae (Fig. 142) are thickest near the middle and have a characteristic bifid tail. All species (as far as is known) feed on grasses or sedges.

Fig. 142. Larva of *Cercyonis pegala* (after Scudder).

KEY TO THE GENERA OF SATYRINAE.

1a FW with bases of veins Sc, Cu and 2V at most slightly swollen...2

1b FW with bases of one or more of above veins (1a) strongly swollen (Fig. 142A) 4

2a Eyes hairy........*Lethe* p. 87

2b Eyes naked.................3

3a DFW and DHW with cream-colored submarginal bands....
............:....*Neominois* p. 94

Fig. 142A. Venation of FW of *Coenonympha*.

3b DFW and DHW without cream-colored submarginal bands........
....*Oeneis* p. 100
4a Eyes naked 5
4b Eyes hairy 8
5a Sc, Cu and 2V all strongly swollen at base....*Coenonympha* p. 93
5b Sc, Cu and 2V not all strongly swollen at base..................6
6a VHW with a submarginal band of lavender flecked with brown...
....*Gyrocheilus* p. 106
6b VHW without such a band....................................7
7a HW with outer margin scalloped to a greater or lesser degree; FW always with at least one ocellus, usually with two largest ocelli subequal, one in cell M$_1$ (subapical), and the other in cell Cu$_1$.......
....*Cercyonis* p. 94
7b HW with outer margin smoothly rounded; FW with or without ocelli, when ocelli are present the largest usually are the subapical pair (in cells M$_1$ and M$_2$), some species with four subequal ocelli......
....*Erebia* p. 96
8a DFW of male with a patch of contrasting dark scales lateral to and behind the cell; VHW with median cross lines sharply irregular (zig-zag)....................................*Paramacera* p. 92
8b DFW of male without contrasting dark patch; VHW with median lines straight, curved or sinuate, never sharply irregular........
....*Euptychia* p. 89

Genus LETHE Hübner

All three of our *Lethe* species have very spotty distributions, sometimes being common in quite restricted areas while being absent from large stretches of similar habitat. The "whys" of such distributions are a challenging problem for the biologist. Our *Lethe* belong to the subgenus *Enodia*.

KEY TO THE SPECIES OF *LETHE*.

1a V brown with pale purple tints; HW margin rather heavily scalloped; V with black spots at least four times the diameter of their white pupils 2

1b V yellowish-brown; HW margin only slightly scalloped; V with black spots at most three times the diameter of their white pupils. Fig. 143................................*Lethe eurydice* Johannson

Range: southern C a n a d a south to northern Florida (mostly in highlands), west to Nebraska and Colorado. Very rare west of 100th meridian, locally common east of it. Found in open marshes and moist meadows.

Fig. 143. *Lethe eurydice* ♂ D. Schiller Pass, Illinois.

2a Male FW pointed and apically produced, with dark androconial patches between veins; both sexes with VFW postmedian band irregular between costa and M_3, sharply produced outward in cell M_1 (this feature is also readily observed on DFW of females); VFW with spot in cell Cu_2 well-developed. Fig. 144.................
....*Lethe creola* Skinner

Range: Manitoba, Illinois, Michigan, southeastward to southern Virginia (Dismal Swamp) and south to Florida and the Gulf Coast. One Kansas record. A butterfly of woodlands and wooded swamps.

Fig. 144. *Lethe creola* ♂ D, ♀ DFW. Suffolk, Virginia.

2b Male FW rounded and not produced, lacking androconial patches;
both sexes with VFW postmedian band essentially straight between costa and M_3, reaching farthest outward in cell M_2 (this
feature is also readily observed on DFW of females); VFW with
spot in cell Cu_2 tiny or absent. Fig. 145......................
....*Lethe portlandia* Fabricius
Range: southern Canada south to Florida and Louisiana and west
to eastern Great Plains. A woodland species.

Fig. 145. *Lethe portlandia* ♂ D, ♀ DFW. Ohio and Illinois.

Genus EUPTYCHIA Hübner

This genus is richly represented in tropical America. It has also
been known as *Neonympha, Megisto,* and *Cissia.*

KEY TO THE SPECIES OF *EUPTYCHIA.*

1a VHW with grayish marginal patch containing small, black marginal ocelli................................subgenus *Cyllopsis* 6

1b VHW without marginal patch, ocelli submarginal................
....subgenus *Euptychia* 2

2a DFW with at least one large ocellus..........................3

2b DFW without ocelli, or at most with very small ocelli..........4

89

3a D ground color orange-brown; DFW with only one ocellus. Fig. 146 ....*Euptychia rubricata* Edwards

Range: Central America north to Texas, New Mexico and Arizona. Food plants: in laboratory *Cynodon dactylon* and *Stenotaphrum secundatum.*

Fig. 146. *Euptychia rubricata* ♂
V. No data.

3b D ground color brown; DFW with two ocelli. Fig. 147 ....
....*Euptychia cymela* Cramer

Range: eastern United States and southeastern Canada. Often abundant. This species has long been known by the specific name *eurytus* Fabricius.

Fig. 147. *Euptychia cymela* ♂
V. Ashville, North Carolina.

4a VFW without distinct ocelli; VHW with ocelli rather elongate on basal-distal axis. Fig. 148 ....
..*Euptychia areolata* J. E. Smith

Range: southeastern United States north to Ocean County, New Jersey.

Fig. 148. *Euptychia areolata* ♂
V. Texas.

4b VFW with distinct ocelli; VHW with ocelli approximately round..5

5a VHW with largest ocellus in the center of a row of six ocelli. Fig. 149...................................*Euptychia mitchellii* French

Range: southern Michigan and Ohio. Reported from northern New Jersey—probably in error.

Fig. 149. *Euptychia mitchellii* ♂
V. Cass County, Michigan.

5b VHW with largest ocelli the second and fifth in a row of six. Fig. 150...................................*Euptychia hermes* Fabricius

Range: southeastern United States north as far as southern New Jersey.

Fig. 150. *Euptychia hermes* ♂
V. Lakeland, Florida.

6a FW of males lacking androconial patch; D homogeneous gray or gray brown; LFW males 15-17 mm., females 17-20 mm. Fig. 151...*Euptychia gemma* Hübner

Range: southeastern United States north as far as southern Illinois, Texas and northern Mexico.

Fig. 151. *Euptychia gemma* ♀
V. Nashville, Tennessee.

6b FW of males with androconial patch; D a brownish-gray with some red suffusion; LFW males 18-22 mm., females 18-25 mm..........7

7a VHW with postmedian band straight, toothed distally, extending to costal margin where it connects with the postmedian band of **VFW.** Fig. 152......................*Euptychia pyracmon* Butler

Range: Panama to Arizona and Colorado. This species is also known as *henshawi* Edwards.

Fig. 152. *Euptychia pyracmon*
♂ V. Paradise, Arizona.

7b VHW with postmedian band irregularly concave outwardly and extending to costa where it appears to meet the submarginal band of **VFW.** Fig. 153...................*Euptychia dorothea* Nabokov

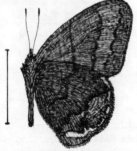

Range: northwestern Arizona and southern Colorado to western Texas and southward.

Fig. 153. *Euptychia dorothea* ♂
V. Davis Mountains, Texas.

Genus PARAMECERA Butler

There is only one species in this genus, *Paramecera xicaque* Reakirt (Fig. 154). It is a Mexican butterfly (common in coniferous forest at 8900 feet, 20 miles east of Toluca, near Mexico City) which crosses our border in southern Arizona.

Fig. 154. *Paramecera xicaque* ♂
V. Paradise, Arizona.

Genus COENONYMPHA Hübner
The Ringlets

Two species of this circumpolar genus are found in North America.

KEY TO THE SPECIES OF *COENONYMPHA*.

1a VHW with five or more distinct dark brown ocelli pupilled with silver and surrounded by dull orange rings. Fig. 155............ ....*Coenonympha haydenii* Edwards

Range: western Colorado and Wyoming, eastern Idaho and southwestern Montana.

Fig. 155. *Coenonympha haydenii* ♂ V. Yellowstone National Park, Wyoming.

1b VHW not so marked. Figs. 156, 157........................... ....*Coenonympha tullia* Muller

Range: circumpolar; California, Arizona and New Mexico north to Alaska and the Hudsonian Zone of Canada as far east as New Brunswick. Recently recorded from extreme northern New York, but otherwise not found in the eastern United States. This is an extremely variable species, and many local varieties have received scientific names.

Fig. 156. *Coenonympha tullia* ♂ V. Brigus, Newfoundland.

Fig. 157. *Coenonympha tullia* ♂ V. Silver Lake, Utah.

Genus NEOMINOIS Scudder

There is only a single species in this genus, *Neominois ridingsii* Edwards (Fig. 158).

Range: Rocky Mountain states westward to eastern California. A species of dry grasslands.

Fig. 158. *Neominois ridingsii* ♂
D. Whitehorn, Colorado.

Genus CERCYONIS Scudder

Wood Nymphs

These widespread and common butterflies present an extremely complex variational picture in the western United States. Just what are or are not species will probably not be settled without extensive breeding or cytogenetic studies. The three segregates given below may not represent genetic species.

KEY TO THE SPECIES OF *CERCYONIS*.

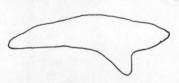

Fig. 159. Valva of *Cercyonis pegala*.

1a Male genitalia with tip of valva curved upward gradually, tapering slowly to a point throughout its entire length (Fig. 159); FW often with broad yellow to orange patch around ocelli (may be entirely absent); generally large (LFW mostly > 24 mm.). Figs. 160, 161........................
......*Cercyonis pegala* Fabricius

Range: our entire area from Mexico north to middle Canada. This is the only *Cercyonis* found east of the Rocky Mountains. Included in this species are, among others, the insects named *C. alope* Fabricius, *C. boopis* Behr, *C. ariane* Boisduval, *C. masoni* Cross, *C. damei* Barnes and Benjamin, and *C. behrii* Grinnel.

Fig. 160. *Cercyonis pegala*
♀ D. Screven County,
Georgia.

Fig. 161. *Cercyonis pegala*
♀ V. Brigham, Utah.

1b Male genitalia with tip of valva rather strongly curved upward, tapering sharply to a point in distal one-half (Fig. 162); FW never with patch around ocelli; generally small (LFW mostly < 24 mm.)..2

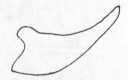

Fig. 162. Valva of *Cercyonis meadii*.

2a VFW with distinct red-orange flush. Fig. 163.....................
....*Cercyonis meadii* Edwards

Range: New Mexico, Arizona, Colorado, Utah, Wyoming and Nebraska. This species appears to be closely related to *Cercyonis sthenele* (see couplet 2b).

Fig. 163. *Cercyonis meadii* ♂
V. Yavapai County, Arizona.

2b VFW without distinct red-orange flush. Fig. 164, 165.............
....*Cercyonis sthenele* Behr

Fig. 164. *Cercyonis sthenele* ♀
V. San Francisco, California.

Range: western Canada and United States except for southern New Mexico and Arizona. The name *sthenele* was originally applied to a local form from the San Francisco region of California, which is now extinct. It is possible that this highly variable assemblage is actually a species complex; genetic studies are badly needed. Included here are *Cercyonis silvestris* Edwards and *C. oetus* Boisduval. The latter form is sympatric with *C. meadii* and does not interbreed with it, so that if *oetus* is correctly placed here, *meadii* and *sthenele* cannot be conspecific in spite of their similarity.

Fig. 165. *Cercyonis sthenele* ♂
V. Custer, South Dakota.

Genus EREBIA Dalman

The Alpines

Our ten species of this Holarctic genus are largely arctic and alpine in distribution. All are single brooded.

KEY TO THE SPECIES OF *EREBIA*.

1a D and V entirely without ocelli................................2

1b Ocelli present on at least VFW................................5

2a V marked with broad, unbroken, contrasting bands. Fig. 166...... ....*Erebia fasciata* Butler

Range: restricted to the treeless northern margins of the continent, flying (early vii) from western-most Alaska to Hudson Bay. Found also in northern Asia. The species is found in low, moist, grassy tundra areas.

Fig. 166. *Erebia fasciata* ♀ V. Eagle Summit, Alaska.

2b V not so marked..3

3a DFW with small orange or orange-red postmedian bars, these bars often forming a postmedian band. Fig. 167.................... ....*Erebia theano* Tauschenberg

Range: mountains of southern Colorado to central Alaska and the southern coast of Hudson Bay. Widely distributed in Siberia. A very local species—colonies are found above treeline in some areas and below in others. vii.

Fig. 167. *Erebia theano* ♂ V. Wind River Mountains, Wyoming.

3b DFW without such markings....................................4

4a DFW with red discal suffusion; VHW strongly mottled with light gray distally. Fig. 168....................*Erebia discoidalis* Kirby

Range: high altitudes in central Asia; central Alaska southward and eastward in the Hudsonian and Canadian Zones of Canada to the Laurentides Park. The only U. S. records are from Minnesota (Itasca Park). vi—vii. *Discoidalis* is often extremely abundant, flying in grassy areas of fields and open woods.

Fig. 168. *Erebia discoidalis* ♂ V. The Pas, Manitoba.

97

4b DFW usually lacking red discal suffusion (present in some far northern specimens); VHW not strongly mottled with gray distally. Fig. 169.............................. *Erebia magdalena* **Strecker**

Range: Colorado, Utah and Wyoming, flying over rock slides high in the mountains. vii. An apparently conspecific form, *Erebia mackinleyensis* Gunder, occurs in central Asia, Alaska and the Yukon Territory. It differs from southern *magdalena* chiefly in its lighter color and reddish discal flush.

Fig. 169. *Erebia magdalena* ♂
V. Boulder County, Colorado.

5a VFW with broad, unbroken, well-defined yellow-orange postmedian band which has a jagged distal edge; FW with two subapical ocelli (in cells M$_1$ and M$_2$) and usually a third ocellus in cell Cu$_1$; VHW with a gray postmedian band. Fig. 170....... *Erebia vidleri* **Elwes**

Range: high Olympics and Cascades of Washington and the mountains of British Columbia.

Fig. 170. *Erebia vidleri* ♀
V. Okanogan County, Washington.

5b. This combination of characters not present.....................6
6a VHW a mottled soft-gray or gray-brown, often approaching blue-gray basally; DFW with only a pair of subapical ocelli. Fig. 171. .... *Erebia callias* **Edwards**

Range: Asia; Colorado, and Wyoming, in alpine meadows above treeline. vii—early viii.

Fig. 171. *Erebia callias* ♂ V.
Berthoud Pass, Colorado.

6b VHW predominently brown; DFW often with three or more ocelli. . 7

7a VHW almost always with a white spot in discal cell near distal
   end and another white spot or area on the costal margin; white
areas may be expanded and border the
dark median band setting it off in striking contrast (especially in Alaskan specimens); DFW with at least a faint
orange tinge basad of ocelli (often pronounced in females); male genitalia
with arms of gnathos spatulate. Fig.
172. . . . . *Erebia disa* Thunberg
   Range: circumpolar; subarctic Alaska
and Canada, from Bering Sea to Ontario, northern Europe and Asia. vi—
early vii.

Fig. 172. *Erebia disa* ♂ V.
Harlan, Saskatchewan.

7b VHW lacking white spots or areas; DFW without orange tinge; male
   genitalia with arms of gnathos pointed. 8

8a DFW lacking any trace of postmedian yellow-orange or orange-
   brown band (ocelli surrounded by yellow-orange rings which may
   be contiguous); some far northern specimens lacking ocelli, leaving
   DFW a uniform brown-black; VHW without ocelli; male genitalia
   with valvae long and slender (length about 5 times width at base)
   with a small, rounded, spined terminus (head). Fig. 173. . . . .
   . . . . *Erebia rossii* Curtis
   Range: Asia and the northern fringe
of the North American continent from
western Alaska to Baffin Island and
(perhaps) northern Labrador, except for
the northern islands of the Canadian
Arctic Archipelago. In the West *rossii*
occurs southward in the mountains to
northern British Columbia and in the
East it is found as far south as The Pas,
Manitoba. Also found in northern and
central Asia. Late vi—early vii. In
Alaska *rossii* is common in the Hudsonian and Arctic Zones.

Fig. 173. *Erebia rossii* ♂ V.
Mount McKinley National
Park, Alaska.

8b DFW with at least a trace of yellow-orange or orange-brown postmedian band (this band may be broken into blocks by strips of
   brown along the veins); VHW with or without ocelli; male genitalia with valvae rather short and stout (length less than four
   times width at base) with a distinct shoulder leading to a flat,
   spined terminus (head). 9

9a DFW with four (rarely five) ocelli, which may be very small, size of the subapical pair equal to or less than that of the others; **VHW** often lacking ocelli. Fig. 174.............*Erebia youngi* Holland

Range: northern and central Yukon Territory and central eastern Alaska. Early vii. *Youngi* flies in the vicinity of treeline.

Fig. 174. *Erebia youngi* ♂ V. Eagle Summit, Alaska.

9b DFW with two to four (rarely five) ocelli, the subapical pair always present and always the largest; **VHW** with ocelli present except in some far northern and high altitude individuals. Fig. 175.
....*Erebia epipsodea* Butler

Range: central Alaska southeastward to southern Manitoba and southward throughout the Rocky Mountains to northern New Mexico (not found in California or coastal Oregon and Washington). vi—viii. Occuring in the Hudsonian, Canadian and Transition Zones.

Fig. 175. *Erebia epipsodea* ♀ V. Lloydminster, Alberta.

Genus OENEIS Hübner

The Arctics

by C. F. dos Passos

These medium to large-size, black, gray or brown butterflies are generally characteristic of arctic, subarctic, alpine and subalpine areas. The life history of many species is unknown, but the larvae of all doubtless live on grasses or sedges. Only one brood a year is known for each species, but there is the possibility of a partial second brood in some.

KEY TO THE SPECIES OF *OENEIS*.

1a Male genitalia with roughly triangular, untoothed valva (Fig.
176); VHW striated, without median band. Fig. 177............
..........*Oeneis uhleri* Reakirt

Fig. 176. Valva of *Oeneis uhleri*.

Range: Rocky Mountains, Colorado to Alberta and Northwest Territories, western Nebraska and South Dakota, Saskatchewan and
Manitoba. Not known from British Columbia.
In Colorado *uhleri* flies mostly below 10,000′.
Oeneis nahanni Dyar is a geographic subspecies of *uhleri*, O. *cairnesi* Gibson is a
synonym of *nahanni*.

Fig. 177. *Oeneis uhleri* ♂ V.
Beulah, Manitoba.

1b Male genitalia with valva not triangular, bearing either one prominent tooth near base of costa or many small teeth on the distal
portion of costa; VHW variable in striation, usually with a median
band 2

2a Male genitalia with valva bearing one prominent tooth near the
base of the costa (Fig. 178).....3

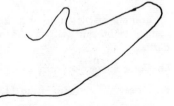

Fig. 178. Valva of *Oeneis
taygete*.

2b Male genitalia with valva bearing many small teeth on distal portion of costa (Figs. 178A, 178B)................................9

Fig. 178A. Valva of *Oeneis polixenes*.

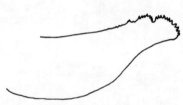

Fig. 178B. Valva of *Oeneis melissa*.

101

3a DFW of male with an often prominent dark patch of scales (androconia) at caudal edge of cell; if androconia not prominent, then LFW < 28 mm..4

3b DFW of male lacking this patch; LFW > 28 mm. Fig. 179........
....*Oeneis macounii* Edwards

Range: northern Minnesota and Michigan, western Ontario to British Columbia and southern Northwest Territories. Late vi, early vii.

Fig. 179. *Oeneis macounii* ♂ D. Harlan, Saskatchewan.

4a Color ashen or tawny...5

4b Color dark gray or gray-brown.................................8

5a Color ashen; restricted to a few counties in California...........
....*Oeneis ivallda* Mead
Range: restricted to the high Sierras in a few counties of north central California (vii). Some authors consider *ivallda* to be a race of *chryxus*.

5b Color tawny or grayish.......................................6

6a Grayish; small (average LFW 20 mm.). Fig. 180................
....*Oeneis alberta* Elwes

Range: Manitoba, Alberta and Saskatchewan (late v—early vi) to Colorado and Arizona (early vi; ix rarely) in isolated colonies. In Colorado *alberta* flies in meadows around 9800', in Arizona around 9000'.

Fig. 180. *Oeneis alberta* ♂ V. Beulah, Manitoba.

6b Tawny; larger (average LFW 26-32 mm.).......................7

7a VFW almost immaculate basally; DFW usually with one or two
   ocelli; size large (average LFW 32 mm.). Fig. 181................
..........................*Oeneis nevadensis* Felder and Felder

Range: northern California to Vancouver Island, none known from British Columbia mainland. vi—vii. For
reasons not at present clear, this species in many areas, flies in numbers
only on even numbered years.

Fig. 181. *Oeneis nevadensis* ♂
D. Modoc County, California.

7b VFW plainly marked with striations basally; DFW usually with
   two to five ocelli; size medium (average LFW 26 mm.). Fig. 182...
.....................................*Oeneis chryxus* Doubleday

Range: widely distributed in Rocky
Mountains (vi—viii) from Arizona to
Alaska, west to Olympic Mountains
of Washington and Sierra Nevada of
California, east to Hudson Bay, Ontario and northern Michigan (late v,
early vi), and the Gaspe (alpine—
early vii). In Colorado *chryxus* flies
from about 8000' to a little above
treeline.

Fig. 182. *Oeneis chryxus* ♂ V.
Silver Lake, Utah.

8a VHW with veins outlined in white. Fig. 183.................
..*Oeneis taygete* Geyer

Range: Europe and North America, Labrador to Alaska, southward to the Gaspe and along the Rocky Mountains to Colorado. vi—vii. Flying above, or north of treeline.

Fig. 183. *Oeneis taygete* ♂ V. Wolstenholme, Quebec.

8b VHW with veins not outlined in white. Fig. 184.................
..*Oeneis bore* Schneider

Range: northern Europe; Hudson Bay to Coronation Gulf and southward to McKinley National Park, Alaska. O. *hanburyi* Watkins and O. *mckinleyensis* dos Passos are geographic forms of *bore*.

Fig. 184. *Oeneis bore* ♂ V. Alaska.

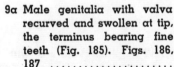

Fig. 185. Valva of *Oeneis polixenes*.

9a Male genitalia with valva recurved and swollen at tip, the terminus bearing fine teeth (Fig. 185). Figs. 186, 187 ....
Oeneis polixenes Fabricius

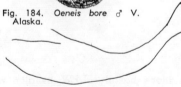

Fig. 186. *Oeneis polixenes* ♂ V. Mount Katahdin, Maine.

Fig. 187. *Oeneis polixenes* ♀ V. Colorado.

Range: Labrador across the continent to Alaska, southward along the Rockies (vii—viii) to New Mexico. There is an isolated colony on Mt. Katahdin, Maine. This species is found above or north of timberline. *Oeneis brucei* Edwards is a geographic race of *polixenes*.

9b Male genitalia with valva not recurved and swollen at tip, the terminus bearing rather coarse teeth (Fig. 188).................10

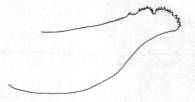

Fig. 188. Valva of *Oeneis melissa.*

10a D with prominent ocelli in light submarginal band; size medium (average LFW 27 mm.). Fig. 189............*Oeneis jutta* Hübner

Range: northern Europe and America, Newfoundland to Alaska, southward to New Hampshire, Michigan and Colorado. vi—vii. Flying in spruce bogs in the East and North, pine woods in Colorado.

Fig. 189. *Oeneis jutta* ♂ D. Chester, Maine.

10b D without ocelli; size small to medium (average LFW 25 mm.). Fig. 190...............................*Oeneis melissa* Fabricius

Range: Newfoundland and Labrador to the Yukon, south to British Columbia and Washington, above or north of timberline. A single isolated colony in the White Mountains of New Hampshire (Mt. Washington and vicinity) is known as O. *semidea* Say. Late vi—vii. *Oeneis beanii* Elwes and O. *lucilla* Barnes and McDunnough are geographic races of *melissa*; O. *simulans* Gibson is a synonym.

Fig. 190. *Oeneis melissa* ♂ V. Clear Creek County, Colorado.

Genus GYROCHEILUS Butler

A single species in our area, *Gyrocheilus patrobas* Hewitson (Fig. 191).

Range: tropical America to southern Arizona.

Fig. 191. *Gyrocheilus patrobas* ♀
V. Ramsey Canyon, Arizona.

Subfamily NYMPHALINAE
The Nymphs

This cosmopolitan group is the largest and most varied subfamily in the Nymphalidae. The Nymphalinae have not been the subject of a modern revision (which is sorely needed) and thus the tribal arrangement used below is, in many places, quite arbitrary, and it has not been practical to give a key to the tribes. The first nine couplets of the generic key below deal with tropical genera only found along our southern borders. They can be ignored when keying specimens from north of our most southern tier of states. A few representative larvae and pupae are shown in Figs. 192, 193.

Fig. 192. Larva and pupa of *Speyeria cybele* (after Scudder).

Fig. 193. Larva and pupa of *Limenitis astyanax* (after Scudder).

KEY TO THE GENERA OF NYMPHALINAE.

1a VHW with black spots or ocelli near the bases of cells M_3 and Cu_1 giving the impression of a figure "8"............*Diaethria* p. 159

1b Not so marked...2

2a VHW with eyespots in cells M_1 and Cu_1, and only in those cells, these eyespots joined by a brown band; D male brassy green; D female brown and white......................*Dynamine* p. 167

2b Not so marked...3

3a D irridescent purplish-blue, cut by blackish transverse bars......
....*Myscelia* p. 158

3b not so marked...4

4a DHW male black with single, large, white, purplish-rimmed spot in postbasal and discal area; DFW female brown with apex and costa black and white subapical spots (mimics danaine).........
....*Hypolimnas* p. 157

4b Not so marked...5

5a D brownish-black, with at least some purple sheen, without prominent markings except for 3-6 white subapical spots on DFW......
....*Eunica* p. 160

5b Not so marked...6

6a D orange-brown; DFW with black apex and a black bar in cell Cu_2; HW with a short, sharp tail starting at end of vein M_3...........
....*Hypanartia* p. 157

6b Not so marked...7

7a Large (LFW > 50 mm.); DFW dark gold basally, with dark brown apex and broad dark brown distal margin (broadest at outer angle); FW apex produced; FW outer margin concave......*Historis* p. 170

7b Not so marked...8

8a D ground color bluish-gray; D with many fine blackish and brownish-gray cross lines and marks; DHW with a row of submarginal ocelli
....*Hamadryas* p. 161

8b Not so marked...9

9a DHW brown, with scalloped outer margin and broad red submarginal band...*Biblis* p. 163

9b Not so marked...10

10a FW twice as long as broad; HW with humeral vein curved anteriorly towards wing base..................................11

10b FW much less than twice as long as broad; HW with humeral vein curved anteriorly away from wing base..................14

11a VHW with silver spots..........................*Agraulis* p. 111

11b VHW without silver spots.............................12

12a HW with discal cell closed.....................*Heliconius* p. 110

12b HW with discal cell open.............................13

13a FW with vein M_3 strongly bent beyond discal cell; male with black androconia along veins............................*Dryas* p. 111

13b FW with vein M_3 scarcely bent beyond discal cell; male without androconia.......................................*Dryadula* p. 112

14a FW with subcostal vein greatly swollen at base......*Mestra* p. 161

14b FW with subcostal vein not swollen at base....................15

15a Antennal club short and stout, three or more times as broad as the rest of the flagellum and more or less abruptly thickened....16

15b Antennal club long and slender, no more than twice as broad as rest of flagellum and more or less gradually thickened.......22

16a Tarsus of metathoracic leg with two rows of spines on ventral side of last tarsomere (except in *Vanessa*); antennal club with three complete longitudinal ridges on underside; eyes sometimes hairy 17

16b Tarsus of metathoracic leg with four rows of spines on ventral side of last tarsomere; antennal club with only one complete longitudinal ridge on underside, or none at all; eyes hairless.......25

17a Eyes hairy 18

17b Eyes hairless 20

18a HW with outer margin round or slightly undulate...*Vanessa* p. 152

18b HW with outer margin bearing a distinct, sharp tail...........19

19a FW with inner margin deeply concave..........*Polygonia* p. 149

19b FW with inner margin straight.................*Nymphalis* p. 147

20a Wings brown with light greenish-white spots and stripes; HW with a short, sharp tail.......................*Metamorpha* p. 155

20b Wings not colored as above, or, if so, without such a tail......21

21a HW rounded, not projecting outward along vein M_3...*Precis* p. 154

21b HW not rounded, projecting outward along vein M_3..*Anartia* p. 156

22a Tarsus of metathoracic leg with four rows of spines on ventral side; ground color of wings black, dark brown, blue, green or purple (rarely orange-brown), sometimes with a prominent white discal band crossing both wings........................*Limenitis* p. 163

22b Tarsus of metathoracic leg with two rows of spines on ventral side; usually not colored as above.................................23

23a HW with humeral vein arising from vein Sc at point where veins Rs and Sc+R_1 part; HW with a long tail.........*Marpesia* p. 167

23b HW with humeral vein arising from vein Sc distad of point where veins Rs and Sc+R_1 part; HW without tail...................24

24a D ground color of both sexes light yellowish-brown; female without a prominent white discal band on both wings..............
....*Asterocampa* p. 170

24b D male ground color dark brown, with an irridescent bluish gloss; both wings of female crossed by a prominent white discal band...
....*Apatura* p. 171

25a Relatively large (LFW > 25 mm.) yellowish brown butterflies with black markings; VHW without silver spots; FW with R_2 originating beyond apex of cell.........................*Euptoieta* p. 112

25b Without this combination of characters.......................26

26a Male genitalia with parts of tegumen membranous; VHW sometimes with silver spots.....................................27

26b Male genitalia without parts of tegumen membranous; VHW never with silver spots...28

27a Large (LFW almost always much > 25 mm.); male genitalia with aedeagus open basally.........................*Speyeria* p. 113

27b Small (LFW almost always much < 25 mm.); male genitalia with aedeagus closed basally.........................*Boloria* p. 119

28 NOTE: David L. Bauer is the author of couplets 28-32.

28a Male genitalia with valva bearing a two-pronged process (clasp) on inner face, upper prong often very short; a spined, padlike structure articulating with the lower edge of this process; valva lacking other posterior projections or processes. (Fig. 193A) ....*Euphydryas* p. 127

Fig. 193A. Inner face of valva of *Euphydryas editha.*

28b Male genitalia with valva bearing a simple process (clasp) on inner face; without a spined, padlike process; valva with at least one other posterior projection or process (Fig. 193B)...........29

29a Male genitalia with process (clasp) of inner face of valva thornlike, curved and usually short, originating close to the base of a similar projection from the lower posterior edge of the valva; valva triangular or quadrilateral, not long and narrow (Fig. 193B).......30

Fig. 193B. Inner face of valva *Poladryas pola.*

29b Male genitalia with process (clasp) of inner face of valva long, straight or curved, not associated at base with a similar structure; valva rarely quadrilateral, usually long, narrow, with posterior edge drawn out into a tapering process (Fig. 193C).........................32

Fig. 193C. Inner face of valva of *Phyciodes tharos.*

30a Male genitalia with valva bearing only one projection on its lower posterior edge, this projection similar to clasper in structure and bifid at its apex.................................*Poladryas* p. 130

30b Male genitalia with valva bearing two projections on its lower posterior edge, one similar to the clasper and the other varied in shape and location...31

31a Male genitalia with second posterior projection of valva variable in position and form; female genitalia with "genital plate" (lamella antevaginalis + lamella postvaginalis) simple, only slightly concave; body slender, with abdomen extending well past the caudal limit of the HW; small (LFW 10-16 mm.)...........*Microtia* p. 131

31b Male genitalia with second posterior projection arising just dorsad of first (the first being the one similar and adjacent to the clasper), curving sharply dorsad and inward until it roughly parallels the posterior edge of the valva; female genitalia with "genital plate" complex, strongly concave; body not unusually slender, with abdomen not extending beyond caudal limit of HW...*Chlosyne* p. 132

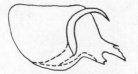

Fig. 193D. Inner face of valva of *Mellicta athalia*.

32a Male genitalia with valva roughly quadrilateral, not tapering to a posterior process (Fig. 193D); a Palaearctic genus with one species doubtfully credited to our fauna..........*Mellicta* p. 140

32b Male genitalia not quadrilateral, narrow and tapering to a single long posterior projection which is sometimes armed with secondary spines (Fig. 193C); well represented in Nearctic...*Phyciodes* p. 141

Tribe HELICONIINI
Genus HELICONIUS Kluk
The Long Wings

The members of this genus presumably have acrid body fluids which make them distasteful to predators. They are mimicked by species of other butterfly families, as well as by moths, and they also mimic one another. This genus is primarily tropical, but one species has a rather wide range in the southern United States.

KEY TO THE SPECIES OF *HELICONIUS*.

1a D wings brown or black, crossed by several longitudinal yellow stripes. Fig. 194....*Heliconius charitonius* Linnaeus. Zebra Butterfly.

Range: South and Central America and the Antilles to Florida, the Gulf Coast and Texas, straying northward (Kansas). Food plant: *Passiflora* (passion flower).

Fig. 194. *Heliconius charitonius* ♂ D. Miami, Florida.

1b D wings brownish-black; DFW with a transverse red stripe; DHW with a yellow stripe in basal costal area. Fig. 195...............
.................................*Heliconius petiveranus* Doubleday.

Range: southern Texas, southward.
Food plant: *Passiflora* (passion flower).

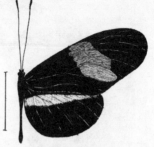

Fig. 195. *Heliconius petiveranus* ♂
D. Nonte, Mexico.

Genus AGRAULIS Boisduval and Leconte

There is only a single, widespread species in this genus, *Agraulis vanillae* Linnaeus (Fig. 196).

Range: southern half of United States, straying northward occasionally (Nebraska—rare). Food plant: *Passiflora* (passion flower).

Fig. 196. *Agraulis vanillae* ♂ V.
Miami, Florida.

Genus DRYAS Hübner

This genus contains only one species, *Dryas julia* Fabricius (Fig. 197).

Range: widely distributed in Neotropical Region, ranging northward to southern Florida and southern Texas. One Nebraska record, almost certainly an import. Food plant: *Passiflora* (passion flower).

Fig. 197. *Dryas julia* ♂ D. Key Largo, Florida.

111

Genus DRYADULA Michener

The single species in this genus, *Dryadula phaetusa* Linnaeus (Fig. 198), is widespread in Central and South America and has been recorded vaguely from the United States.

Fig. 198. *Dryadula phaetusa* ♂ D. Sierra Bianco, Mexico.

Tribe ARGYNNINI
Genus EUPTOIETA Doubleday

There are three species in this genus, two of which are found in the United States.

KEY TO THE SPECIES OF *EUPTOIETA*.

1a DHW with distinct dark markings in basal half. Fig. 199........
....*Euptoieta claudia* Cramer.

Range: Southern New England (strays) south to Mexico and Central America, west to Nebraska and southern California. Food plants: *Viola* (violets and pansies), *Passiflora* (passion flower), *Podophyllum* (May apple), *Sedum* (stone crop), *Meibomia* (beggar-ticks), *Portulaca* (purslane), *Menispermum* (moonseed).

Fig. 199. *Euptoieta claudia*
♂ D. Donna, Texas.

1b DHW without distinct dark markings in basal half. Fig. 200......
....*Euptoieta hegesia* **Cramer.**

Range: widespread in the tropics, breeds in southern Texas.

Fig. 200. *Euptoieta hegesia*
♂ D. Mexico.

Genus SPEYERIA Scudder
The Fritillaries
by L. P. Grey

This strictly North American genus is closely related to the Palae-arctic *Argynnis* (with which some authors consider it congeneric). The latter name is used in most older works. The group presents many systematic problems, some of which probably will yield only to intensive breeding experiments, cytotaxonomic studies, serological analysis, and the like.

The dark larvae have the upper spines of the first thoracic segment smaller than those on the abdomen. All species are nocturnal and feed on violets (*Viola*). The adults usually are found coursing rapidly through meadows, visiting thistles and other flowers.

Since the species found in the eastern United States and Canada are easy to separate, a superficial key to specimens taken in this area is given first.

KEY TO THE SPECIES OF *SPEYERIA* IN THE EASTERN UNITED STATES AND CANADA (EAST OF THE MISSISSIPPI RIVER).

1a VHW with basal two-thirds nearly uniform in color. (See Figs. 205, 206.).....................................*Speyeria diana* **Cramer.**

1b VHW with basal two-thirds sprinkled with silvered or whitish spots **2**

2a DHW with one (male) or two (female) rows of whitish spots. (See Fig. 209.).................................*Speyeria idalia* **Drury.**

2b DHW not so marked...**3**

3a D wing margins usually almost solid black; generally rather small (LFW usually < 31 mm.). (See Fig. 215)...*Speyeria atlantis* **Edwards.**

3b D wing margins tending to fulvous between ends of veins; generally rather large (LFW usually > 32 mm.).....................**4**

4a D males with veins M₁ — 2V appearing widened because of dark scaling along them; DHW females without rosy-tinged patch in median area towards inner margin; V both sexes tending to brownish coloration of pattern. (See Fig. 204.)..*Speyeria cybele* Fabricius.

4b D males with veins not appearing widened; DHW females with a rosy-tinged patch in median area towards inner margin; V both sexes tending to reddish coloration of pattern. (See Fig. 203)....
....*Speyeria aphrodite* Fabricius.

KEY TO ALL SPECIES OF *SPEYERIA*, REGARDLESS OF LOCALITY.

1a Female genitalia with bursa copulatrix constricted so as to form a secondary anterior sac (Fig. 201)......
..........subgenus *Semnopsyche* 2

Fig. 201. Lateral outline of bursa copulatrix of *Semnopsyche*.

1b Female genitalia with bursa copulatrix simple, ovoid (Fig. 202)..............
................subgenus *Speyeria* 4

Fig. 202. Lateral outline of bursa copulatrix of *Speyeria*.

2a DFW with scaling of veins M₁ — 2V roughly the same in both sexes. Fig. 203.............................*Speyeria aphrodite* Fabricius.

Range: transcontinental in southern Canada, south in the East to North Carolina and in the West to Arizona (rare). Does not penetrate most of Great Plains (one old Kansas record) or the Great Basin—Sierra—Cascade country.

Fig. 203. *Speyeria aphrodite* ♂ V. Jefferson County, Colorado.

2b DFW male with distinctly wider dark scaling along veins, M₁ — 2V than DFW female...3

3a VHW with many silver spots in discal area. Fig. 204...........
.............Speyeria cybele Fabricius. Great Spangled Fritillary.

Range: transcontinental from Canadian taiga to North Carolina, Georgia,
Arkansas, Oklahoma, New Mexico
and California.

Fig. 204. *Speyeria cybele* ♂
V. Douglas County, Kansas.

3b VHW essentially without silver spots in discal area. Figs. 205, 206
......................................Speyeria diana Cramer

Fig. 205. *Speyeria diana* ♂
D. Fayette County, West
Virginia.

Fig. 206. *Speyeria diana* ♀
D. Evansville, Indiana.

Range: Austral-Transition Zones from Virginia coastal plain to eastern Mississippi Valley, Arkansas to Illinois. Local, strongholds in higher
foothills of Blue Ridge-Piedmont belt, West Virginia to Georgia. The
female presumably mimics the distasteful *Aristolochia* swallowtail, *Battus philenor*.

Fig. 207. Tip of uncus of Speyeria idalia.

4a Male genitalia with uncus comparatively wide, ventrally excavate near tip (Fig. 207).....................5

Fig. 208. Tip of uncus of Speyeria edwardsii.

4b Male genitalia with uncus more uniformly tapering to clawlike terminus (Fig. 208).............6

5a DHW with submarginal band very dark (blackish). Fig. 209......
...........................Speyeria idalia Drury. Regal Fritillary.

Range: Maine to North Carolina and Arkansas, west to Rocky Mountains in Upper Austral and Transition Zones. Local and erratic, perhaps most common in prairie states. Prefers wet meadows.

Fig. 209. Speyeria idalia ♀ V. Canton, Ohio.

5b DHW with submarginal pale band reddish or straw colored. Fig. 210.....................................Speyeria nokomis Edwards.

Range: Colorado to California (including Great Basin) south to Mexico, replacing S. idalia in similar environments.

Fig. 210. Speyeria nokomis ♂ V. Utah.

6a Male genitalia with valva bearing a long process, this process three to four times as long as broad (Fig. 211). Fig. 212................ ....*Speyeria edwardsii* Reakirt.

Range: Manitoba, Alberta, western Nebraska, western South Dakota, Montana, Wyoming, Colorado, and southern Canadian Prairie foothills, showing a strong affinity for the area of the Continental Divide (east slope mostly).

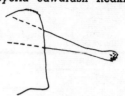

Fig. 211. Tip of valva of *Speyeria edwardsii.*

Fig. 212. *Speyeria edwardsii* ♂ V. Boulder County, Colorado.

6b Male genitalia with valva bearing a relatively short process (Fig. 213).....................7

Fig. 213. Tip of valva of *Speyeria mormonia.*

7a DFW with scaling of veins $M_1 - 2V$ roughly the same in both sexes. Fig. 214..........................*Speyeria mormonia* Boisduval.

Range: widely distributed over western United States, Canada and Alaska. Rather tolerant ecologically, ranging through many life zones. It is the highest flying *Speyeria*, reaching above tree line in Colorado (and extending downward to 9,000 feet).

Fig. 214. *Speyeria mormonia* ♂ V. Lloydminster, Saskatchewan.

7b DFW male with distinctly wider dark scaling along veins M₁ — 2V than DFW female. "callippe group."

Fig. 215.................................*Speyeria atlantis* Edwards.

Fig. 216...*S. egleis* Behr.

Fig. 217..................................*S. callippe* Boisduval.

Fig. 218....................................*S. zerene* Boisduval.

Fig. 219...*S. coronis* Behr.

Fig. 220..................................*S. hydaspe* Boisduval.

This is a western complex of six extremely variable species which can only be separated with assurance by experts who have long series from many localities for comparison. One species *(atlantis)* occurs also in the eastern United States and Canada, where it may be identified with the superficial key. Figures of specimens of each species are given, and clues given below will help to sort out some specimens of *coronis* and *hydaspe*. Material with which you have difficulty may be sent to Mr. L. P. Grey, Rt. 1, Box 216, Lincoln, Maine, who will determine season catches in papers for the privilege of examination. *Be sure to write before sending specimens.* Speyeria *coronis*—always with silver spots, generally large in size (LFW often > 32 mm.). *Speyeria hydaspe*—outside of Northern California, this is the only species with a reddish-melanic cast and delicate lavender overscaling of VHW discal area. The *callippe* group, in its entirety, is very complex because of the large amount of geographic variation in each species. They are widely sympatric, and there are numerous cases of parallel variation involving first one pair of species, and then another. Fortunately local naturalists have their problems reduced, since most localities will yield only a few of the species in the complex. To know the region is to know the species; experienced collectors will get definite help from ecological and temporal segregation of the species.

Fig. 215. *Speyeria atlantis* ♂ V. Boulder County, Colorado.

Fig. 216. *Speyeria egleis* ♂ V. Polaris, Montana.

Fig. 217. *Speyeria callippe* ♂ V. Blaine County, Idaho.

Fig. 218. *Speyeria zerene* ♂ V. Brewster, Washington.

Fig. 219. *Speyeria coronis* ♂ V. Ketchum, Idaho.

Fig. 220. *Speyeria hydaspe* ♂ V. Wind River Mountains, Wyoming.

Genus BOLORIA Moore
The Lesser Fritillaries
by A. B. Klots

These medium-sized, orange-brown and black butterflies occur in open spaces from Arctic tundra to mountaintops, meadows and marshes southward. Some have quite fast, flickering flights. Most of the species have many geographic subspecies and local forms that are sometimes very different from each other, and they also show much individual variation. All but five of the species occur also in Europe and Asia. The life histories of nearly all are only slightly, or not at all, known. European food plant records are given, including some which are merely suspected, as possible clues to those in North America. Most

119

species have only one generation a year, but the southern ones may have two or three.

KEY TO THE SPECIES OF *BOLORIA*.

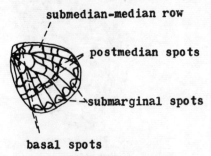

submedian-median row

postmedian spots

submarginal spots

basal spots

Fig. 221. Outline of VHW of *Boloria selene*, showing position of markings.

1a Dark spots in submarginal areas of VHW in cells Rs—Cu$_2$ and of VFW in cells R$_5$—M$_2$ regularly round or oval and sharply defined, with light yellow, white or silvery centers; VHW with distal margin of light spot of submedian-median r o w (Fig. 221) in cell Cu$_2$ convex. Fig. 222. . . . .
. . *Boloria eunomia* Esper.

Fig. 222. *Boloria eunomia* ♂ V. Nominingue, Quebec.

Range: chiefly in true sphagnum bogs, Canadian Zone forest, from subarctic Alaska across Canada to Labrador; southward in mountains to Colorado and Maine; Europe and Asia. Food plants: *Viola* (violets) and *Polygonum* (knotweed) in Europe; in North America, *Polygonum viviparum* (knotweed). Previously known as *Boloria aphirape* Hübner.

1b Dark spots in submarginal areas of VHW in cells Rs—Cu$_2$ and of VFW in cells R$_5$—M$_2$, when present usually indistinctly outlined, not clearly light yellow, white or silvery centered; VHW with distal margin of light spot of submedian-median row in cell Cu$_2$ usually concave, indented, or double, extending farther distad along veins Cu$_2$ and 2V than in median area of cell. 2

2a VHW with all postmedian light spots prominent and silvery. Fig. 223. . . . .*Boloria selene* Schiffermüller.

Fig. 223. *Boloria selene* ♂ V. Brokenhead, Manitoba.

Range: subarctic Alaska and Canada east to Newfoundland; southward in Rocky Mountains to Colorado; in lowland meadows to Iowa, Nebraska, southern Illinois and Maryland, and in mountains to North Carolina; Europe and Asia. This species is most often found in wet meadows. Food plants: in Europe *Viola* (violets), *Fragaria* (strawberries) and *Vaccinium uliginosum* (bilberry); in North America *Viola*. This species and *Boloria toddi* are the commonest and most widespread of the North American *Boloria*.

2b VHW with all postmedian light spots never prominent and silvery..**3**

3a Outer margin of HW slightly angled distad at tip of M_3, somewhat straight anterior and posterior to this; VHW with median light spot at end of discal cell white or pearly within the cell, but yellowish or brownish distad of the cell like the adjacent spots of the submedian-median series; D ground color of females notably paler and duller than bright orange-brown of males. Fig. 224........
..................................*Boloria napaea* Hoffmannsegg

Range: Alaska, western arctic Canada, northern British Columbia and Alpine Zone in Wyoming (Wind River Mountains) in grassy tundra and meadows; Europe and Asia. Food plants: in Europe, *Viola* (violets) and *Vaccinium?* (bilberry or cranberry). Formerly called *B. pales* Denis and Schiffermüller.

Fig. 224. *Boloria napaea* ♂ V. Mount McKinley National Park, Alaska.

3b Outer margin of HW more evenly curved, not angled distad at tip of M_3; VHW with median spot at end of discal cell not as in 3a, the portions of it within the discal cell and distad of the cell being concolorous (often both portions white or contain white); D ground color of females not notably duller than males (except in some *B. chariclea* and *B. polaris*)..**4**

4a VHW with light spots of submedian-median series, especially those in cells Rs, M_1, M_3, and Cu_1, largely filled with dark scaling, never all clear yellow or whitish....................................**7**

4b VHW with all light spots of submedian-median series (cells Sc—Cu_2) clear yellow to pearly white, containing very few, if any, darker scales except along lower discocellular vein....................**5**

5a Marginal dark markings of DFW and DHW a pair of thin, parallel lines, the space between which is often almost solidly filled with dark; marginal markings little expanded at vein tips, wing margin therefore more evenly dark with little checkering; VHW with submedian-median row of light spots pearly to silvery white; Canadian Rockies and Washington at high elevations above timberline. Fig. 225...................................*Boloria astarte* Doubleday.

Range: Canadian Rockies (Alberta) and Washington (Cooney Mt., near Methow Valley, J. C. Hopfinger); Siberia. A denizen of high, barren windswept ridges.

Fig. 225. *Boloria astarte* ♂ V. Banff, Alberta.

5b Marginal dark markings of DFW and DHW considerably expanded
at vein tips, narrower between veins, so that wing margin is definitely checkered; VHW with submedian-median light spots yellow,
never all white or pearly or silvery white.....................6

6a FW and HW with submarginal dark markings between veins forming angled lines or triangles with their apices pointing basad; VHW
with a complete or nearly complete series of clearly defined submarginal light spots; VHW with postbasal spot in discal cell seldom
large and conspicuous, if so, then yellowish or whitish with black
center. Fig. 226...........................*Boloria titania* Esper.

Range: central Alaska eastward through
Canada to Labrador and New Brunswick,
and southward in mountains to Washington, Utah and New Mexico; Mt. Washington, New Hampshire; Europe and Asia.
Found in meadows and along roadsides
in subarctic and Canadian Zone forest.
Food plants: in Europe, *Polygonum* (knotweed); in North America, arctic willows
(*Salix arctica* and *S. herbacea*)? and knotweed (*Polygonum viviparum?*). *Boloria
helena* Edwards and *B. montinus* Scudder
are geographic forms of this species.

Fig. 226. *Boloria titania*
♂ V. Savanne, Ontario.

6b FW and HW with submarginal dark markings between veins forming angled lines or triangles with their apices pointing distad; VHW
with no series of clearly defined submarginal light spots; postbasal
spot in discal cell large and conspicuous, black with light center.
Fig. 227...............................*Boloria kriemhild* Strecker.

Range: Great Basin regions of Idaho, Montana, Wyoming and Utah in mountain
meadows.

Fig. 227. *Boloria kriem-
hild* ♂ V. Soda Springs,
Idaho.

7a Small (LFW 15-20 mm.); D ground color dark and dull; dark markings blurred and indistinct. Fig. 228.......*Boloria improba* Butler.

Range: Alaska, northern British Columbia and eastward to Baffin Island north of or above timberline; arctic Europe and (?) Asia. Food plant: in Europe, *Salix herbacea*? (arctic willow).

Fig. 228. *Boloria improba* ♂ V. Eagle Summit, Alaska.

7b Larger (LFW 19-25 mm.); D ground color usually bright orange-brown; dark markings, though often very extensive, clearly contrasting with ground color.....................................8

8a FW with outer margin not evenly curved, but somewhat angled distad at tip of M₂. Fig. 229.................*Boloria toddi* Holland.

Range: Canadian Zone of British Columbia eastward across Canada to Maritime Provinces; southward in Rocky Mountains to Colorado; southward at low elevations to Nebraska, Minnesota, Wisconsin, Illinois, Maryland and, in the mountains, North Carolina. Food plant: *Viola* (violets). This and *selene* are the commonest and most widespread American *Boloria*.

Fig. 229. *Boloria toddi* ♂ V. Red Lodge Park, Alberta.

8b FW with outer margin evenly curved, not noticeably angled distad at tip of M₂.....................................9

9a V with all markings and colors dull, dingy, and non-contrasting, with no white, yellow, black or orange-brown markings or areas. Fig. 230.................................*Boloria alberta* Edwards.

Range: Rocky Mountains of Alberta, on high, barren ridges.

Fig. 230. *Boloria alberta* ♂ V. Laggan, Alberta.

9b V usually with many, always with at least some clearly defined contrasting markings or areas...............................10

10a FW and HW with submarginal dark markings clearly forming angled lines or triangles with their apices pointing basad......11

10b FW and HW with submarginal dark markings forming angled lines or triangles with their apices pointing distad, or forming spots and blotches of various shapes, but never angled lines or triangles with their apices pointing basad.................14

11a VHW with light spots of postmedian series (except, occasionally, that in cell M₂) clearly defined, white or satiny white; light submarginal spots white, forming a row of thin lines more or less expanded basad lying at right angles to the wing margin......12

11b VHW with light spots of postmedian series indistinct, often discernable only in cells Sc, Rs, Cu₁ and Cu₂, and only then as light shades (never pure white); light submarginal spots longer on axis parallel to wing margin than at right angles to it......13

12a VHW with spots of submedian-median series, except those in cells Sc and M₂, with very little white except for very narrow basal and distal edging; basal and postbasal light spots in discal cell usually absent or indistinct; white spots of postmedian series usually run together forming a band, definitely separated from the dark spots of the submarginal area; general tone of VHW usually yellowish-brown; area distad of white postmedian spots in cells Rs and M₁ almost always forming a yellowish-brown patch. Fig. 231...........................*Boloria freija* Thunberg.

Range: arctic America, from Alaska to Ellesmere Island and Labrador, southward in boggy areas in Canadian Zone forest to Ontario (Geraldton) and Quebec (Laurentides Park); southward in Rocky Mountains at and above timberline to Colorado; northern Europe and Asia; Mt. Daisetsu, Japan. Food plants: *Arctostaphylos uva-ursi* (bearberry) and *Empetrum nigrum* (crowberry) in Europe; *Rhododendron aureum* in Japan (M. Inoue).

Fig. 231. *Boloria freija* ♂ V. Geraldton, Ontario.

12b VHW with nearly all spots of submedian-median series except those in cells Sc and M$_2$, prominently white-edged both basally and distally; basal and postbasal light spots in discal cell, particularly the latter, usually prominent, white; white spots of postmedian series prominent, but usually separate and distally partly enclosing the dark spots in the submarginal area; general tone of **VHW** warm chocolate to orange-brown; area distad of white postmedian spots in cells Rs and M$_1$ not forming a distinct light patch. Fig. 232.........................*Boloria polaris* Boisduval.

Range: tundra north of, or above, timberline, arctic Alaska and Canada, eastward to Greenland; arctic Europe and Asia. With *B. chariclea*, one of the most arctic of butterflies.

Fig. 232. *Boloria polaris* ♂ V. Eagle Summit, Alaska.

13a VHW with basal spot in cell Cu$_2$ and submedian-median spots in cells Sc, M$_2$ and Cu$_2$ prominent, white to silvery white, that in cell M$_2$ (at end of discal cell) usually extending distad as a long, tapering point; other spots in submedian-median series usually much filled-in with the darker color of adjacent areas; light spots of submedian-median row seldom prominently margined basally and distally with dark brown or black; D of females with duller ground color and more dark suffusion than males. Fig. 233.....
.....................................*Boloria chariclea* Schneider.

Range: true Arctic only, Alaska and Canada to northernmost land in Ellesmere Island and Greenland; arctic Europe and Asia. Food plant: perhaps *Salix arctica* (arctic willow). This is the most northern of all butterflies; it and *B. polaris* are two of the five species of butterflies known from Greenland.

Fig. 233. *Boloria chariclea* ♂ V. Kotzebue, Alaska.

13b VHW with no spots of submedian-median series ever pure white or silvery white; some or all may be yellowish, brownish-white, or yellow; most are usually more or less invaded by the darker colors of adjacent areas, and prominently margined basally and distally with dark brown or black; D of females seldom duller colored and more dark suffused than males. (See Fig. 226.)......
...........................*Boloria titania* Esper (see couplet 6a.).

14a VHW with submarginal and postmedian series of light spots complete in cells Sc-Cu$_2$, white and clearly defined; light spots of submedian-median series distally strongly concave, extending distad along the veins as long, tapering points. Fig. 234.........
....*Boloria distincta* Gibson.

Range: Alaska and Yukon mountains, on high, barren ridges. This is the rarest American *Boloria*.

Fig. 234. *Boloria distincta* ♂ V. Richardson Mountains, Northwest Territories.

14b VHW with no distinct, clearly defined, submarginal or postmedian light spots; light spots of submedian-median series mostly convex distally, never strongly concave and extending distad along the veins 15

15a VHW with considerable blue-gray to violet gray; basal and submedian light spots of cell Sc usually whitish to violet-gray and so fused together along veins Sc and Rs as to enclose a dark patch; the more distal of these spots prolonged distad below vein Sc; DFW and DHW with basal third to half considerably, often almost entirely, heavily clouded with dark scales; FW of male slightly narrower and more pointed apically than that of female. Fig. 235......................*Boloria frigga* Thunberg.

Range: arctic and subarctic tundra, Bering Sea to Baffin Island and Labrador; southward in mountain bogs to British Columbia and Colorado, and in true sphagnum bogs to central Ontario (Geraldton) and northern Michigan; arctic Europe and Asia. Food plants: in Europe, *Rubus chamaemorus*? (salmonberry) and sallow (*Salix*?).

Fig. 235. *Boloria frigga* ♂ V. Big Delta, Alaska.

15b VHW chiefly brownish-yellow to reddish-brown, with little or no blue-gray to violet-gray; basal and submedian light spots in cell Sc usually yellow or yellowish, seldom fused together so as to enclose a dark patch; DFW and DHW with dark markings usually narrow and clear-cut, and with little or no dark basal suffusion; FW of male not noticeably narrower or more pointed apically than that of female. Fig. 236.......... *Boloria epithore* **Edwards.**

Range: southern British Columbia, Alberta, Montana, Washington, Oregon and California, in meadows. Food plant: *Viola* (violets).

Fig. 236. *Boloria epithore* ♂ V. Polaris, Montana.

Tribe MELITAEINI
Checker Spots, Crescents, and Patch Butterflies
by David L. Bauer
Genus EUPHYDRYAS Scudder

The great majority of colonies of *Euphydryas* will fit in one of the species (or species groups) keyed below. In some localities two or more species may fly together, making careful comparison of the wing pattern, coloring, and male genital structures necessary for proper determination. Differences in the genitalia are usually accompanied by differences in coloration. There is variation in the genitalia, but it is not as extreme as that present in the pattern and coloration. This is a most difficult genus; it is hoped that the key will be helpful.

KEY TO THE SPECIES OF *EUPHYDRYAS.*

1a VHW with postmedian series of spots pale yellow or white in color. Fig. 237............................. *Euphydryas phaeton* **Drury.**

Range: Minnesota and Kansas in the West to Georgia and north Atlantic coast north to Maritime Provinces of Canada. Food plant: *Chelone glabra* (turtlehead), also rarely a few other plants. One brood (v-vi). Very local, found only around food plant.

Fig. 237. *Euphydryas phaeton* ♂ V. Knauers, Pennsylvania.

1b VHW with postmedian series of spots or postmedian band prominently colored some shade of red or orange-brown, or at least a dot of red or orange-brown in each spot......................2

2a D with a wide, prominent orange-brown postmedian band, median spot band white or pale yellowish and marginal and submarginal bands reduced in size (almost obsolete on HW of some specimens). Fig. 238.............................*Euphydryas gillettii* Barnes.

Range: Yellowstone National Park area north through Montana to Glacier National Park. Food plant: unknown. One brood (vii-viii).

Fig. 238. *Euphydryas gillettii* ♂ D. Soldier County, Montana.

2b D not as in 2a (with our present knowledge of the remaining species, wing pattern and coloration are of little value in identification) 3

Fig. 239. Inner face of valva of *Euphydryas editha.*

3a Male genitalia: clasp of valva with two prongs directed at a wide angle (more than 90°) from each other; upper prong heavily armed with tiny spines (Fig 239); food plants predominantly Plantaginaceae. Fig. 240.............................*Euphydryas editha* Boisduval.

Range: Baja California to British Columbia and Montana; not found in Arizona, New Mexico or Colorado. Food plants: Plantaginaceae. One brood, ii-viii, depending on locality.

Fig. 240. *Euphydryas editha* ♂ V. Lake Hodges, California.

3b Male genitalia: clasp of valva with two prongs at right angles to each other, or upper prong curved downward and often running roughly parallel to lower prong; food plants predominantly Scrophulariaceae....4

4a Male genitalia: upper prong of clasp at right angles to lower, or slightly curved down; very short to medium in length and covered with very minute spines, especially near the apex (Fig. 241). Fiç. 242.............*Euphydryas chalcedona* Doubleday and Hewitson.

Range: extreme southern Oregon, all of California, extreme western Nevada, and across Arizona from northwestern to southeastern corners. Food plants: many genera and species of Scrophulariaceae. One brood in north and on coast, often two in desert and in Arizona (ii-vii and ix-x).

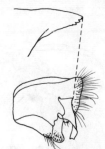

Fig. 241. Inner face of valva of *Euphydryas chalcedona*, tip of upper prong of clasp magnified at top.

Fig. 242. *Euphydryas chalcedona* ♀ V. Oakland, California.

4b Male genitalia: upper prong not as in 4a......................5

5a Male genitalia: upper prong of clasp without minute spines on either outer or inner edge; length of prong variable, when short only upper edge curved downward. (Fig. 243)........................
.....................................*Euphydryas colon* Edwards.

Range: Sierra Nevada of California north through Cascades to British Columbia and mountains of Idaho and Montana. Food plant: *Pentstemon* species. One brood, v-ix depending on elevation.

Fig. 243. Inner face of valva of *Euphydryas colon*.

5b **Male genitalia: upper prong of clasp strongly toothed on inner edge or at least with minute spines near apex on inner edge, none on outer edge; upper prong long and generally strongly curved downward, often parallel to lower prong (Fig. 244)...............**
.....................Euphydryas anicia Doubleday and Hewitson.

Range: British Columbia and Alberta south into the Cascade Mountains of Washington (not known from Oregon Cascades or Sierra Nevada of California?) and through eastern Washington and Montana to northern Arizona and New Mexico. Food plant: various species of Pentstemon. One brood, v-viii, depending on elevation.

Fig. 244. Inner face of valva of *Euphydryas anicia*.

Genus POLADRYAS Bauer, new genus

Type Species: *Melitaea pola* Boisduval 1869.

The two species of this new genus superficially resemble members of the Palaearctic genus *Melitaea* Fabr. but are placed in a separate genus because the male genitalia are a modified *Chlosyne* type (see couplet 30a of generic key, and Fig. 245), and the female genitalia (Fig. 246) are very simple as in *Euphydryas* Scudder with the genital plate simple and flat, and the bursa arising from the middle. There are numerous local variations but the key will enable recognition of the two species.

Fig. 245. Inner face of valva *Poladryas pola*.

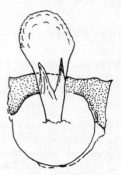

Fig. 246. Female genitalia of *Poladryas pola*, dorsal (internal) view.

1a VHW margined with black at base of fringe so that creamy-white marginal band is margined with black on both inner and outer edges. Fig. 247.......................*Poladryas minuta* Edwards.

Range: Texas south into Mexico, Chihuahua, Coahuila, and Nuevo Leon. Food plant: *Pentstemon* sp.

Fig. 247. *Poladryas minuta* ♀ V. Texas.

1b VHW not margined with black at the base of fringe, so that marginal band and fringe blend. Fig. 248....*Poladryas pola* Boisduval.

Range: western Nebraska to Sierra Nevada Mountains, California; and Wyoming to Sonora, Mexico. Inhabits deserts and alpine meadows. Food plant: *Pentstemon* sp. Two broods (iv-vii and ix).

Fig. 248. *Poladryas pola* ♂ V. El Paso County, Colorado.

Genus MICROTIA Bates

Originally erected by Bates as a monotypic genus for *Microtia elva* Bates. In recent years two additional species have been found to share the simple female genital structure, the fragile elongate wing shape, and the slender lengthened abdomen typical of *elva*. One of these species is found along our southern border and is included with *elva* in the genus. The other species is entirely Mexican.

KEY TO THE SPECIES OF *MICROTIA*.

1a D and V dark brown; FW with a subapical transverse orange band from costa to outer margin, and a median orange patch on inner margin extending to, or a little past, vein Cu$_1$; HW with a median band from costa to inner margin; D orange, V cream tinged with orange. Fig. 249............................*Microtia elva* Bates.

Range: southern Arizona to southern Texas thence south through Central America. Food plant: unknown. Multiple brooded.

Fig. 249. *Microtia elva* ♂ D. Guerrero, Mexico.

1b D various shades of orange-brown broken into spot bands by dark scaling along veins and transverse dark lines; there is considerable geographical variation in the extent of the dark scaling; VHW banded with alternating bands of cream or white and orange brown, which are irregular and broken in basal area; unique among American Melitaeini in having a distinct orange-brown marginal band on VFW, and except in rare instances only a black marginal line on VHW. Fig. 250...................*Microtia dymas* Edwards.

Range: Imperial Valley area California through southern Arizona to southern Texas and northern Mexico. Food plant: in west *Beloperone californica*. Multiple brooded (ii-xi).

Fig. 250. *Microtia dymas* ♂ V. Baboquivaria Mountains, Arizona.

Genus CHLOSYNE Butler

This is a large and varied genus, and is further enlarged in this key to include the American species, which formerly were placed in the Palaearctic genus *Melitaea* Fabricius, but are now known to have the *Chlosyne* male and female genital structure. The Palla group is a difficult group to make a key for, because of the geographical variation and the limits of our knowledge. For positive identification one should check localities carefully, and reference to the technical literature may be necessary.

132

Range: central Arizona to central Texas and throughout most of Mexico. Food plant: in Mexico Compositae species. Multiple brooded. This species is in the subgenus *Texola* Higgins. Food plant: in Texas *Siphonoglossa pilosella*, (Acanthaceae); in Mexico compositae species.

Fig. 251. *Chlosyne elada* ♂ V. Burnet, County, Texas.

Range: from Manitoba, Canada to Mexico in the west, and from New England to Georgia in the east. Food plants: various species of *Aster* and *Helianthus* (sunflower). Multiple broods in the south, only one brood in the north.

Fig. 252. *Chlosyne gorgone* ♂ V. Lawrence, Kansas.

5a V marginal band rarely all the same color; usually pale cream colored at the apex of FW and on costa of HW, rest of marginal band some shade of orange-brown often clouded with dusky scales in cells M_1 and M_2 on HW, and cells M_1 and M_2 on FW; VHW has submarginal spot in cell M_3 much larger than rest of series and submarginal spot in cell M_2 nearly always obsolete and replaced by dark scaling; very little if any orange-brown in basal half of wing, the dominant color being pale yellowish often mixed with shining white. Fig. 253..............*Chlosyne nycteis* Doubleday.

Range: southern Canada from Manitoba to Maritime Provinces thence south to eastern Arizona, Texas, and Georgia. Food plants: various species of *Aster* and *Helianthus* (sunflower). One brood in the north and multiple brooded in south.

Fig. 253. *Chlosyne nycteis*
♂ V. Lawrence, Kansas.

5b V with marginal band always entirely orange-brown and prominent; VHW with submarginal spot in cell M_3 only slightly larger than rest of series, and spot in cell M_2 not greatly reduced or obsolete; VHW always has some orange-brown scaling in basal half of wing, and commonly the orange-brown spots are conspicuous; D very variable. Fig. 254..............*Chlosyne harrisii* Scudder.

Range: southern Canada from Manitoba to Maritime Provinces south to northern Illinois, Ohio, West Virginia, and New Jersey. Food plant: *Aster* (aster). One brood (vi-vii).

Fig. 254. *Chlosyne harrisii* ♂ V. Center Ossipee, New Hampshire.

6a VHW light areas dull white or lustrous pearly white (this is the Acastus group, and each species is so variable that no characters can be said to be typical of or restricted to any one of them, hence locality and habitat are the best key characters known to date)....7

6b VHW light areas yellow to creamy white never pearly (this is the Palla group, containing only two species which can be separated with certainty only by the male genitalia).....................10

7a VHW light areas lustrous or pearly white; D maculation and coloring bright and clear not dull and clouded......................8

7b VHW light areas dull white, sometimes with a yellowed cast; maculation on all surfaces of the wings usually dull and clouded. Fig. 255...............................*Chlosyne damoetas* Skinner.

Range: High alpine species found along crest of Sierra Nevada Mountains in California and Rocky Mountains of Colorado at 11,000-12,000 feet north through Wyoming to Alberta and British Columbia at 8,000-10,000 feet. Food plant: Composite species?. One brood (vi-vii).

Fig. 255. *Chlosyne damoetas* ♂ V. Colorado.

8a D ground color orange-brown with a complete pattern of dark horizontal and transverse lines....................................9

8b D ground color ruddy orange-brown; dark maculation weak or obsolete in discal area of all wings. Fig. 256......................
...................................*Chlosyne neumoegeni* Skinner.

Range: Mojave and Colorado deserts of California and western Arizona. Food plant: *Aster tortifolius* and other Asters. Two broods (iii-iv, and ix).

Fig. 256. *Chlosyne neumoegeni* ♀ D. Mojave Desert, California.

9a Coastal mountains and valleys of California; VHW submarginal and postmedian spot bands, and basal spots, lustrous pearly white. Fig. 257.....................................*Chlosyne gabbii* Behr.**

Range: Coastal mountains and valleys of California from Monterey south to northern Baja California. Food plant: *Corethrogyne filaginifolia* (wooly-aster), *Hazardia squarrosa*. Spring brood (iii-vi) depending on elevation, and rarely a second brood (vii or viii).

Fig. 257. *Chlosyne gabbii* ♀ D. Glendora, California.

9b Great Basin and Rocky Mountain area; VHW all light areas lustrous white; duller in the north and often pearly in the south. Fig. 258.....................................*Chlosyne acastus* Edwards.**

Range: from southeastern Oregon to western Nebraska on the north to southeastern Arizona on the south. Food plant: various species of *Aster*. One brood.

Fig. 258. *Chlosyne acastus* ♀ V. Arizona.

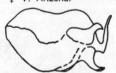

Fig. 259. Inner face of valva of *Chlosyne palla.*

10a Posterior process of the valva of the male genitalia long and not stoutly joined to the valva (Fig. 259); an extremely variable species. Fig. 260...............*Chlosyne palla* Boisduval.**

Range: southern California north to southwestern Oregon, then east of Cascades north to British Columbia, also eastward through central Oregon and Idaho to the Rocky Mountains, where it flies from Montana to northern New Mexico. Food plant: *Castileja* sp. and *Aster* sp., one brood (iii-vii).

Fig. 260. *Chlosyne palla* ♂ V. Santa Cruz, California.

10b Posterior process of the valva short and stoutly joined to the valva
(Fig. 261); D median band conspicuously wider than other bands
and paler than outer portion of wings; basal third of wings
mostly dark blackish brown in marked
contrast to median band; dark markings on outer portion commonly obsolete in postmedian area; this description good only for Sierra Nevada specimens as Washington specimens
greatly resemble males of *palla*; check
the male genitalia to be sure. Fig. 262.
............*Chlosyne hoffmanni* Behr.

Fig. 261. Inner face of valva of *Chlosyne hoffmanni*.

Range: subalpine areas of Sierra
Nevada and Scott Mountains, etc. of
California north up the Oregon Cascade Mountains and along the east
slope of the Washington Cascades to
Canadian border. Food plant: not
known. One brood (v-viii).

Fig. 262. *Chlosyne hoffmanni* ♀ D. Eldorado County, California.

11a VHW with at least a spot of orange-brown in the discal cell, but
usually with a band of orange-brown in the submedian area...12

11b VHW without any red or orange-brown in the discal cell or in the
submedian area 15

12a VHW postmedian series of spots all orange-red and forming a band
from the anal angle to costa...............................14

12b VHW postmedian series of spots not all the same color, those in
cells Cu_1, Cu_2, M_1, and M_2 being orange-brown but the middle
spot in cell M_3 is whitish...................................13

13a FW postmedian series of spots orange-brown, blending with the
median series to form a broad band. Fig. 263................
.....................................*Chlosyne definita* Aaron.

Range: west Texas south into Mexico.
Food plant: not known. Multiple broods.

Fig. 263. *Chlosyne definita* ♂ V. Texas.

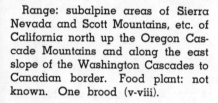

**13b FW postmedian series of spots reduced to a series of white dots in a brownish black ground. Fig. 264.........................
...........................Chlosyne endeis Godman and Salvin.**

Range: extreme southern Texas south into Mexico. Food plant: not known. Multiple broods.

Fig. 264. *Chlosyne endeis* ♀ V. Pharr, Texas.

14a FW with postmedian series of pale spots outlined with blackish. Fig. 265............................Chlosyne theona Menetries.

Range: southern Arizona, New Mexico, Texas south into Mexico. Food plant: *Castileja* sp. and *Verbena* sp. Multiple broods.

Fig. 265. *Chlosyne theona* ♂ V. Arizona.

**14b FW suffused tawny; lacking postmedian spots. Fig. 266........
.................................Chlosyne chinatiensis Tinkham.**

Range: mountains of Big Bend area in Texas. Food plant: not known. Multiple broods.

Fig. 266. *Chlosyne chinatiensis* ♂ V. Terlingua, Texas.

15a **VHW without a trace of red or orange-brown; ground color very pale yellow to almost white, veins scaled in black, a postmedian black band enclosing six spots same color as the ground; various amounts of black in submedian area sometimes forming a transverse band. Fig. 267** ....
........*Chlosyne leanira* **Felder and Felder, and related species.**

Range: *C. leanira* from central Oregon south through California to northern Baja California. This is an extremely variable insect varying from very dark specimens with reduced yellow spots and almost no red to specimens in which the black is almost entirely absent and replaced by orange. This species is single brooded, and the food plant is *Castileja*. *C. alma* Strecker (=*fulvia* Edwards) from Southern Utah through Arizona, and New Mexico into west Texas. This is a much more constant species with a dimorphic female that is always much more orange-brown

Fig. 267. *Chlosyne leanira* ♀ V. Glendora, California.

than the male. Multiple brooded (iii-x). In extreme southeastern Arizona is *C. cyneas* Godman and Salvin, a dark species without light spots in the basal area on the D. surface of the wings. I have been unable to make a key for this group that did not result in keying out similar specimens from all the species rather than separating the species.

15b **VHW with red or orange-red patches or spots on the outer half of the wings, or at least a tinge of orange color** **16**
16a **VHW at least a patch or trace of red or orange-red in cell 2V at the anal angle** **17**
16b **VHW no red or orange in cell 2V at anal angle; but a large basal yellow patch with black dots and spots in it edged with a band of red extending from vein 2V to M₁; DFW black with numerous**

white dots; DHW with a large discal patch of orange-red surrounded by black which is widest along the outer margin. This is a large insect; LFW male 28 mm., female 34 mm. Fig. 268 ....
.....*Chlosyne janais* Drury.

Range: southern T e x a s south through Central America. Food plant: not identified. Multiple broods.

Fig. 268. *Chlosyne janais* ♀ D. Cochise County, Arizona.

17a VFW discal cell always washed with, or wholly orange; VHW inner margin orange; FW and HW submarginal spots tinged with orange; D with a broad orange median band and submarginal spots orange. Fig. 269..............*Chlosyne californica* Wright.

Range: southern Nevada, southeastern California, southern Arizona, northern Sonora, and all of Baja California. Food plant: various species of Compositae—sunflowers, etc. Multiple broods (ii-x).

Fig. 269. *Chlosyne cali-fornica* ♂ D. Congress, Arizona.

17b VFW discal cell without any orange coloring and VHW always with at least a spot of red-orange in cell 2V at the anal angle; an extremely variable species, if you have a specimen that you have keyed out this far and fits the above two characters, it is proba· bly one of the multitude of color variations of this species. D may be plain black with white bands and spots, or with yellow, orange, red-orange, or separate white and deep red median bands (and every gradation between these). Some lack a median band on the secondaries and other specimens have wide discal patches of the above colors; these are some of the northern color forms, in the tropics there are still others. Fig. 270....*Chlosyne lacinia* Geyer.

Range: from southern California through Arizona and New Mexico to Texas thence south to Argentina. This is the most widely distributed species of the genus. Food plants: numerous Compositae, especially sunflowers. Multiple broods (iii-x).

Fig. 270. *Chlosyne lacinia* ♀ D. Sarita, Texas.

Genus MELLICTA Billberg
There is only one species *Mellicta athalia* Rottemburg (= *mayi* Gunder) credited to North America (Fig. 271) and it has not been col-

lected for many years. It has been taken at Banff, Alberta and Smithers, British Columbia. The male genitalia (Fig. 272) are identical with those of the Japanese specimens of *Mellicta athalia ambigua* (Menetries) and it is now thought that the original specimens of *M. mayi* Gunder were mislabeled Japanese specimens. It is included here just in case someone again turns up some specimens, as it would be easy for a species to be lost in the wilds of northern British Columbia where very little collecting has been done.

Fig. 271. *Mellicta athalia* ♂ V. Europe.

The specimen before me labeled Smithers, B.C. Canada, may be described as follows: VFW evenly orange-brown with black transverse lines, and a few paler spots in the apical area; VHW marginal band dull cream colored with a hint of orange-brown: postmedian area dull dusky orange-brown except for a series of crescentic brighter orange-brown spots in distal portion from anal angle to vein Rs; D typical Melitaeine pattern of dark lines on an orange-brown ground.

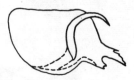

Fig. 272. Inner face of valva of *Mellicta athalia*.

Genus PHYCIODES Hübner

There are three subgenera of the genus *Phyciodes*. Because of the difficulty involved in making a key for these essentially similar, but confusingly variable insects, each subgenus will be keyed separately.

Several of the species formerly placed in the genus *Phyciodes* have been found to have the *Chlosyne* male and female genital structures and are included in the key to that genus. If care is not taken these species could be keyed out under the genus *Phyciodes*, but a check of the male genital structure (Fig. 273) using the key to the genera will settle the question conclusively.

Fig. 273. Inner face of valva of *Phyciodes tharos*.

KEY TO THE SUBGENERA OF *PHYCIODES*.

1a Male genitalia with two posterior projections of tegumen not armed with single hooks or clusters of spines...........*Tritanassa* p. 146

1b Male genitalia with two posterior projections of tegumen armed with single hooks or clusters of spines..........................2

2a Male genitalia with two posterior projections of tegumen armed with single incurved hooks (except *vesta*, which has two or three)......
....*Phyciodes* p. 142

141

2b Male genitalia with two posterior projections of tegumen armed with an elaborate cluster of spines.........................*Eresia* p. 146

Subgenus PHYCIODES Hübner

This is the Tharos group, which has its greatest development in the United States. Because of the numerous species in the U.S. and their great individual, seasonal, altitudinal and geographical variation, it is impossible to make a workable key that is more than about 75% efficient. To expedite the use of the key and identification of specimens,

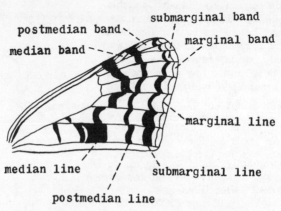

Fig. 273A. Pattern elements of *Phyciodes* FW.

Fig. 273a, giving the nomenclature of the maculation of bands and lines used in the key is given.

KEY TO THE SPECIES OF *PHYCIODES* (*PHYCIODES*).

Fig. 274. *Phyciodes vesta* ♂ V. Texas.

1a VFW submarginal and postmedian lines black and connected by black scaling along veins between them, resulting in the postmedian band being broken into separate spots particularly in cells M_3, Cu_1, Cu_2. Fig. 274.... ....*Phyciodes vesta* Edwards

Range: Texas to Guatemala. Food plant: *Siphonoglossa pilosella* (Acanthaceae). Multiple broods.

1b VFW with the postmedian line in limbal area absent or deep orange-brown, not black..2

2a VFW males with discal and limbal areas extensively and usually evenly colored a brighter orange-brown than rest of wing; postmedian line obsolete in limbal area resulting in a broad unmarked

expanse; DFW with apical, subapical, and marginal areas largely black with a prominent orange-brown spot in cell M_3; DHW males with a broad marginal black band; VHW with a chocolate brown area centered around the submarginal spot in cell M_3, this chocolate area sometimes reduced to a few spots. Fig. 275. . . . .
. . . .*Phyciodes tharos* Drury.

Range: all of North America from southern Canada to mountains of southern Mexico, except the Pacific Coast west of the Sierra Nevada and Cascade Mountains. Food plant: Asters. Multiple broods except in the north.

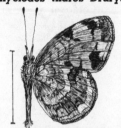

Fig. 275. *Phyciodes tharos* ♂ V. Lawrence, Kansas.

2b VFW with discal and limbal areas not evenly colored bright orange-brown; but marked with lighter spots, sometimes pale yellow, and darker lines of orange-brown. 3

3a D predominantly bright orange-brown; DFW submarginal spots in cells R_4 and R_5 always present and clear and distinct, usually DFW submarginal series is complete. 4

3b D not predominantly bright orange-brown, but marked with heavy black lines and spots, FW marginal areas generally black; DFW submarginal spots of males either absent or indistinct except in cell M_3. 6

4a DFW males with median band lighter than postmedian band, often markedly so, with pale bar near end of discal cell; in specimens approaching *P. mylitta* in appearance the marginal band is also orange-brown; Sierra Nevada Mountains of California at high altitudes. . . . .*Phyciodes campestris* Behr (see couplet 8a).

4b DFW males median band not lighter than postmedian series of spots; bar near end of discal cell same shade as other orange-brown spots; FW and HW marginal band thin and predominantly black in color; when postmedian line becomes obsolescent it becomes ruddy orange-brown in limbal area. 5

5a Insect large, LFW averages 19.6 mm. in male, 21.8 mm. in female; D black lines and spots often obsolete, sometimes almost entirely so, except for median line in cell Cu_2 which is expanded to a prominent spot and very persistent; VHW in females with submarginal spots whitish to shining white and rarely clouded with brown even in cells M_2 and Cu_1. Fig. 276..........*Phyciodes barnesi* Skinner.

Fig. 276. *Phyciodes barnesi* ♂ D. Cochise County, Arizona.

Range: from British Columbia and Washington along the eastern foothills of the Cascade Mountains southeastward to Colorado and north rim of Grand Canyon, Arizona. Food plant: probably Thistle. One brood (v-vii). This has been regarded as a subspecies of *P. mylitta,* but in Washington and British Columbia it broadly overlaps the range of *mylitta.* In the same area *mylitta* is multiple brooded and *barnesi* single.

5b Insect smaller than preceding; LFW male averages 16.3 mm., female averages 17.2 mm.; D black lines are much more constant, and median line not commonly expanded into prominent black spot in cell Cu_2 except in Arizona specimens; VHW in females with a prominent chocolate brown area centering around submarginal spot in cell M_3, this chocolate brown area less prominent in Arizona specimens. Fig. 277...................*Phyciodes mylitta* Edwards.

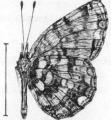

Fig. 277. *Phyciodes my-litta* ♂ V. Oakland, California.

Range: northern Baja California and Guatemala north to southern British Columbia in Canada. Food plant: Thistle. Multiple brooded throughout range (iii-x).

6a V maculation as in *P. mylitta;* size, as large or larger than *P. barnesi;* D heavy black marking on an essentially *mylitta* pattern; DFW in male orange-brown spots all about the same shade; shape of wings as in *mylitta;* rare. Fig. 278....*Phyciodes orseis* Edwards.

Fig. 278. *Phyciodes orseis* ♂ D. California.

Range: very limited in coastal mountains of northern California from San Francisco area north. Food plant: not known. One brood (iii-vi).

6b DFW median band lighter in color than postmedian band either strongly contrasting or at least a shade lighter.................7

7a V ground color dull orange-yellow; VHW with rusty orange-brown lines and spots..8

7b V ground color pale yellowish in summer generation—whitish and much mottled with various shades of brown in spring and fall generations; VHW not marked with rusty orange-brown, but with black or chocolate brown...9

8a VFW with black coloring reduced and replaced by rusty orange-brown; western North America from Canada to Mexico; usually a pale bar across discal cell near end. Fig. 279.....................
....*Phyciodes campestris* Behr.

Range: reported from shores of Arctic ocean in Canada south to the mountains of Mexico west of the Great Plains. Food plant: not known. Single brood in north, two or more in the south (iv-ix). *P. montana* Behr is the high altitude form of this species (see couplet 4a).

Fig. 279. *Phyciodes campestris* ♂ V. Echo Lake Drive.

8b VFW with black coloring more extensive, median line usually complete, or nearly so; inhabits eastern area; bar across discal cell near end usually clouded with orange-brown and indistinct. Fig. 280....
....*Phyciodes batesii* Reakirt.

Range: southeastern Canada and U.S. from Nebraska to New Jersey. Food plant: Aster. One brood (v-vi).

Fig. 280. *Phyciodes batesii* ♂ V. Douglas Lake, Michigan.

9a VFW large apical area of clear pale yellow, and in male submarginal spots in cells M_3 and M_2 separated from yellow apical area by dark line. Fig. 281..............*Phyciodes picta* Edwards.

Range: Arizona to Nebraska and south into Mexico. Food plant: Asters. Multiple broods.

Fig. 281. *Phyciodes picta* ♂ V. No data.

145

9b VFW small apical spot of pale yellow or white limited to sub-marginal spots in cells R_4 and R_5 and marginal area adjacent thereto; VFW in male submarginal spot in M_3 isolated by spots immediately above and below, being obscured by chocolate brown (summer) or gray brown (winter); bar near end of discal cell obscured by orange-red color of discal area. Fig. 282..............
....*Phyciodes phaon* Edwards.

Range: Georgia to Kansas and south-eastern California thence south through Cuba and to Guatemala. Food plant: *Lippia lanceolata* and *L. nodiflora.* Multiple broods.

Fig. 282. *Phyciodes pha-on* ♂ V. Indian River, Florida.

Subgenus ERESIA Doubleday

There is only one species of this subgenus, *Phyciodes frisia* Poey (Fig. 283), found in the United States, but in Central and South America there are several dozen.

Range: southern Florida, southern Texas to Arizona, south to Panama. Food plant: unknown. Multiple broods.

Fig. 283. *Phyciodes frisia* ♀ D. Miami, Florida.

Subgenus TRITANASSA Forbes

Only one species is recorded from our area, but others come close to the Rio Grande and may eventually be taken in the United States. Our species is *Phyciodes texana* Edwards (Fig. 284).

Range: Georgia, Florida, Kansas to Arizona and south to Guatemala. Multiple broods. Food plants: *Beloperone guttata, Jacobinia carnea, Siphonoglossa pilosella, Ruellia drummondiana,* and *R. occidentalis* (all Acanthaceae).

Fig. 284. *Phyciodes tex-ana* ♂ V. Santa Rita Mountains, Arizona.

Tribe NYMPHALINI
Genus NYMPHALIS Kluk
The Tortoise Shells

Like the *Polygonia*, these butterflies hibernate as adults. They may be seen flying on warm days in mid-winter.

KEY TO THE SPECIES OF *NYMPHALIS*.

1a D with light marginal band contrasting with dark ground color. Fig. 285...........*Nymphalis antiopa* Linnaeus. The Mourning Cloak.

Range: Hudsonian Zone of Alaska and Canada south to the southern limits of the Temperate Zone. Food plants: *Ulmus* (elm), *Salix* (willow), *Populus* (poplar), *Celtis* (hackberry) and many other plants.

Fig. 285. *Nymphalis antiopa* ♂ D. Oak Creek Canyon, Arizona.

1b D without contrasting light marginal band......................2
2a D with a sharply outlined yellow and orange submarginal band. Fig. 286............................*Nymphalis milberti* Latreille.

Range: Newfoundland to the Canadian Pacific Coast, south to West Virginia, Colorado and California. Food plant: *Urtica* (nettle).

Fig. 286. *Nymphalis milberti* ♂ D. Saskatchewan.

2b D without a sharply outlined submarginal band.................3

3a Large (LFW 32 mm.); D with broad basal areas of brown. Fig. 287.
.................*Nymphalis vau-album* Denis and Schiffermüller.
The Compton Tortoise Shell.

Range: Alaska and Canada,
south in wooded areas to North
Carolina, Missouri, and Colorado. Never an abundant species. Food plants: *Salix* (willow), *Betula alba* (northern white
birch), and *Populus* (poplar). This
has long been known as *Nymphalis j-album* Boisduval and
Leconte.

Fig. 287. *Nymphalis vau-album* ♂ D
Center Ossipee, New Hampshire.

3b Small (LFW 27 mm.); D without broad basal areas of brown, yel-
lowish-orange ground color covering DHW almost to base. Fig. 288.
.................................*Nymphalis californica* Boisduval.

Range: Colorado to Montana west to
California and Oregon. Occasionally
found in the East, due probably to ac-
cidental importation. Food plant: *Ceanothus*.

Fig. 288. *Nymphalis californica* ♀ D. Mariposa, California.

Genus POLYGONIA Hübner
The Angle Wings
by C. F. dos Passos and Paul R. Ehrlich

These butterflies strongly resemble leaves when they rest with their wings folded. They rarely visit flowers. Like the *Nymphalis* and *Vanessa*, *Polygonia* hibernate as adults. In some of the species which are double-brooded the individuals of the summer generation are considerably darker than those which overwinter. The relationships of the various western "species" are little understood, and the following key admittedly leaves much to be desired.

KEY TO THE SPECIES OF *POLYGONIA*.

1a Silvery mark on VHW at end of cell ("comma line") consisting of curved line and separate dot. Fig. 289..........................
..........*Polygonia interrogationis* Fabricius. **The Question Mark**.

Range: entire United States and southern Canada, east of the Rocky Mountains. Food plants: *Urtica* (nettles), *Ulmus* (elm), *Celtis* (hackberry), *Humulus* (hops), *Boehmeria* (false nettle), and others.

Fig. 289. *Polygonia interrogationis* ♂
V. Douglas County, Kansas.

1b Comma line a single unit, not a curved line and dot.............2
2a D often with a greenish sheen; V often with submarginal greenish spots; D with very contrasting dark brown borders; DFW with large, dark, discal spots; D generally "heavily marked"; wing margins extremely irregular. Fig. 290...........*Polygonia faunus* Edwards.

Range: southern Canada south to northern Georgia in the mountains, west to northern California (not found in Great Plains). Food plants: *Betula lenta* (black birch), *Salix humilis* (willow), *Alnus* (alder), *Ribes* (currant), *Azalea occidentalis*. A closely related form, *Polygonia hylas* Edwards is placed here tentatively. Specimens labeled *"hylas"* usually have the ventral surface a more uniform pale gray than more typical *faunus*.

Fig. 290. *Polygonia faunus* ♂
D. Germania, Pa.

2b Without greenish coloring; markings and outline of wing variable..3

3a V a bright, warm, brown, tending to yellow-brown; DHW with dark
border very narrow or almost absent. Fig. 291.................
....*Polygonia satyrus* Edwards.

Range: western North America (usually in mountains) extending eastward along the Canadian border
states and provinces to New York,
Ontario, Quebec and Newfoundland.
Food plants: *Urtica* (nettle) and perhaps *Ulmus* (elm).

Fig. 291. *Polygonia satyrus* ♂
V. Oakland, California.

3b V dull or dark brown, or gray—if tending towards yellow-brown,
then DHW with dark border at least twice as wide as that of DFW..4

4a V with light gray postmedian band strongly contrasting with dark
basal area; comma line not hooked or enlarged at either end. Fig.
292......................*Polygonia gracilis* Grote and Robinson.

Range: Alaska, southern Canada, and
the most northern parts of the northeastern United States. Frequently visits
flowers of *Gnaphalium* (everlasting).

Fig. 292. *Polygonia gracilis*
♂ V. New Brunswick.

4b V lacking strongly contrasting postmedian band; comma line may
taper at both ends or it may be enlarged and/or hooked........5

5a V brownish; comma line enlarged or hooked at both ends. Fig. 293.
.............................*Polygonia comma* Harris. Comma.

Range: eastern United States and Canada south in the mountains to the Carolinas and west to the Great Plains (Texas to Dakotas). Food plants: *Urtica* (nettles), *Ulmus* (elm), *Humulus* (hops), *Boehmeria* (false nettle).

Fig. 293. *Polygonia comma* ♂ V. Barberton, Ohio.

5b V gray or brownish-gray; comma line tapered at both ends, not enlarged or hooked...6

6a DHW with broad, dark brown border broken by small yellow dots; border occupying distal ½ of wing. Fig. 294.....................
....*Polygonia progne* Cramer.

Range: Alaska to Nova Scotia, south in the mountains to North Carolina and west to Kansas and Nebraska. Southern limits in far West unknown. Food plant: *Ribes* (currant and gooseberry) and (rarely) *Ulmus* (elm).

Fig. 294. *Polygonia progne* ♂ D. Lexington, Michigan.

6b DHW with relatively narrow brown border, or, if border wide, it is broken by large yellow spots (spots about 1/3 width of border). Fig. 295............................*Polygonia zephyrus* Edwards.

Range: United States west of Great Plains and Canada as far east as Riding Mountains (Manitoba). Food plants: *Ulmus* (elm), *Ribes* (currant and gooseberry), *Azalea*, *Rhododendron*. Two forms whose status is in doubt are included here (*P. oreas* Edwards and *P. silenus* Edwards). The latter has the V wings very dark, and is found in the Pacific Northwest.

Fig. 295. *Polygonia zephyrus* ♂ D. No data.

Genus VANESSA Fabricius
The Thistle Butterflies

Butterflies of this genus are characteristically wide ranging. Several species habitually migrate.

KEY TO THE SPECIES OF *VANESSA*.

1a DFW with orange or red color confined to a single band. Fig. 296. ....*Vanessa atalanta* Linnaeus. Red Admiral

Range: all of North America south of the Arctic as well as much of Europe, western Asia and North Africa. Food plants: *Urtica* (nettle), *Boehmeria* (false nettle), *Humulus* (hops), *Parietaria* (pellitory), and probably other Urticaceae.

Fig. 296. *Vanessa atalanta* ♂ D. Lawrence, Kansas.

1b DFW with orange or red color not confined to a single band.....2

2a VHW with two large submarginal eye spots, each as broad or broader than the cell in which it is centered. Fig. 297............
...............*Vanessa virginiensis* Drury. The Painted Beauty.

Range: transcontinental in southern Canada and the United States, south to Central America. Food plants: *Gnaphalium* (cudweed), *Antennaria* (everlasting), *Artemisia* (sage) and other composites.

Fig. 297. *Vanessa virginiensis* ♂ V. Lawrence, Kansas.

2b VHW with 3 or 4 submarginal eye spots, none as broad as the cell in which it lies...3

3a DFW with subapical bar white. Fig. 298.................*Vanessa cardui* Linnaeus. Cosmopolite, Painted Lady, Thistle Butterfly.

Range: cosmopolitan in our area except for the arctic. This is the most widespread of butterflies, found in virtually every corner of the world except the arctic, antarctic, parts of South America and most of southeast Asia and the East Indies. In Australia and New Zealand it is replaced by a closely related species, *Vanessa kershawi* McCoy. Food plants: numerous composites, rarely other plants (Malvaceae). This species often migrates.

Fig. 298. *Vanessa cardui* ♀ V. Richfield, Kansas.

3b DFW with subapical bar reddish brown. Fig. 299................
....................*Vanessa carye* Hübner. The West Coast Lady.

Range: British Columbia to Patagonia, east to Colorado. Food plant: *Malva* (mallow), *Lupinus succulentus* (lupine), *Althaea rosea* (hollyhock).

Fig. 299. *Vanessa carye* ♂
V. Santa Cruz, California.

Genus PRECIS Hübner
Peacock Butterflies

Two species of this tropical genus occur north of the Mexican border.

KEY TO THE SPECIES OF *PRECIS*.

1a DHW eyespot nearest costal margin much larger than largest eyespot on DFW. Fig. 300....................*Precis lavinia* Cramer.

Range: New England and southern Canada southward past the southern border of our area. Food plants: *Plantago* (plantain), *Antirrhinum* (snapdragon), *Gerardia*, *Sedum* (stonecrop), *Ludvigia* (false loosestrife), *Verbena prostrata*, and others. This species has also been known as *Precis coenia* Hübner.

Fig. 300. *Precis orithya*
♂ D. Lawrence, Kansas.

1b DHW eyespot nearest costal margin at most the same size as the largest eyespot on DFW (never distinctly larger). Fig. 301.......
....*Precis genoveva* Stoll.

Range: southern Florida, southern Texas, southern Arizona, to South America. Food plant: *Lippia* (in Cuba).

Fig. 301. *Precis genoveva* ♂
D. Houston, Texas.

Genus METAMORPHA Hübner
The Malachites

One species occurs in our area, *Metamorpha steneles* Linnaeus (Fig. 302).

Range: American tropics north to southern Texas and Florida, rarely straying north as far as Kansas. Food plant: *Blechum brownei* in Cuba and Puerto Rico, *Blechum blechum* in Cuba.

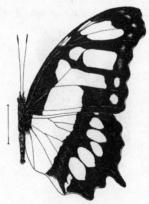

Fig. 302. *Metamorpha steneles* ♂ D. Texas.

Genus ANARTIA Doubleday

Two common tropical species of this genus are found north of the border.

KEY TO THE SPECIES OF *ANARTIA.*

1a Ground color white. Fig. 303........*Anartia jatrophae* Johannson.

Range: southern Texas and Florida, rarely straying northward (Kansas, southern New England). Food plants: *Jatropha manihot* (in Brazil), *Lippia* (in Cuba), *Bacopa* (in Puerto Rico).

Fig. 303. *Anartia jatrophae* ♂ D. Miami, Florida.

1b Ground color brownish. Fig. 304..........*Anartia fatima* Fabricius.

Range: in our area only southern Texas, where it is a permanent resident.

Fig. 304. *Anartia fatima* ♂ D. Acapulco, Mexico.

Genus HYPANARTIA Hübner

This small genus is primarily tropical American, but several species are found in Africa. One supposedly occurs in our area in southern Texas, *Hypanartia lethe* Fabricius (Fig. 305).

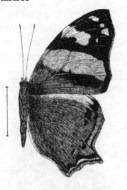

Fig. 305. *Hypanartia lethe* ♂ D. "Texas."

Genus HYPOLIMNAS Hübner
Tropic Queens

One species of this Old World genus has been introduced into the Western Hemisphere, *Hypolimnas misippus* Linnaeus (Figs. 306, 307).

Range: Africa, southern Asia, introduced long ago into the Antilles and northern South America. A few specimens have been captured in Florida. Food plants: Malvaceae (mallows), *Portulaca* (purslane), *Ipomaea* (morning glory).

Fig. 306. *Hypolimnas misippus* ♂ D. No data.

Fig. 307. *Hypolimnas misippus* ♀ D. No data.

Tribe ERGOLINI
Genus MYSCELIA Doubleday

These beautiful butterflies are common south of the border, but occur in our area only as strays.

KEY TO THE SPECIES OF *MYSCELIA*.

1a Male DFW with bluish marks extending into discal and limbal areas; female DFW with white spots in discal and limbal areas. Fig. 308. . . . .*Myscelia ethusa* Boisduval.

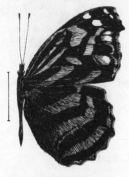

Range: a tropical species which occurs as a straggler in extreme southern Texas.

Fig. 308. *Myscelia ethusa* ♂ D. Huichihuayan, S.L.P., Mexico.

1b Male DFW with bluish marks limited to basal and postbasal areas; female DFW without white spots in discal and limbal areas. Fig. 309. . . . .*Myscelia cyananthe* Felder.

Range: another tropical species found occasionally in southern Texas.

Fig. 309. *Myscelia cyananthe* ♂ D. Guerrero, Mexico.

158

Genus DIAETHRIA Billberg

Two members of this large tropical genus penetrate our southern borders on rare occasions.

KEY TO THE SPECIES OF *DIAETHRIA*.

1a VHW (right) with central markings closely resembling the number "89"; VHW (left) mirror image of same. Fig. 310................
...................................*Diaethria clymena* Hübner.

Range: there is at least one genuine record of this species from Royal Palm Park, Florida.

Fig. 310. *Diaethria clymena* ♂ V. "Florida."

1b VHW not so marked. Fig. 311. . . *Diaethria asteria* Godman and Salvin.

Range: common in northern Mexico, has been taken a number of times in Texas.

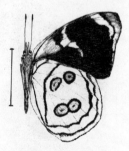

Fig. 311. *Diaethria asteria* ♂ V. Alamo, Texas.

Genus EUNICA Hübner
Purple Wings

Of the over sixty species of this tropical genus, only two are found in the United States.

KEY TO THE SPECIES OF *EUNICA*.

1a DFW with seven prominent white spots; D with a strong purple sheen. Fig. 312.....................*Eunica tatila* Herrich-Schaeffer.

Range: southern Florida (often common) and southern Texas (rare) straying north to Kansas.

Fig. 312. *Eunica tatila* ♂
D. Florida.

1b DFW with less than seven white spots, usually only three prominent; D with faint purple sheen. Fig. 313...*Eunica monima* Cramer.

Range: occurring sparingly in southern Texas and Florida, straying north as far as southern Kansas. Food plant: in Mexico, *Zanthoxylum pentamon* (a tropical prickly ash).

Fig. 313. *Eunica monima*
♂ D. Brownsville, Texas.

Genus MESTRA Hübner

One species of this genus is a resident of the United States, another has been recorded doubtfully.

KEY TO THE SPECIES OF *MESTRA*.

1a FW gray at base and margin only, white discally. Fig. 314.......
.....................................*Mestra amymone* Menetries.

Range: southern Texas (abundant), moving northward during summer to establish itself in southern Kansas (where it is wiped out each winter). Recorded from Colorado and Nebraska. Food plant: *Tragia*.

Fig. 314. *Mestra amymone* ♂ D. Bluntzer, Texas.

1b FW almost entirely gray. Fig. 315.........*Mestra cana* Erichson.

Range: recorded from Florida, but records of doubtful authenticity.

Fig. 315. *Mestra cana* ♂ D. "Florida."

Genus HAMADRYAS Hübner
The Calicoes

The butterflies of this tropical genus habitually rest head downward on tree trunks with their wings spread. An apparatus on the wings permits them to make a clicking noise in flight. Four species have been recorded from our area, but two of these almost certainly do not occur here. These are keyed out without comment—it is possible that sooner or later they will turn up.

KEY TO THE SPECIES OF *HAMADRYAS*.

1a VHW yellow. Fig. 316............
........*Hamadryas fornax* Hübner.

Range: common in Mexico, strays into southern Texas.

Fig. 316. *Hamadryas fornax* ♂ V. No data.

1b VHW whitish...2

2a VFW with relatively solid markings at apex; VHW with ocelli lacking any reddish or rusty-brown coloring. Fig. 317......................
......*Hamadryas feronia* Linnaeus.

Range: same as *H. fornax*.

Fig. 317. *Hamadryas feronia* ♂ V. "Texas."

2b VFW with dark markings at apex well-penetrated by ground color; VHW with reddish or rusty-brown markings in ocelli (especially in caudal pair)..3

162

3a DFW with whitish ground color very prominent over distal 2/3.
..................................*Hamadryas ferox* Staudinger.

3b DFW with whitish ground color not prominent in distal 2/3......
..................................*Hamadryas februa* Hübner

Genus BIBLIS Fabricius

A common tropical species, *Biblis hyperia* Cramer (Fig. 318) is found on occasion in extreme southern Texas.

Fig. 318. *Biblis hyperia*
♂ D. Victoria, Mexico.

Tribe LIMENITINI
Genus LIMENITIS Fabricius
Admirals and Sisters

The larvae of the subgenus *Limenitis* overwinter in tubes (hibernacula) formed by rolling a leaf and tying it with silk threads. The chrysalis has a distinctive prominent mid-dorsal projection. There is considerable justification for considering the subgenus *Adelpha* as being of full generic status.

KEY TO THE SPECIES OF *LIMENITIS.*

1a DFW without a prominent subapical orange spot...............
..................................subgenus *Limenitis* 2

1b DFW with a prominent subapical orange spot (ground color not orange).....................................subgenus *Adelpha* 6

2a D with orange ground color, veins and border dark brown. Fig. 319 . . . .*Limenitis archippus* **Cramer. The Viceroy.**

Fig. 319. *Limenitis archippus* ♂
D. Harrisburg, Pennsylvania.

Range: entire United States east of Rocky Mountains, southeastern and south central Canada, New Mexico, Arizona, southern Utah and southwestern California. Food plant: *Salix* (willow), *Populus* (poplar and cottonwood), *Quercus* (oak), *Malus* (apple), *Prunus* (plum), and others. This species mimics *Danaus plexippus* and *D. gilippus*, but can be easily separated from them by the presence on the HW of a narrow black postmedian band paralleling the outer margin. The geographic variation of *archippus* is correlated with the distribution of the *Danaus* species it mimics (*plexippus* over most of the East, a dark form of *gilippus* in most of peninsular Florida, a pale desert *gilippus* in the southwest).

2b Not so marked **3**

3a D without prominent white banding. Fig. 320 . . . .
. . . .*Limenitis astyanax* **Fabricius. The Red-spotted Purple.**

Fig. 320. *Limenitis astyanax* ♂
V. Barberton, Ohio.

Range: eastern United States north to southern Canada, west to Rocky Mountains, southwest to Arizona. Food plants: a wide variety, especially of Rosaceae, including also *Salix* (willows), *Populus* (poplars), *Crataegus* (hawthorn) and (?) *Vaccinium* (deerberry). This species is considered by some to be conspecific with the more northern *L. arthemis*, with which it hybridizes in a narrow zone in southern New England, New York, northern New Jersey, Pennsylvania, Michigan and Wisconsin. The continued distinctness of the parental types in the area of overlap, however, suggests that they are best considered distinct species.

3b D with prominent white banding **4**

4a DFW with apex orange bordered (rarely faint). Fig. 321...........
.......................*Limenitis lorquini* Boisduval and Leconte.

Range: West Coast from British
Columbia to California, east to
Colorado. Commonly found in
river bottoms overgrown with willows. Food plants: *Salix* (willow),
Populus (poplar, cottonwood), *Prunus* (choke-cherry).

Fig. 321. *Limenitis lorquini* ♂ V.
Oakland, California.

4b DFW not so marked...5

**5a DHW with blue marginal and submarginal markings; VHW with
reddish basal marks (no prominent light basal streaks). Fig. 322.
...*Limenitis arthemis* Drury. The Banded Purple or White Admiral.**

Range: southern Canada and northeastern United States as far south as
northern New Jersey, Pennsylvania,
west past the Great Lakes to the
Canadian prairies. Food plants: *Betula* (birch), also *Salix* (willow), *Crataegus* (hawthorne) and others. This species is characteristic of the Canadian
Zone, and is frequently found along
woodland watercourses and in clearings. Its relationship with *L. astyanax*
is discussed under that species.

Fig. 322. *Limenitis arthemis* ♀
V. Germania, Pennsylvania.

5b DHW without blue marginal and submarginal markings; **VHW** with prominent light basal streaks (no reddish basal marks). Fig. 323...
..................................*Limenitis weidemeyerii* Edwards.

Range: Eastern California and Idaho eastward to New Mexico, Colorado, Kansas (strays), Nebraska, South Dakota (Black Hills), and Montana. Food plants: various *Populus* (aspens and other poplars), *Salix* (willows).

Fig. 323. *Limenitis weidemeyerii* ♂ V. Salt Lake City, Utah.

6a DFW with unbroken white median band reaching costa. Fig. 324....
.......*Limenitis fessonia* Hewitson.

Range: occurs as a stray in southern Texas.

Fig. 324. *Limenitis fessonia* ♂ D. Victoria, Mexico.

6b DFW with white median band ending well before costa, broken into spots. Fig. 325...
................Limenitis bredowii Geyer. The California Sister.

Range: California, Nevada, Arizona, New Mexico, southwestern Colorado, western Texas, south to central Mexico. Rarely straying to Kansas. Food plant: *Quercus,* especially *Q. chrysolepis* (oaks).

Fig. 325. *Limenitis bredowii* ♂ D. Water Canyon. New Mexico.

Genus DYNAMINE Hübner

This large genus is considered by various authors to be related to the Admirals (*Limenitis*), in spite of the superficial distinctness of the two groups. Only one species, *Dynamine dyonis* Geyer (Fig. 326), has been taken in our area (southern Texas).

Fig. 326. *Dynamine dyonis* ♂ V. Victoria, Mexico.

Genus MARPESIA Hübner
The Dagger Wings

Four species of this tropical genus have been found in the United States, but only one is a permanent resident.

KEY TO THE SPECIES OF *MARPESIA.*

1a D marked with fine dark lines crossing both wings............2

1b D with broad bands crosisng both wings, or without lines or bands 3

2a FW not sharply produced at apex; DFW with line crossing cell end angled sharply basad. Fig. 327........*Marpesia eleuchia* Hübner

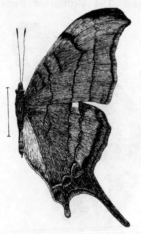

Range: an Antillean species listed by Seitz as occurring in Texas and Florida. As a member of our fauna its status is in doubt.

Fig. 327. *Marpesia eleuchia* ♂ D. Sierra Maestra, Cuba.

2b FW sharply produced at apex; DFW with line crossing cell and continuing straight to margin. Fig. 328....*Marpesia petreus* Cramer.

Range: southern Florida and Texas southward. Rarely straying north as far as Kansas and Colorado. Food plants: *Ficus* (figs) and *Anacardium*, in Brazil.

Fig. 328. *Marpesia petreus* ♂ D. Miami, Florida.

3a V with basal half of wings silky-white, distal half brownish, the two halves sharply contrasting, joining in a straight line with no blending; DFW without white markings. Fig. 329..............
..*Marpesia coresia* Godart.

Range: a tropical species, occasionally found in southern Texas.

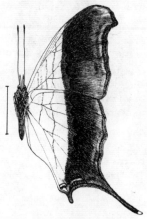

Fig. 329. *Marpesia coresia* ♂ V. "Texas."

3b V not so marked; DFW with subapical white spots. Fig. 330.......
......................................*Marpesia chiron* Fabricius.

Range: South America, Antilles. Mexico, sometimes found in southern, Florida and Texas, and very rarely straying northward (one Kansas record).

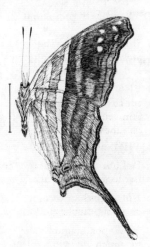

Fig. 330. *Marpesia chiron* ♀ V. Brownsville, Texas.

Genus HISTORIS Hübner

Historis odius Fabricius (Fig. 331), which is common in tropical America, has been found occasionally in Florida. A very similar species, *Historis acheronta* Fabricius, has been recorded vaguely from Florida. It can be readily separated from *odius* by the possession of a short, sharp tail on the HW. Seitz records the food plant of *H. odius* (in Brazil) as "Embauba".

Fig. 331. *Historis odius* ♂ D. "Southwestern Texas."

Tribe APATURINI
Genus ASTEROCAMPA Röber
Hackberry Butterflies

All three of our species feed on hackberry (*Celtis*), and they are frequently seen flying rapidly around these trees.

KEY TO THE SPECIES OF *ASTEROCAMPA*.

1a DFW with a prominent black eyespot in cell Cu_1...............2

1b DFW without a prominent black eyespot in cell Cu_1. Fig. 332.....
.....................*Asterocampa clyton* Boisduval and Leconte.

Range: New England westward to Michigan, Iowa and Nebraska and south to Texas and the Gulf States.

Fig. 332. *Asterocampa clyton* ♂ D. Bethlehem, Pennsylvania.

2a DFW with two continuous zig-zag bars in discal cell. Fig. 333....
.....................................*Asterocampa leila* Edwards.

Range: southern Texas, New Mexico, Arizona
and southward.

Fig. 333. *Astero-
campa leila* ♂
D. Sabino Can-
yon, Arizona.

**2b DFW with a zig-zag bar (distal) and two spots (basal) in discal
cell. Fig. 334..........*Asterocampa celtis* Boisduval and Leconte.**

Range: southern Canada southward east
of the Rocky Mountains, southwest to New
Mexico and Arizona. Rare north of Pennsylvania in the East.

Fig. 334. *Asterocampa
celtis* ♂ D. Reading,
Pennsylvania.

Genus APATURA Fabricius

One species of this largely tropical genus,
Apatura pavon Latreille (Fig. 335), is taken
regularly in extreme southern Texas. The
female of this species superficially resembles
a member of the subgenus *Adelpha* of the
genus *Limenitis*.

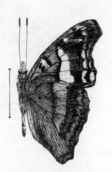

Fig. 335. *Apatura pa-
von* ♂ V. Cairo,
Costa Rica.

171

Subfamily CHARAXINAE

Only one genus of this small, tropicopolitan subfamily is found in our area. With the exception of one tropical nymphaline genus (*Stibochiona*) these are the only true butterflies with sclerotized parapatagia (Fig. 335A).

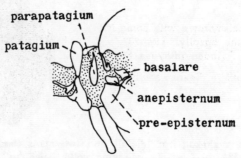

Fig. 335A. Cervix, prothorax and cephalic portion of mesothorax of *Anaea andria*.

Genus ANAEA Hübner
The Leaf Wings

These are very fast flying butterflies that ordinarily do not visit flowers, although they are often attracted to feces, dead animals, decaying fruit and the like. The underside of the wings is very dull and leaf-like. Many tropical species which have brilliant upper sides seem to disappear when they alight and fold their wings, exposing only the protectively colored lower surfaces.

KEY TO THE SPECIES OF *ANAEA*.

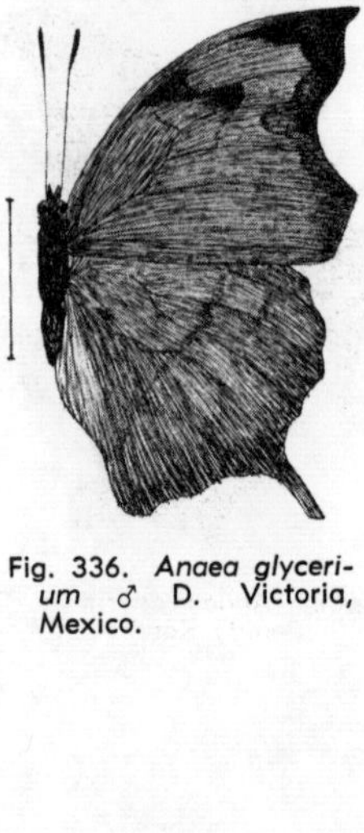

1a FW margin very irregular, strongly curved outward at vein Cu_2. Fig. 336. ....*Anaea glycerium* Doubleday.

Range: Mexican, straying into south Texas.

Fig. 336. *Anaea glycerium* ♂ D. Victoria, Mexico.

1b FW margin not strongly irregular (may be finely serrate), not strongly curved outward at vein Cu_2.............................2

2a DFW blackish-brown with some irridescent blue basally. Fig. 337.....
............*Anaea pithyusa* Felder.

Range: southern Texas, southward.

Fig. 337. *Anaea pithyusa* ♂ D. Valles, Mexico.

2b DFW not so marked...3

3a Wing margins smooth; DFW of male with essentially no pattern in discal area except for bar at end of cell. Fig. 338..............
.....................*Anaea andria* Scudder. Goatweed Butterfly.

Range: Texas north to Illinois, Iowa and Nebraska and east to Ohio, Tennessee, and Georgia (not found in southern Florida). Food plant: *Croton* (croton or goatweed).

Fig. 338. *Anaea andria* ♀ D. Smith County Kansas.

3b Wing margins finely serrate or sinuate; DFW of male with pattern in discal area in addition to bar at end of cell. Fig. 339...........
....*Anaea aidea* Guerin.

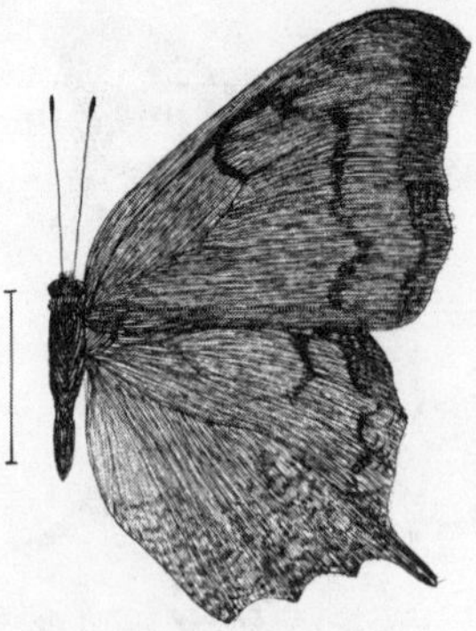

Range: southern California, Arizona, Texas, southern Florida, southward to Honduras. Rarely straying north (Kansas). Food plant: *Croton* (croton or goatweed).

Fig. 339. *Anaea aidea* ♂
D. Miami, Florida.

Family LIBYTHEIDAE
Snout Butterflies

This is the smallest family of butterflies, containing one genus and somewhat over a dozen species, two of which are found in our area. Our species can be readily separated from all other North American butterflies by the great development of the labial palpi. The male prothoracic legs are reduced in size; those of the female fully developed. The family is closely related to the Nymphalidae.

Genus LIBYTHEA Fabricius

The American species of *Libythea* form a structurally distinct group, the subgenus *Libytheana* Michener.

KEY TO THE SPECIES OF *LIBYTHEA*.

1a HW distinctly projected in anal region; FW with anterior discal white markings broken into two distinct spots, the posterior one well laterad of the anterior; FW with orange in cell not extending almost to base of wing. Fig. 340....
...........*Libythea carinenta* Cramer.

Range: recorded from southern Texas and Arizona.

Fig. 340. *Libythea carinenta* ♂ D. Brazil.

1b HW not distinctly projected in anal region; FW with anterior discal white markings usually forming a white bar between costa and vein M$_3$, if broken into two spots the posterior one only slightly laterad of the anterior; FW with orange in cell extending almost to base. Fig. 341..................*Libythea bachmani* Kirtland.

Range: New England and southern Ontario south to Florida and west to Rocky Mountains, southern Arizona and southeastern California; Mexico. Food plants: *Celtis* (hackberry) and *Symphoricarpos occidentalis* (wolfberry). This species sometimes migrates in vast numbers.

Fig. 341. *Libythea bachmani* ♂ D. Versailles, Kentucky.

Family LYCAENIDAE
Blues and Metal-marks

This is a very large, cosmopolitan family of medium to very small butterflies. Many are marked with irridescent or metallic colors.

Structurally the adults are very distinctive. The face is flat between the eyes, and the latter are almost always emarginate at the antennae (Fig. 342). The patagia are always membranous, and the lamella of the mesodiscrimen curves downward to the base of the furca (unique in the butterflies). The prothoracic legs of the males are (with rare exceptions) somewhat reduced in size; those of the females are fully developed.

eye emarginate at antenna

Fig. 342. Front view of head of *Lycaena helloides*.

The larvae are mostly slug-shaped (Fig. 343) and have small heads. They are usually attended by ants, which take from them a sweet glandular secretion, and give them varying degrees of care and protection.

Fig. 343. Larva of *Callophrys gryneus* (after Scudder).

Fig. 344. Pupa of *Callophrys gryneus* (after Scudder).

The pupae (Fig. 344) are short, stout, and rounded, and usually lack sharp projections. They are usually tightly lashed to the substrate by a silken girdle.

Two of the three subfamilies are found in our area (ignore couplet 1 of the following key if your specimen is from North America).

KEY TO THE SUBFAMILIES OF LYCAENIDAE.

1a Mesothoracic anepisternum absent, or, if present, not strongly convex; labial sclerite completely sclerotized; male prothoracic tarsi usually neither segmented or bearing claws....................2

1b Mesothoracic anepisternum a prominent, strongly convex, separate sclerite; labial sclerite sclerotized principally behind (strongly) and between (lightly) the palpal sockets; male prothoracic tarsi segmented and bearing a claw each; a monobasic subfamily from the Peruvian Andes..Styginae

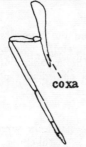

coxa

Fig. 345. Prothoracic leg of ♂ *Apodemia nais.*

2a Male prothoracic coxae extending spinelike below the articulation of the trochanter (Fig. 345); male prothoracic legs less than one-half length of pterothoracic legs; HW often with a vein along the basal part of costal margin; HW with humeral vein usually present (when absent vein on costal margin present); mesothoracic anepisternum always a distinct, separate sclerite..Riodininae p. 242

2b. Male prothoracic coxae not extending spinelike below articulation of trochanter; male prothoracic legs more than one half length of pterothoracic legs; HW without vein along basal part of costal margin; HW with humeral vein usually absent; mesothoracic anepisternum usually not a distinct separate sclerite.....Lycaeninae p. 176

Subfamily LYCAENINAE
Blues, Coppers, Harvesters and Hairstreaks

The majority of the lycaenids belong to this subfamily. The lycaenines fold their wings over their backs when they alight; the closely related riodinines usually hold them spread.

KEY TO THE TRIBES OF LYCAENINAE.

by Harry K. Clench

1a FW radius three-branched, none stalked; HW often with one or two tails; DFW male often with scent pad......................
....Theclini (Strymoniti) p. 178

1b FW radius four-branched, the last two stalked; DFW male never with a scent pad 2

2a Meso- and metathoracic tibiae without spurs ...... Gerydini p. 220

2b Meso- and metathoracic tibiae each with one pair of spurs 3

3a Tarsal claw always without inner tooth; male genitalia with uncus lobes (labides) long and digitate; males D purple or coppery orange, rarely bright blue, occasionally gray; DFW females usually with postmedian line present .... Lycaenini p. 220

3b Tarsal claw nearly always with inner tooth (except Brephidium, Zizula, in the Plebejini); uncus lobes short, inconspicuous (the few apparent exceptions have tarsal claws with distinct inner teeth); males D usually blue; DFW females seldom with distinct postmedian line 4

4a Large (LFW usually > 18 mm.); stout-bodied; HW tailed ....
.... Theclini (Thecliti) p. 177

4b Smaller (LFW usually < 18 mm.); body rather slender; nearly always tail-less (when tailed, LFW usually < 15 mm.). Plebejini p. 228

Tribe THECLINI
Hairstreaks
by Harry K. Clench

These are the familiar hairstreaks, with representatives all over the world, particularly in the tropics. There are indications that it is not a natural group, though the two subtribes in North America are certainly natural.

KEY TO THE SUBTRIBES OF THECLINI.

1a FW with 2 radial veins (R_3, R_5) stalked; male genitalia with an anellus present .... Thecliti p. 177

1b FW with all radials free from cell, the last one occasionally connate or short stalked with M_1; male genitalia without an anellus ......
.... Strymoniti p. 178

Subtribe THECLITI

Our two genera are each monotypic, and probably derived from the Palearctic where the majority of the genera of the subtribe occur today. In common with most hairstreaks the external structural details of the two American genera are remarkably similar, but the male genital structures are widely different and fully confirm the striking diversity of color and pattern.

KEY TO THE GENERA OF THECLITI.

1a D and V brown; uncus of male genitalia single, broadly triangular; falces lightly arched, simple .... Habrodais p. 178

1b D purple and black, V gray; uncus double, two long slender rods; falces abruptly angulate, anterior edge of fore-arm serrate ....
.... Hypaurotis p. 178

Genus HABRODAIS Scudder

There is only one species, *Habrodais grunus* Boisduval (Fig. 346).

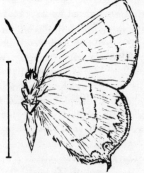

Range: Northern Oregon to southern California, eastward to southern Idaho and western Nevada. Foodplant: *Quercus chrysolepis*. Two broods (vi, vii-viii, vic. San Francisco), the first much less common. Fond of perching on the leaves of its foodplant, apparently little attracted to flowers. Crepuscular flying is apparently usual (both dawn and dusk).

Fig. 346. *Habrodais grunus* ♂V. Los Angeles, California.

Genus HYPAUROTIS Scudder

There is only one species, *Hypaurotis crysalus* Edwards (Fig. 347).

Range: Montane, from central Colorado southward to New Mexico, westward to Utah and Arizona, straying to southern California. Food plant: probably *Quercus gambelii*. One brood (chiefly vii). Settles on leaves, especially of oaks, and seems to avoid flowers.

Fig. 347. *Hypaurotis crysalus* ♀ V. Salt Lake City, Utah.

Subtribe STRYMONITI

This is a preeminently New World group, enormously developed in the tropics. The several Palearctic members seem to have been derived from our fauna. The classification of this subtribe presented below is new, and is based for the most part on the structures of the male genitalia. It represents a considerable change from what has been published previously, with an unfortunate but inescapable increase in number of genera employed, as well as the reshuffling of these into assemblages which appear to be far more natural than those hitherto used. Because the generic characters are thus largely internal, requiring preparation of the genitalia to study them, two keys have been prepared. One is based on these genital characters and is intended primarily for the specialist. It follows the natural sequence and relationship of the genera so far as can be determined. For greater ease in identification to species, however, it was thought necessary to add a "pattern key," using external traits visible without dissection, usually to the unaided eye. It follows no natural sequence, being based on characters selected for the unambiguity, clarity and ready visibility. Where possible it leads to genera (under which keys to the included species will be found). In several cases, however, this was not possible, and the key runs out to individual species.

TECHNICAL KEY TO THE GENERA OF STRYMONITI.

1a Tibiae without spurs; falx with process at elbow....*Eumaeus* p. 188

1b Mid and hind tibiae each with 1 pr. of spurs; no process on falx...2

2a Cornuti terminal, usually 2, at least one of them usually dentate; aedeagus tip usually distinctly flared and slightly upturned.....3

2b Cornutus far within shaft (with rare exceptions), though capable of exsertion with vesica, single, almost never dentate; tip of aedeagus usually not flared or upturned..........................14

3a Tip of aedeagus with ventral lamellar keel, serrate to serrulate ventrally 4

3b No such ventral keel...7

4a Valvae contiguous to tips.....................................5

4b Valvae distinctly divergent distally............................6

5a Tips of valvae with a mesial fringe of fine hair-like processes; one cornutus....................................*Chlorostrymon* p. 189

5b Tips of valvae without mesial hair-like fringe; 2 cornuti..........
....*Phaeostrymon* p. 190

6a One cornutus.............................*Chrysophanus* p. 191

6b Two cornuti.................................*Satyrium* p. 192

7a One cornutus..8

7b Two cornuti 11

8a Valvae apically divergent for at least half their lengths.........9

8b Valvae contiguous for most or all of their lengths.............:.10

9a Saccus over 4 times as long as width at middle (saccus length measured from anterior border of vinculum, next to the base of the valvae, to posterior tip); anterior edge of vinculum laterally without processes.............................*Ministrymon* p. 196

9b Saccus about 2 times as long as width at middle; anterior edge of vinculum with large triangular process laterally at middle, one on either side....................................[new genus] p. 198

10a Valvae with truncate tips; falx with longitudinal lamella on forearm..*Calycopis* p. 198

10b Valvae regularly tapering to tips; falcal fore-arm without lamella
....*Tmolus* p. 199

11a Valvae contiguous, or very close, for their whole length..........
....*Callophrys* p. 200

11b Valvae divergent distally (rarely touching again at tips)......12

12a Saccus about 8 times as long as its width at middle; anterior edge
of vinculum with marked process about middle......*Atlides* p. 211

12b Saccus usually not much more than twice as long as width at
middle, rarely up to 4 times.................................13

13a Valva with ventrolateral process at middle, conical, acuminate...
....*Dolymorpha* p. 212

13b Valva without such a process.................*Euristrymon* p. 212

14a Cornutus very blunt distally, truncate.........................15

14b Cornutus acuminate or bluntly pointed......................16

15a Saccus at least twice as long as width at middle.............
....*Hypostrymon* p. 214

15b Saccus distinctly less than twice as long as wide, even absent....
....*Panthiades* p. 214

16a Tip of valva with surface covered with minute basally directed
teeth...*Strymon* p. 215

16b No such teeth...17

17a Tip of valva excurved in a blunt hook; cornutus long acuminate;
aedeagus subterminally with an acuminate, distally directed tooth
....*Erora* p. 218

17b Tip of valva not excurved; cornutus bluntly pointed; aedeagus
simple...*Electrostrymon* p. 218

PATTERN KEY TO STRYMONITI EXCLUDING *CALLOPHRYS (INCISALIA)* (Fig. 348).

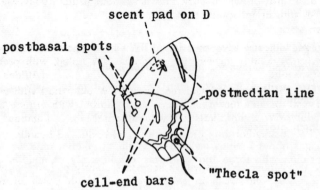

Figure 348

1a V. especially HW, dominantly green or blue-green...............2

1b V not green, though some green marks may be present..........8

2a D with some purple, blue or green (a small tornal mark only, *Erora* male HW)...3

2b No such color; D gray or brown, with or without some fulvous....6

3a VHW postmedian line coppery red, of considerably dislocated bars ....*Erora* p. 218

3b VHW postmedian line not red................................4

4a VHW with a row of terminal maroon patches between veins, or with a large uninterrupted patch shaded, especially inwardly, with maroon or red...5

4b VHW with no row of maroon or red markings.................
.....................................*"Strymon" facuna* (?) p. 220

5a VHW terminal patch connected, uninterrupted; male D purple or reddish purple.............................*Chlorostrymon* p. 189

5b VHW with dull maroon patches between veins only, male D blue..
.................................*Callophrys (Cyanophrys)* p. 211

6a HW tailed......................*Callophrys (Mitoura)* (part) p. 205

6b HW without tails..7

7a VHW terminal white line nearly as thick as the heavy post-median white line, which is rather smoothly convex throughout; VFW disk fulvous almost to costa......*Callophrys (Sandia)* p. 205

7b VHW terminal white line absent or very faint; postmedian white line usually irregular, dentate, and faint to absent; but when heavy and convex, never with any discal fulvous VFW................
.................................*Callophrys (Callophrys)* p. 209

8a D with at least some blue or green..........................9

8b D without blue or green (disregard any tiny bluish or bluish gray bars near DHW tornus.....................................26

9a V dark gray-brown to dark brown, without usual transverse lines; VHW with green spots or bars................................10

9b Not so 11

10a VFW with red spot at base; VHW 2 red spots at base and a series of metallic green bars at tornus; HW tailed, with prominent tornal lobe.......................................*Atlides* p. 211

10b VFW, VHW without basal red spots; VHW outer half with a series of rows of metallic green spots; inner margin with orange spot at middle; HW without tails and without tornal lobe...*Eumaeus* p. 188

11a VHW postmedian line prominently edged with red basally......12

11b Not so 17

12a VHW postmedian line with 2 segments clearly concave outwardly (cells Cu_1 and Cu_2), in cell Cu_2 usually with patch of red, or darker gray, in concavity.......................*Calycopis* p. 198

12b VHW postmedian line outwardly clearly concave in cell Cu$_2$ only; no red distad of this line in concavity.........................13

13a VHW no post-basal marks at all (except, rarely, numerous fine cross-striae) 14

13b VHW with post-basal series of red marks, occasionally faint....15

14a Large (LFW 12 mm. or over); male D bright metallic purplish blue, with large black patch in middle FW; V ground with numerous fine darker cross-striae all over...........*Hypostrymon* p. 214

14b Small (LFW 11 mm. or less); D blue feeble, neither purplish nor metallic; no large discal black patch on DFW male; V ground not cross-striate. See Fig. 378.................*Tmolus azia* p. 200

15a VHW postmedian line with distal white very narrow and sharp, the gray ground beyond it as dark as ground basad; post-basal red marks slender and faint................................16

15b VHW postmedian line with distal white distally diffused, the ground just distad of red thus much paler than ground basad; post-basal red marks heavy, nearly round. See Fig. 373........
.....................................*Ministrymon clytie* p. 197

16a VHW post-basal red marks very slender and faint; postmedian line segments all narrow and linear, subequal in thickness throughout; D blue of male rather pale and not shining. See Fig. 372....
....*Ministrymon leda* p. 197

16b VHW post-basal marks prominent, large and rounded; postmedian line segments very irregular in thickness, tending to be rounded; D blue of male deep, rather lustrous. See Fig. 377..............
....*Tmolus echion* p. 200

17a No tails; VHW mottled various shades of brown, without orange capped "Thecla spot"......................................18

17b HW, one or two tails; VHW usually with prominent orange or red capped "Thecla spot"......................................19

18a DHW male with extensive discal patch of blue; VHW both sexes, no subterminal black spot in cell Cu$_1$. See Fig. 418.............
....*Strymon bazochii* p. 217

18b DHW male without blue; VHW with subterminal black spot in cell Cu$_1$. See Fig. 415.........................*Strymon cestri* p. 217

19a HW with unusually produced tornal lobe; VHW markings chiefly long mustard-colored bands convergent on tornus, on cream ground...*Dolymorpha* p. 212

19b Not so...20

20a VFW cell-end bar white and prominent on the red-brown ground; DFW with blue in both sexes; VHW with fulvous lunule of "Thecla spot" small, indistinct; VFW, VHW postmedian line heavy, white, continuous..........................*Callophrys (Mitoura)* p. 205

20b Not with that combination of characters.....................21

21a VHW postmedian line tornally "W" shaped, the segment in cell Cu$_2$ outwardly concave....................................22

21b VHW postmedian line not "W" shaped, the segment in cell Cu$_2$ straight, slightly sinuate or outwardly convex..................24

22a Large (LFW > 14 mm.), V brown, HW "Thecla spot" with very large bright red lunule; D male bright lustrous blue..........23

22b Small (LFW < 12 mm.), V gray, HW "Thecla spot" at most with slight trace of pale orange, usually none; D blue rather dull. See Fig. 371.................................*Ministrymon ines* p. 197

23a D (both sexes) blue very dull and grayish, in female shading distally to dirty gray on HW; DHW female with red tornal lunule in cell Cu$_1$..[new genus] p. 198

23b D male with blue very intense; in female less so, but never grayish and not shading to dirty gray on HW; DHW female without tornal lunule...................................*Panthiades* p. 214

24a VHW postmedian line continuous, straight, very heavily white-edged; no post-basal spots. See Fig. 410...*Strymon martialis* p. 215

24b VHW postmedian line irregularly disjunct, faintly white-edged..25

25a VHW with a post-basal spot in base at cell Sc post-median line segments rather rounded, spot-like, especially costad; male without blue above. See Fig. 417..............*Strymon columella* p. 217

25b VHW, no post-basal spot; postmedian line of rather distinct bars, not at all rounded.........................[new genus] p. 198

26a HW without tails; VHW a subterminal row of thick red spots, subequal in size (incl. cell Cu$_2$)..............*Chrysophanus* p. 191

26b HW with 1 or 2 tails (except *cestri, dryope, adenostomatis,* which have little or no red VHW); if a subterminal row of red or orange spots is present VHW, they diminish in size costad and the one in cell Cu$_2$ is much smaller or absent.......................27

27a V ground gray; postmedian line both wings straight, white; VHW with 2 prominent white post-basal spots, one below Sc, one in cell. See Fig. 411...............................*Strymon acis* p. 215

27b Not so..28

28a VHW postmedian line heavily edged with red, in cells M$_1$ and M$_2$ the red as thick as an interspace width; outwardly concave segment of postmedian line in cell Cu$_2$ usually encloses a red patch in concavity (the patch may be darker gray than ground, instead of red); VHW no post-basal marks.............*Calycopis* p. 198

28b VHW postmedian line without red, or red is thin, or post-basal marks are present; never any red distad of line in cell Cu$_2$.....29

29a HW without tails, without tornal lobe; D uniformly brownish gray, usually dark; V ashy gray, markings usually feeble; without fulvous or red marks or patches above or below. See Fig. 358......
....................................*Satyrium fuliginosum* p. 192

29b Not so..30

30a HW without tails; D with bright fulvous discal patches, often occupying most of area, on both wings of both sexes; V ashy brown with white-edged dark markings, irregularly disposed, and VHW with a single, usually feeble, fulvous lunule subterminally in cell Cu$_1$. See Fig. 359......................*Satyrium behrii* p. 192

30b Not so; usually with HW tails; D mostly without fulvous above discally, though not invariably...............................31

31a V ground brownish gray; VHW with post-basal linear transverse shade of off-white from Sc well across cell and beyond; postmedian line thinly edged basad with red; VFW cell-end bar prominent, pale, not dark-lined. See Fig. 416.....*Strymon yojoa* p. 217

31b Not so..32

32a VHW with prominent post-basal mark (cell Sc) or series of marks 33

32b No such marks...36

33a VHW post-basal spots and postmedian line red. See Fig. 377....
....*Tmolus echion* p. 200

33b These marks brown......................................34

34a VHW post-basal mark single (in cell Sc), linear, faint to absent...
....*Euristrymon* p. 212

34b A series of post-basal marks, rounded, prominent..............35

35a Tail-less; VHW "Thecla spot" without orange at all; post-basal spot in cell nearer to base than to cell-end. See Fig. 415.......
....*Strymon cestri* p. 217

35b Tailed; VHW "Thecla spot" nearly always with at least some orange (faint in southwest); post-basal spot in cell nearer to cell-end than to base. See Fig. 417.........*Strymon columella* p. 217

36a VHW postmedian line segments in cells CU$_1$ and Cu$_2$ both deeply concave outwardly; V postmedian lines prominently white-edged, thin, continuous, on FW continuous and as prominent below Cu$_2$ as above....................................*Phaeostrymon* p. 190

36b VHW postmedian line concave only in cell Cu$_2$ or not at all....37

37a D both sexes uniform coppery brownish orange, without darker borders (except dark fringe). See Fig. 361..*Satyrium saepium* p. 193

37b Not so: when orange present above it is as a discal suffusion or as spots, never uniform over all of both wings................38

38a VFW postmedian line segment below Cu$_2$ deeply disjunct basad, as much as width of cell Cu$_1$; males with small accessory scent patch DFW on vein between bases of M$_3$ and Cu$_1$; V ground usually dark brown to purplish..............................39

38b Not so: VFW postmedian line segment below Cu$_2$ either more or less in line with rest of line, or else faint to absent; no such accessory scent patch; V ground variable....................40

39a VFW postmedian line distinctly duplex, very broad, and so dislocated that the outer edge of segment in cell Cu$_2$, inner edge of segments in cells M$_3$ and Cu$_1$, and outer edge of cell-end bar are all in line; VHW postmedian line segment in cell Cu$_2$ with costal end pulled strongly basad to point to basal part of cell-end bar. (Note: individuals from Manitoba and the Rockies have all marks below faintly defined; they must be looked at carefully to discern these traits.) See Fig. 363...............*Satyrium liparops* p. 194

39b VFW postmedian line less distinctly duplex, occasionally not at all; never aligned as above; VHW postmedian line segment in cell Cu$_2$ not so strongly pulled basad, usually pointing to distal part of cell-end bar or even more distad. See Fig. 364..........
....*Satyrium kingi* p. 194

40a V both wings, postmedian line with red in it.................41

40b No red in postmedian line.....................................44

41a DHW a definite and sometimes prominent subterminal black spot capped with orange or red (sometimes faint, when black spot is smallest) in cell Cu$_1$; D never with large orange discal areas; VHW postmedian line does not form a definite "W".........42

41b DHW with no such orange capped black spot; D wings often with large orange or orange-yellow areas; VHW postmedian line in cubital region forming a well-marked "W"...*Electrostrymon* p. 218

42a VHW postmedian line remote from orange of "Thecla spot" (as far as or farther than inner edge of orange is from termen).......43

42b VHW postmedian line usually touches, and always comes close to, orange of "Thecla spot." See Fig. 412..*Strymon melinus* p. 216

43a V ground gray; VHW orange of "Thecla spot" very faint; V postmedian line of both wings faintly edged with red (Santa Catalina Id., California, only). See Fig. 413......*Strymon avalona* p. 216

43b V ground tinged brownish; VHW "Thecla spot" with orange well developed; V postmedian line of both wings strongly edged with red (southern Texas southward). See Fig. 414...................
......................................*Strymon rufofusca* p. 216

44a V postmedian line not broken into rings, each segment transverse, or else line very indistinct.....................................50

44b V postmedian line sharp and clear, broken into a series of dots or rings...45

45a V ground lighter or darker brown; postmedian spots darker brown, not black, nearly always showing slightly lighter centers; DFW never with any fulvous.....................................46

45b V ground gray to white; postmedian spots black, solid; DFW often with more or less fulvous suffusion....................47

46a VHW postmedian spots above M₃ very ring-like; orange marks
pure orange, the subterminal orange lunules extending costad to
M₁; orange streak on inner margin near tornus heavy and extends along edge of blue patch in cell Cu₂ to beyond middle of
patch. See Fig. 366..................*Satyrium edwardsii* p. 195

46b VHW postmedian spots nearly always elongate transversely;
"orange" marks red-orange to red, subterminal lunules extending costad rarely beyond M₃; orange streak on inner margin thin,
touches blue patch in cell Cu₂ only at inner end of patch. See
Fig. 365...............................*Satyrium calanus* p. 194

47 *Note:* The following four species (*acadica, californica, sylvinus,
dryope*) are very difficult to separate in some instances, especially
in the Great Basin and Rocky Mts. regions.

47a Tail-less; V ground nearly white (Californian Sierras and Coast
Ranges near San Francisco). See Fig. 370..*Satyrium dryope* p. 196

47b With tails 48

48a V ground pearl gray; D gray brown (grayer when fresh), completely without fulvous suffusion; DHW with rather sharp subterminal fulvous lunule in cell Cu₁ and occasionally smaller,
fainter ones adjoining; VHW orange subterminal marks bright,
extensive, reaching costad to Rs at least; blue patch in cell Cu₂
with thick orange cap. (Rockies eastward to the Atlantic.) See
Fig. 369................................*Satyrium acadica* p. 196

48b V ground various, almost never pearly; D brown, usually with
some discal fulvous suffusion on FW, HW or both; often the subterminal lunules vague and suffused; VHW orange subterminal
marks variable (Rockies to the Pacific).....................49

49 *Note:* I am reasonably certain of the separation of these two species only in S. California. Elsewhere (where pattern characters
may be very unreliable) foodplant association if known may help.

49a V ground nearly white; VHW subterminal orange restricted to
"Thecla spot" in cell Cu₁; larva feeds on willow. See Fig. 367....
.................................*Satyrium sylvinus* p. 195

49b V ground gray; VHW subterminal orange extensive, reaching
costad at least to M₃ and with a prominent cap over the blue
patch in cell Cu₂. Larva on oak. See Fig. 368.................
.................................*Satyrium californica* p. 195

50a V ground pearly gray (rarely darker gray) to nearly white; D
ground very dark uniform gray DHW with subterminal orange
lunule in cell Cu₁, rarely smaller ones adjoining; no defined scent
pad in male. See Fig. 412..............*Strymon melinus* p. 216

50b V ground gray-tan or ocher to brown or nearly black; D ground
variable, subterminal orange lunule HW often absent; scent pad
present in male DFW cell-end................................51

51a VHW distal white edge of postmedian line suffused distad as a white dusting; orange lunule of "Thecla spot" small and pale, almost the ground color. See Fig. 362........................
.................................*Satyrium adenostomatis* p. 193

51b VHW distal white edge of postmedian line sharp and linear or absent; orange of "Thecla spot" variable.....................52

52a VHW postmedian line forms a "W," the segment in cell Cu_2 angularly concave outwardly, usually rather deeply so (slight and faint in Arizona specimens of *ontario*)..............*Euristrymon* p. 212

52b VHW postmedian line not forming a clear "W," the segment in cell Cu_2 transverse or only feebly inangled..................53

53a VHW fulvous lunule of "Thecla spot" faint to absent; V ground ocher; postmedian line usually faint; DFW female usually with fulvous suffusion (Calif. only). See Fig. 360....................
....*Satyrium auretorum* p. 193

53b VHW fulvous lunule of "Thecla spot" orange to red-orange, bright and prominent; V ground tan to dark brown, never ocher; postmedian line prominent; DFW never suffused with fulvous......54

54a V ground tan or pale gray tan; marks at cell-end faint pale streaks, hardly noticeable (Texas, rare)...............[new genus] p. 198

54b V ground brown to dark brown, rarely gray-brown (Colo.); marks at cell-end (FW, HW) duplex whitish streaks, usually with darker brown edging inward, prominent............................55

55 *Note:* The following two species are separable with certainty only by means of the male genitalia. The pattern characters given are helpful, but by no means infallible.

55a Male genitalia with a prominent spiculate projection on each side, arising on vinculum just below falx and directed mesad (Fig. 349); V postmedian line distinctly duplex, thickening costad on each wing to about an interspace width; VHW postmedian line segment in cell Sc displaced basad, in line with cell-end duplex bar; VHW fulvous lunule of "Thecla spot" orange, small (not thicker than the black spot it encloses); DFW scent pad of male about half as wide as discal cell...........*Satyrium caryaevorus* p. 194

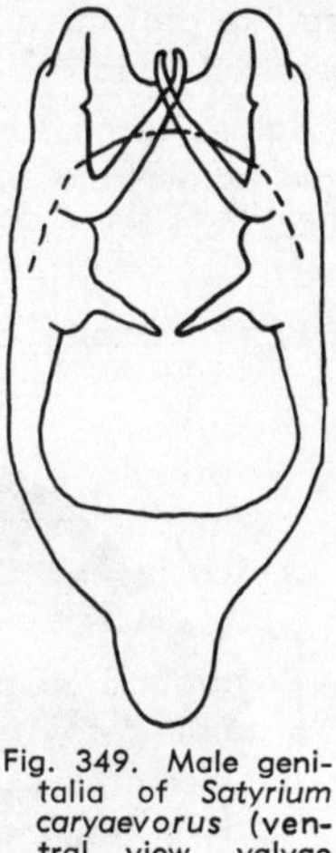

Fig. 349. Male genitalia of *Satyrium caryaevorus* (ventral view, valvae removed).

55b Male genitalia without spiculate projection (Fig. 350); V postmedian line not usually duplex, not usually thickening costad; V postmedian line segment in cell Sc about midway between next segment and cell-end bar; VHW fulvous lunule of "Thecla spot" red-orange, nearly always thicker than the enclosed black spot; DFW scent pad of male more than half as wide as discal cell. See Fig. 365..........Satyrium calanus p. 194

Fig. 350. Male genitalia of *Satyrium calanus* (ventral view, valvae removed).

Genus EUMAEUS Hübner

Hind wing without tails, tornus rounded; male without scent pad. Mid and hind tibiae without spurs. Abdomen of male near end with a pair of very large, long, eversible tufts, each normally withdrawn into a deep pocket completely within body cavity. Male genitalia: aedeagus somewhat flared at tip, apparently lacking cornuti; each falx with a spur-like projection at the elbow, more digitate in *atala* than in *minyas*; valva subquadrate; saccus about twice as long as width at middle.

Rather large for lycaenids, the rounded dark wings with metallic spots below and orange patch on hind wing inner margin being unmistakable. A tropical group barely within our limits.

KEY TO THE SPECIES OF *EUMAEUS*.

**1a Fringe wholly black, concolorous with ground. Fig. 351.........
....*Eumaeus atala* Poey.**

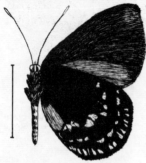

Range: Cuba, the Bahamas and southern Florida. In the latter area formerly common but now nearly extinct. Food plant: *Zamea integrifolia*. Multiple brooded (i-xi).

Fig. 351. *Eumaeus atala* ♂ V. Miami, Florida.

1b Fringe contrastingly pale, nearly white. Fig. 352..............
......................................*Eumaeus minyas* Hübner

Range: Extreme southern Texas
(probably only as a rare stray) southward to South America. Life history
unknown.

Fig. 352. *Eumaeus minyas* ♂ V.
No data.

Genus CHLOROSTRYMON Clench, new genus
Type species: *Thecla telea* Hewitson 1868

Hind wing tailed; male without scent pad. Male genitalia: aedeagus
with one terminal cornutus; tip of aedeagus with mid-ventral keel,
edged with a row of extremely minute teeth; valvae contiguous throughout, tips with a fringe of very fine hairlike processes (nonsocketed cuti-
cular outgrowths).

Smaller than average hairstreaks with iridescent upper surfaces
and green ground color below; essentially tropical, the three species
in our fauna are at the extreme northern limit of their ranges.

KEY TO THE SPECIES OF *CHLOROSTRYMON*.

1a VFW postmedian line thick, white; male D deep reddish purple.
Fig. 353.........................*Chlorostrymon simaethis* Drury.

Range: Widespread from Bolivia and
Brasil northward to southern Texas, Arizona and southern California. Life history
unknown. Perhaps only single brooded
(x-xii, Texas). Not as rare as *telea* (below)
but still quite uncommon and local.

Fig. 353. *Chlorostrymon
simaethis* ♂ V. Victoria,
Mexico.

**1b VFW postmedian line black (without white) or faint to absent;
male D purple (not reddish)**.....................................**2**

**2a VHW terminal patch extends costad to M₁; postmedian line makes
a distinct "W"; VFW postmedian line very faint to absent (Texas).
Fig. 354**...........................*Chlorostrymon telea* **Hewitson.**

Range: Bolivia and Brasil northward to southern Texas (Laredo, vi, one specimen only). Habits
and life history unkown. Nearly everywhere uncommon to rare. It is closely related to *maesites*
(below) and is apparently its continental representative, and accordingly often considered a
subspecies; the two, however, are different in
many traits and seem best considered full
species.

Fig. 354. *Chlorostry-
mon telea* ♂ V. Pa-
rana, Brazil.

**2b VHW terminal patch extends costad to M₃; postmedian line does
not make a "W"; VFW postmedian line black (Florida). Fig. 355.**
........................*Chlorostrymon maesites* **Herrich-Schäffer**

Range: Chiefly West Indies, occurring very
locally in southern Florida, from Miami southward. Life history unknown. Apparently
double-brooded (i-ii; vii). Despite its small
size one of the most brilliantly beautiful butterflies in North America. It occurs in ham-
mocks, visiting flowers readily.

Fig. 355. *Chlorostry-
mon maesites* ♂ V.
Miami, Florida.

Genus PHAEOSTRYMON Clench, new genus
Type species: *Thecla alcestis* Edwards 1871

Hind wing tailed; male with a minute elongated scent pad. Male
genitalia; aedeagus flared at tip, with a serrated ventral keel and two
slender terminal cornuti; valvae contiguous to tips, without mesial

terminal fringe; saccus short (about as long as wide), vinculum without shoulder process.

A single species is known, *Phaeostrymon alcestis* Edwards (Fig. 356).

Range: Southern Kansas south through Oklahoma to Texas, west to Arizona. Food plant: *Melia* (Chinaberry). Single brooded (iv-vii). Seems to prefer flying about hedgerows, perching on leaves.

Fig. 356. *Phaeostrymon alcestis* ♂ V. Caldwell, Kansas.

Genus CHRYSOPHANUS Hübner

Hind wing without tails; male with a prominent scent pad. Male genitalia: aedeagus apically flared, with a serrate midventral keel and a single stout, dentate cornutus; valvae contiguous to middle, then abruptly and widely divergent; saccus short (about as long as wide) but prominent because of the slenderness of the vinculum adjacent to it; posterior edge of vinculum with a stout serrate process arising just below the falx.

Only a single known species, *Chrysophanus titus* Fabricius (Fig. 357).

Range: Over most of North America from southern Canada southward, except southern Florida, the lower Gulf states and the southwest. Food plants: *Prunus* (plum, wild cherry); also *Quercus* (oak) and *Eupatorium coelestinum* (mistflower). Larva myrmecophilous. One brood: (late vi-viii). Not common westward, but widespread and common in the east, particularly fond of flowers (especially *Asclepias*), occurring in open scrub land and fields near woods.

Fig. 357. *Chrysophanus titus* ♀ V. Chicago, Illinois.

191

Genus SATYRIUM Scudder

Hind wing usually tailed, but tails may be very long to completely absent; male scent pad usually well developed, but may be small or absent entirely; tornal lobe of hind wing usually well developed but it, too, varies from prominent to completely absent. Male genitalia: aedeagus flared at tip, with a ventral serrated keel; two terminal cornuti present, usually with at least one dentate; valvae contiguous proximally, distally abruptly divergent; vinculum laterally broad, abruptly becoming very slender toward the saccus; saccus small (about 1 to 2 times as long as breadth at middle) but prominent due to the slenderness of the adjacent vinculum.

A large and almost exclusively holarctic genus, nearly as well developed and diversified in the palaearctic as in the nearctic. Several subgenera are indicated but not applied here due to absence of detailed study of the palaearctic species.

Our species are keyed out in the "pattern key" above.

Fig. 358...............................*Satyrium fuliginosum* Edwards.

Fig. 358. *Satyrium fuligino-sum* ♂ V. Modoc County, California.

Range: Western montane (ca. 7-9000 ft., Wyoming), in scattered groups of colonies, from southern Alberta and British Columbia south to the middle Sierras, Wyoming and northwestern Colorado. Strangely unreported from many states: Oregon, Idaho, Montana, most of Nevada, Utah; in most or all of which it should occur. Food plant: *Lupinus*. Single brooded (late vi-early viii). Common along roadsides and in grassy fields.

Fig. 359................................*Satyrium behrii* Edwards.

Fig. 359. *Satyrium behrii* ♂ V. Modoc County, California.

Range: Western montane, in scattered groups of colonies, in southern British Columbia and Washington; northeastern California and the Sierras with an isolated colony in the San Bernardino Mts.; northwestern Wyoming southward to northern New Mexico, with an isolated colony in Palo Duro Canyon, Texas. As with *fuliginosum* above, strangely unrecorded from several states where it should occur: Oregon, Montana, Arizona and Nevada. Food plants: *Lupinus, Lotus, Astragalus*, perhaps also *Purshia*. One brood (vi-viii). Fond of flowers, especially wild buckwheat.

Fig. 360.............................*Satyrium auretorum* Boisduval.

Range: California in the Sierras and southern mountains. Food plant: probably oaks. Single brooded (vi-vii, southern mts.). Rare and very local.

Fig. 360. *Satyrium auretorum* ♀ V. Cajon Pass, California.

Fig. 361...............................*Satyrium saepium* Boisduval.

Range: Southern British Columbia southward through the Rocky Mts. to Colorado, westward to the coast. Food plant: *Cercocarpus betuloides* (hardtack or mountain mahogany), *Ceanothus cuneatus* (buckbrush), *Ceanothus macrocarpus*. One brood (v-vi, lower elevations in California; vii-viii, Rockies and higher elevations in California). Flies in the foothills and lower mountains, apparently common and generally distributed in California, somewhat rarer and more local elsewhere. *S. chalcis* Edw. is a synonym.

Fig. 361. *Satyrium saepium* ♂ V. Salem, Oregon.

Fig. 362.....................*Satyrium adenostomatis* Henry Edwards.

Range: California, chiefly in the south, northward to Mendocino and Modoc counties, but rare and spotty northward, unreported for many localities. Food plant: *Cercocarpus betuloides*. One brood (vi-vii).

Fig. 362. *Satyrium adenostomatis* ♀ V. Los Angeles, California.

Fig. 363......................*Satyrium liparops* Boisduval & Leconte.

Range: Widely distributed from southern Canada southward to northern Florida, Kansas and Colorado, from the Atlantic westward to the Rockies. Food plants many: *Quercus* (oak), *Salix* (willow), *Amelanchier* (shadbush), *Malus* (apple), *Prunus* (plum), *Vaccinium* (blueberry), *Rubus* (blackberry), *Crataegus* (hawthorn), the latter in Colorado. Single brooded (vi, vii). Local and mostly uncommon to rare; open woods and fields, occasionally on flowers but mostly on leaves.

Fig. 363. *Satyrium liparops* ♂ V. Galena, Illinois.

Fig. 364...........................*Satyrium kingi* Klots and Clench.

Range: So far found only in coastal Georgia and in upland areas of South Carolina, Georgia, Alabama and Mississippi. Food plant unknown. Probably single brooded (v near the coast; vii-viii inland). This species is local, rare and difficult to capture; much more information about it is still needed.

Fig. 364. *Satyrium kingi* ♂ V. Atlanta, Georgia.

Fig. 365.................................*Satyrium calanus* Hubner.

Range: Widely distributed from southern Canada to central Florida, westward to the Rocky Mountains where it reaches southward to New Mexico. Food plants: *Quercus* (oak), *Carya* (hickory), *Juglans* (butternut). Single brooded in the north (v-vi, Texas; late vi-vii, most of remaining area), possibly double brooded in Florida (iii-iv; (?) vi). Occurs chiefly on leaves in sunlit openings in deciduous forest; occurs also, but usually much less frequently, on flowers (chiefly *Asclepias*, *Melilotus alba*) in fields near such forest. Widespread and not uncommon, occasionally abundant. *S. falacer* Godart is a subspecies of *calanus*.

Fig. 365. *Satyrium calanus* ♂ V. Willow Springs, Illinois.

See Fig. 349.....................*Satyrium caryaevorus* McDunnough.

Range: Occupies an elongated oval territory from Vermont and Connecticut westward to upper peninsular Michigan, Minnesota, south to northwestern Ohio, Kentucky and western Pennsylvania. Food plants:

Carya (hickory), *Fraxinus nigra* (black ash), *Crataegus* (hawthorn). One brood (late vi-vii). Has the same habits as *calanus* does in its area, and the two usually fly together, though *caryaevorus* is usually very rare.

Fig. 366...............................*Satyrium edwardsii* Saunders.

Range: Southern New England west to Manitoba and Nebraska, southward to upland Georgia and Texas. Food plant: *Quercus ilicifolia* (scrub oak), larva myrmecophilous. Single brooded (v, Texas; late vi-vii, most of range). Habits much as in *calanus* (found on sunlit leaves in forest openings, on flowers in fields near woods) but not often occurring with it. Common and generally distributed in the northeast, becoming spotty, local and rather rare southward and westward.

Fig. 366. *Satyrium edwardsii* ♀
V. Palos Park, Illinois.

Fig. 367...............................*Satyrium sylvinus* Boisduval.

Range: Western, from Colorado and New Mexico west to the coast, north possibly to Washington, south into extreme northern Mexico (Baja California). Food plant: *Salix* (willow). Common but rather local, occurring along open streams, or in wet meadows at higher elevation, where its food plant grows. This species has the same larval food as *acadica*, but resembles that species less than *californica* does. These three species, as well as *dryope*, need much careful study; they are often, especially in the Rockies and Great Basin regions, extremely difficult, even impossible, to discriminate.

Fig. 367. *Satyrium sylvinus* ♂ V. Los Angeles, California.

Fig. 368...............................*Satyrium californica* Edwards.

Range: Western, from southern British Columbia southward to Colorado, west to the coast. Food plants: *Ceanothus; Quercus* is also suspected and possibly certain Rhamnaceae. One brood (vi-vii, occ. viii). Found in the foothills and very partial to flowers, where it may be taken easily. Northern individuals are often difficult to distinguish from *acadica* and the two might conceivably intergrade in certain places. See under *sylvinus* above.

Fig. 368. *Satyrium californica* ♂ V. Los Angeles, California.

195

Fig. 369...............................*Satyrium acadica* Edwards.

Range: Occurs in a comparatively narrow belt from Nova Scotia south to New Jersey, and west to the Rockies, as far south as Colorado. Food plant: *Salix* (willows); larva myrmecophilous. Single brooded (late vi-vii). The relationship of *acadica* to the western species *sylvinus* and *californica* is not well understood (see above under those species). Local in fields near streams where low shrubby willows abound, generally not uncommon; westward colonies are fewer and widely separated. Fond of flowers, especially *Asclepias*.

Fig. 369. *Satyrium acadica* ♂ V. Ontario.

Fig. 370...............................*Satyrium dryope* Edwards.

Range: California in the Sierras (south to Tehachapi) and coastal ranges between Monterey and Lake counties. Food plant unknown, but oaks are suspected. Single brooded (v-vi). Very similar to *sylvinus* but recognizable in the field (aside from key characters) by its association with oak rather than with willow. See comments under the preceding three species.

Fig. 370. *Satyrium dryope* ♂ V. Santa Clara County, California.

Genus MINISTRYMON Clench, new genus
Type species: *Thecla leda* Edwards 1882

Hind wing tailed; male scent pad small but present. Male genitalia: aedeagus not flared apically, without ventral keel but with two small erect ventral teeth near tip; a single slender curved cornutus is present, terminal; valvae divergent for nearly their whole length; vinculum without process on anterior edge, broadly joining saccus which is long and slender (about 4.5 times as long as width at middle).

A small genus of smaller than average hairstreaks of homogeneous appearance. The only species definitely known to belong are the three listed below (separated in the pattern key above), though others may be found among the tropical Theclas.

Fig. 371.................................*Ministrymon ines* Edwards.

Range: Southern California to southern Arizona and probably south into Mexico. Life history unknown. Multiple brooded (v, Arizona; ix-x, California). This has been listed as a form (presumably seasonal) of *leda*, but the absence of intermediates and the simultaneous occurrence of both (in comparable condition) in several localities makes their specific distinctness much more likely. The two, however, seem to enjoy a virtually identical range, though *ines* is much the rarer.

Fig. 371. *Ministrymon ines* ♂ V. Arizona.

Fig. 372.................................*Ministrymon leda* Edwards.

Range: Southern California to southern Arizona, southward into Baja California and Sonora. Food plant: *Prosopis juliflora* var. *glandulosa* (honey mesquite). Multiple brooded (v, vi, vii, viii, Arizona). Locally may be rather common—much more so than *ines*.

Fig. 372. *Ministrymon leda* ♀ V. La Puerta Valley, California.

Fig. 373.................................*Ministrymon clytie* Edwards.

Range: Southern Texas (and Arizona?) south into Mexico. Life history unknown. Multiple brooded and seasonally dimorphic, the dark winter form occurring x-ii, the lighter summer form, iii-ix. Locally not uncommon.

Fig. 373. *Ministrymon clytie* ♂ V. Brownsville, Texas.

Genus ? (new genus)

Hind wing tailed; male with a rather large bipartite scent pad. Male genitalia: aedeagus slightly flared at tip if at all, without ventral keel or ventral teeth, with a single sinuate terminal cornutus, distally expanded and dentate; valvae divergent from about the middle; vinculum with a large triangular process from anterior border at about the middle on each side, broadly joining the saccus which is about twice as long as its width at middle.

In the absence of an identified genotype it would be imprudent to bestow a name on this group, the more so as the species concerned barely enter our fauna.

Fig 374.................................."Thecla" spurina Hewitson.

Fig. 374..................................."Thecla" zebina Hewitson.

The tangled situation in the middle of which these two names are found is impossible to unravel at the present time. Several different, but very similar and apparently hitherto confused, species are involved, further complicated by the difficulty of associating females (on which some names have been based) with males (on which other names have been based). Two specimens have been taken in southern Texas, one referred to one of these, and one to the other. Their true identity remains uncertain.

Fig. 374. "Thecla" spurina or zebina ♂ V. Barretal, Mexico.

Genus CALYCOPIS Scudder

Hind wing tailed; males without scent pad. Male genitalia: tip of aedeagus without ventral keel, but ventral edge slightly upturned terminally; a single terminal cornutus, curved and slender; valvae contiguous for their whole length, with truncated tips; forearm af falx slightly sinuate, with a longitudinal lamella; vinculum without anterior processes, broad, broadly joining the moderate saccus.

A rather large tropical genus, with two species occurring in North America.

1a VHW "Thecla spot" in cell Cu$_1$ subterminally with pale lunule bright red, as thick as or thicker than the small black spot it encloses; VFW red of postmedian line much thinner throughout than corresponding red on HW at costa. Fig. 375.. *Calycopis beon* Cramer.

Fig. 375. *Calycopis beon* ♂ V. Fort Worth, Texas.

Range: East-central Texas (a stray taken as far north as Kansas), southward over most of Central and South America. Food plant unknown. Broods not worked out (iii-viii, xi; in Texas); possibly seasonally slightly dimorphic. In extreme eastern Texas largely replaced by *cecrops*, but the two have been taken together in some areas. They are similar and may be difficult to separate, though unquestionably distinct.

1b VHW "Thecla spot" with pale lunule variable in amount of red (from none to bright red), but always much thinner than the black spot it encloses; VFW red of postmedian band about as thick as costal end of corresponding red of HW. Fig. 376.................
....................................*Calycopis cecrops* Fabricius.

Fig. 376. *Calycopis cecrops* ♂ V. Highlands, Florida.

Range: Southeastern United States, resident as far north as southern New Jersey, West Virginia, the Ohio River region to eastern Oklahoma and Texas. Strays have been taken as far north as southwestern Michigan. Food plants: *Croton; Rhus copallina* (dwarf sumac), the latter in New Jersey and possibly favored northward. Broods not worked out, possibly two (iv-v; ix-xi; Florida. iii-iv, vi-viii; Texas). Very local in the north, widespread and common southward, favoring open country near woods, perching on low plants and shrubs.

Genus TMOLUS Hübner

Hind wing tailed; male with scent pad. Male genitalia: aedeagus terminally more or less upturned, without ventral keel, with a single terminal cornutus; valvae distally regularly tapering, contiguous throughout; vinculum broad, more or less broadly connected to the very long saccus.

A tropical genus of smaller than average hairstreaks, probably more closely allied to *Ministrymon* than its position here would intimate. Most of the species are tropical, two barely entering our fauna. They are keyed out in the pattern key above.

Fig. 377......................................*Tmolus echion* Linnaeus.

Range: From South America northward, rarely straying into southern Texas, where a single specimen has been taken.

Fig. 377. *Tmolus echion* ♂
V. Presidio, Vera Cruz,
Mexico.

Fig. 378......................................*Tmolus azia* Hewitson.

Range: South America north into southern Texas and southern Arizona. Life history unknown. Possibly only single brooded in Texas (iv-v), where it is not common.

Fig. 378. *Tmolus azia*
♂ V. Rio Grande
City, Texas.

Genus CALLOPHRYS Billberg

Hind wing tailed or not; male nearly always with a well developed scent pad. Male genitalia: aedeagus more or less flared at tip, without ventral keel, with two dentate terminal cornuti; valvae contiguous for their whole length; vinculum rather broad dorsally, abruptly slender ventrally, joining the rather long saccus.

A large and very diversified group widely distributed over three continents. The several subgenera have mostly been considered full genera heretofore.

KEY TO SUBGENERA OF *CALLOPHRYS*.

1a Valvae "capped" (tips thickened, with the thickened zone set off sharply by a transverse line)..................................2

1b Valvae not "capped"...4

2a HW tailed................................subgenus *Xamia* p. 205

2b HW tail-less...3

3a Palpi twice as long as vertical diameter of eye; V green.........
....subgenus *Sandia* p. 205

3b Palpi about one and one-half as long as vertical diameter of eye; V brown...............................subgenus *Incisalia* p. 201

4a Male genitalia with cornuti slightly spatulate; HW tailed; D without blue, or, when blue, V brown . . . . .subgenus *Mitoura* p. 205

4b Male genitalia with cornuti not spatulate; V green 5

5a D usually metallic blue; HW usually tailed . . . .
. . . . .subgenus *Cyanophrys* p. 211

5b D without blue; HW tail-less . . . . .subgenus *Callophrys* p. 209

Subgenus INCISALIA Scudder

Hind wing nearly always without tails; male scent pad absent in one species only; ends of androconial scales entire, rounded or dentate; wings below brown. Palpi approximately 1.5 times as long as vertical eye diameter. Tips of valvae "capped" (with a sharply delimited terminal thickening). Most highly developed in North America, but with a number of species in the eastern Palaearctic as well.

KEY TO THE SPECIES OF *CALLOPHRYS* (Incisalia).

1a VFW with terminal hoary band; VHW with extensive hoary shading in terminal half; HW fringe checkered, feebly crenulate, but not lobed at vein-ends; HW costa distally straight but not recurved. Fig. 379 . . . . *Callophrys polios* Cook & Watson.

Range: Eastern Alaska and the lower Mackenzie R., southeast through Canada to Nova Scotia, south to New Jersey, Virginia (mountains) and Michigan; westward extending far south to New Mexico in the Rockies but not south of Washington on the Pacific coast. Food plant: *Arctostaphylos uva-ursi* (bearberry); perhaps also *Epigaea repens* (ground laurel), according to an observed association in central Pennsylvania. Single brooded (iv-vi, New Jersey; v-vi, Colorado and also the lower Mackenzie River). Closely associated with its food plant, it rarely visits flowers.

Fig. 379. *Callophrys polios* ♀ V. New Hampshire.

1b VFW without hoary terminal shading 2

2a HW with terminal projection at Cu_2, distinctly longer than those on any other veins, occasionally forming a true tail; HW costa strongly recurved distally; VHW terminal area extensively hoary shaded . . .3

2b HW with terminal projection at Cu_2 not longer than those at other veins; HW costa rarely recurved distally; terminal area usually without extensive hoary shading 4

3a Male with long scent pad at cell-end DFW; VHW with "Thecla spot"; VHW basal area usually ruddy brown with a basal hoary patch. Fig. 380..........................*Callophrys irus* Godart.

Range: A rather limited bipartite area: southern New England to South Carolina, westward in north to Michigan and northwestern Indiana; and secondly, east-central Texas. The subspecies in the latter area (*hadros* Cook & Watson) has usually been considered a good species. Food plants: *Lupinus perennis, Baptisia tinctoria.* Single brooded (iv-v, New Jersey). Local and generally rather uncommon.

Fig. 380. *Callophrys irus* ♂
V. Scranton, Pennsylvania.

3b Male without scent pad; VHW without "Thecla spot," without basal hoary patch, the basal area uniform, usually very dark brown (nearly black) except in Texas. Fig. 381........................
..........................*Callophrys henrici* Grote & Robinson.

Range: The most unusual in the subgenus: Central Florida to Texas, north to about Lat. 40° west of Appalachians; in and east of these mountains extending north to Nova Scotia, thence west to northern Michigan. Food plants: *Prunus, Vaccinium (corymbosum* and probably *vacillans)* and *Gaylussacia* in the east; *Cercis canadensis,* probably also *Prunus,* in the west. In Texas also reported associated with cedars. Single brooded (iii-iv, Mississippi; v, New Jersey). Local and in the east uncommon to rare; westward it is sporadically and locally abundant.

Fig. 381. *Callophrys henrici* ♂ V. St. Louis, Missouri.

4a Fringe of both wings strongly checkered (alternating black and white), on HW strongly crenulate; VHW pattern bold, of irregularly disjunct bars and angular lines; VFW dots of terminal row usually black, sharp and cuneiform.....................................6

4b Fringe, especially FW, feebly or not at all checkered, on HW weakly or not at all crenulate; VHW pattern more diffuse and usually consisting of dark basal, paler postmedian and darker subterminal areas; VFW subterminal dots usually gray or brownish, often diffuse and indistinctly or not at all cuneiform....................5

5a VHW with a terminal, often crenulate, white line; subterminal band mahogany red, yellowish or hoary gray, rarely if ever brick red; basal field usually with trace of an inwardly white-edged black line, often angled. Figs. 382, 383....*Callophrys fotis* Strecker.

Range: Western montane, from the Rocky Mts. westward to the Pacific, from southern British Columbia south to Arizona, but spotty and unreported from many regions. Larva on *Sedum* (Vancouver Id.). Single brooded (iv-v, rarely late iii, Colorado). The several races may be grouped into three assemblages each of which has heretofore been considered a full species: (a) typical *fotis*, in the desert areas of the Southwest, very gray, hoary-looking below; (b) *mossii* Hy. Edwards (with *schryveri* Cross) from Vancouver to Colorado along the Rockies, rich mahogany red below, larger and richer northward; and (c) *doudoroffi* dos Passos (with *windi* Clench), respectively in the coast ranges south of Monterey and in the central Sierras, of California, similar to *mossii* but paler, more yellowish, especially below. The species as a whole is quite local, often rather rare.

Fig. 382. *Callophrys fotis* ♂ V. Coal Creek, Colorado.

Fig. 383. *Callophrys fotis* ♀ V. Salt Lake City, Utah.

5b VHW without terminal white line; subterminal band usually brick red, occasionally gray infuscated, never mahogany or gray; basal field rarely with traces of a dark bar, never white-edged. Fig. 384.
....................................*Callophrys augustinus* Kirby.

Range: Upland Mississippi, Alabama and Georgia north to Newfoundland, and Labrador, westward through Canada (including Michigan and northern Minnesota), north to lower Mackenzie River; reaching coast near Vancouver Id. and south in Rockies and coastal states to New Mexico, Arizona, California and northern Mexico. Food plants: *Vaccinium (vacillans, corymbosum, pennsylvanicum)* and less commonly *Arctostaphylos* in the east; *Cuscuta, Ceanothus,* also *Malus* (!), *Gaultheria, Arbutus* and perhaps *Sedum,* in west. Single brooded (iv-v, Mass.; much earlier southward, espe-

Fig. 384. *Callophrys augustinus* ♀ V. Nekoosa, Wisconsin.

cially in southern California). In many areas much the commonest *Incisalia,* usually flying low over and about its food plant, generally ignoring flowers. The western group of subspecies has usually been treated as a distinct species (*iroides* Boisduval).

6a VHW with "Thecla spot," contrasting with markings in other cells; HW costa definitely recurved distally; small; LFW rarely over 11 mm. Fig. 385.................Callophrys lanoraieensis Sheppard.

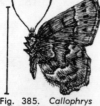

Fig. 385. *Callophrys lanoraieensis* ♂ V. Lincoln, Maine.

Range: So far known only from near Lincoln, Maine, and Lanoraie, Quebec. A reported capture near Ithaca, New York, is unverified as to identity and doubtful. Food plant: *Picea nigra*. Single brooded (v-vi). Occurs in bogs or muskegs where black spruce is found. Near Lincoln not uncommon, but apparently rare at Lanoraie.

6b VHW cells subterminally with substantially the same markings in each; HW costa distally straight but not recurved; larger, LFW > 12 mm...7

7a VHW subterminal angular black line much more shallowly angled between M_3 and Cu_2 than elsewhere; VHW termen narrowly shaded with hoary from tornus to M_3 or M_2; VFW with 2 transverse bars in cell; eastern. Fig. 386...............Callophrys niphon Hübner.

Fig. 386. *Calloyhrys niphon* ♂ V. Rumford, Rhode Island.

Range: Northern Mississippi, Alabama and Georgia north to Nova Scotia, thence west through southern Canada and Michigan to southern Manitoba; also Colorado (strays?). Food plant: "hard" pines (*Pinus rigida*, probably *banksiana* and others as well). Single brooded (iii-iv, Mississippi; late iv-early vi, New Jersey). A more frequent flower visitor than other *Incisalia*, and flies generally a little later.

7b VHW subterminal line as deeply angled between M_3-Cu_2 as elsewhere; VHW normally with little or no terminal hoary shading; VFW with only a single distinct bar at cell-end; western. Fig. 387..............................Callophrys eryphon Boisduval.

Fig. 387. *Callophrys eryphon* ♀ V. Salt Lake City, Utah.

Range: Western, chiefly montane (6-10,000 feet, Colorado), from central California (coast range and Sierras), eastern Arizona and New Mexico, north to southern British Columbia, eastward to Rockies, Nebraska and northern Manitoba. Food plant: Pines (*P. ponderosa, contorta*). Single brooded (late v-early vii, Colorado).

Subgenus SANDIA Clench and Ehrlich

Hind wing without tails; male scent pad well developed; androconial scales dentate; wings below, especially hind wing, green. Palpi approximately 2 times as long as vertical eye diameter (unique in the genus). Tips of valvae "capped" (see *Incisalia* above).

Only one recently discovered species is known, *Callophrys mcfarlandi* Ehrlich and Clench (Fig. 388).

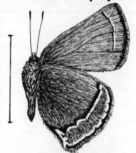

Range: known only from the Sandia Mts., near Albuquerque, New Mexico, and the Davis Mts. of Texas. Probably much more widespread. Food plant: *Nolina microcarpa* (beargrass). Apparently multiple brooded, though flight periods still not determined accurately. There is one flight approximately during the first 2 weeks of May, and a second emergence during June. Local but not uncommon.

Fig. 388. *Callophrys mcfarlandi* ♂ V. Paratype. Sandia Mountains, New Mexico.

Subgenus XAMIA Clench, new subgenus

Hind wing tailed; male scent pad well developed; androconial scales dentate; wings below, especially hind wing, green. Palpi approximately 1.5 times as long as vertical eye diameter. Tips of valvae "capped" (see *Incisalia*).

The type species is the single known species, *xami*. It is keyed out under *Mitoura* below.

Fig. 389. . . . .*Callophrys xami* **Reakirt.**

Range: From Jalapa and Mexico City, Mexico, north barely into the United States in southern Texas and southern Arizona. Life history unknown. Probably at least three broods (iv, vi-vii, x-xii, Texas). Rare in the north, commoner southward.

Fig. 389. *Callophrys xami* ♂ V. Mexico City, Mexico.

Subgenus MITOURA Scudder

Hind wing tailed; male scent pad well developed; androconial scales rounded apically; wings below either green or brown. Palpi about 1.0-1.5 times as long as vertical eye diameter. Tips of valvae not "capped"; cornuti rather spatulate (unique in the genus).

A wholly American group, best developed in the southwestern United States.

KEY TO THE SPECIES OF CALLOPHRYS (Mitoura).

1a VHW with post-basal marks....................................2

1b No such marks..4

2a VFW most of wing brown, the green limited to small terminal patch near apex and a costal area towards base, not filling cell; VHW postbasal marks connected, area between them and postmedian line nearly filled with brown, contrasting with green ground. Fig. 390......................................*Callophrys loki* Skinner.

Range: Southern California (south of Riverside) south into northern Baja California (Valle de la Trinidad). Food plant: *Juniperus (californica)*. Single brooded (iii-vi). Apparently local, uncommon, and closely associated with its food plant.

Fig. 390. *Callophrys loki* ♂ V. Perris, California.

2b VFW mostly green (fresh specimens needed!), which fills cell completely, and extends usually down to M_3, occasionally beyond; VHW postbasal marks not connected, area between them and postmedian line as green as rest of wing........................3

3a VFW usually with white dot or spot in cell near end; VHW with dark brown double patch just distad of postmedian line in cells M_1 and M_2. Fig. 391...........*Callophrys hesseli* Rawson & Ziegler.

Range: Found so far only along the Atlantic Coast, from Massachusetts (Milton) to North Carolina. Food plant: White cedar *(Chamaecyparis thyoides)*. Double brooded (iv-v, vii), flying at the same time as *gryneus*. Flies in close association with its food plant, and seems much more local and uncommon than its sibling relative *gryneus*.

Fig. 391. *Callophrys hesseli* ♂ V. Ocean County, New Jersey.

3b VFW almost never with white mark near cell-end; VHW without such dark brown patch (the area green). Fig. 392.............
..*Callophrys gryneus* Hübner.

Range: Southern New England west through northern Indiana to eastern Kansas, south to central Florida, Mississippi, most of Texas; possibly in southern New Mexico. Food plant: *Juniperus virginiana.* Double brooded in the north (late v-early vi; late vii-early viii: Massachusetts); three broods farther south (iv-v, vi-vii, viii-ix: Oklahoma); but in South Carolina there is a discrete spring brood (iii-early iv) followed by a long continuous summer flight (vii-ix), which may be true of most of the southern part of the species range. Local and often spotty in its occurrence it can nonetheless be extremely common in favored places.

Fig. 392. *Callophrys gryneus* ♂ V. Morris County, New Jersey.

Remains very close to its red cedars (and seems to prefer the lower, more stunted, trees), flying about the tops and perching on branches; strays occasionally to nearby flowers. The subspecies in central Florida (*smilacis* Boisd. & Lec., formerly *sweadneri* Cherm.) has heretofore been considered a good species.

4a D shaded with steel blue, without fulvous; V without green. Fig. 393.............................*Callophrys spinetorum* Hewitson.

Range: Western montane from southern British Columbia south (Rockies westward) to Jalisco, Mexico, but unreported from Oregon, Idaho, most of Nevada, Utah and California (except north and south extremes of the latter). Food plant: various species of *Arceuthobium* (mistletoe) on pines. Single brooded (v-vii, Colorado; vii-viii, Calif.). Fond of flowers and occurs in open or scrubby fields near pine forests. In some areas apparently common, in others very rare.

Fig. 393. *Callophrys spinetorum* ♀ V. Laguna, California.

4b D without blue, usually with some fulvous shading or lunules....5

5a V (especially HW) green...6

5b V brown or purplish brown, without any green..................7

6a VHW postmedian white line abruptly projecting tooth-like distad along veins Cu$_1$ and Cu$_2$, the line nearly straight costad of M$_3$....
........*Callophrys (Xamia) xami* Reakirt (see preceding subgenus)

6b VHW postmedian line throughout angled or disjunct, often sinuous, but not projecting on veins as described. Fig. 394..............
...Callophrys siva Edwards

Range: Rocky Mts. from Montana south through Wyoming, western Nebraska, to Arizona, New Mexico and western Texas; also in southern California. Food plant: various *Juniperus*. Probably double brooded (v-vi, vii-viii: New Mexico; iv-v, vii-viii: California).

Fig. 394. *Callophrys siva* ♂
V. Los Angeles, California.

7a V (especially HW) ground tinged with lilac. Fig. 395.............
...................................Callophrys nelsoni Boisduval.

Range: A rather narrow area along the west coast from southern British Columbia to southern California, east as far as eastern Oregon, western Nevada, montane southward. Also, astonishingly, on Guadeloupe Island (about 150 mi. west of Vizcaino Bay, Baja California). Food plants: reared from *Thuja plicata* in British Columbia; *Libocedrus decurrens* suspected in most of California.

Fig. 395. *Callophrys nelsoni*
♀ V. Yosemite County,
California.

7b V without lilac tint. Fig. 396..........Callophrys johnsoni Skinner

Range: Very localized in the Cascades of Oregon, northern California, norwestern Washington (Seattle) and southern Vancouver Island. Food plant: *Arceuthobium douglassii*. Single brooded (late v-early vi). Apparently rare or very local.

Fig. 396. *Callophrys johnsoni* ♀ V. "Gold Lake,
California."

Subgenus CALLOPHRYS Billberg

Hind wing without tails; male scent pad well developed; scent scales entire, the ends rounded; wings below green. Palpi about 1.5 times as long as vertical eye diameter. Tips of valvae not "capped"; cornuti slender.

More widely distributed (but less diversified) in the Palearctic than in the Nearctic, this is a characteristic and readily recognized group.

KEY TO THE SPECIES OF *CALLOPHRYS (Callophrys)*.

1a VFW with green down to Cu$_2$ or 2V.............................2

1b This green restricted to a more or less broad costal and terminal border, leaving a large central area of gray or brown..........4

2a VHW immaculate, or at most with a very faint indication of a postmedian line: usually a row of obscure whitish dashes. Fig. 397.................................*Callophrys affinis* Edwards.

Range: Curiously disjunct: northern Utah and Wyoming; then central Washington and southern British Columbia. There is no apparent reason why it should not turn up in the intervening area. Life history unknown. Possibly double brooded, but this is not certain. This may intergrade with (and hence be conspecific with) *apama*.

Fig. 397. *Callophrys affinis* ♂ V. Utah.

2b VHW with either a prominent postmedian white line or with a series of distinct pure white dashes or dots...........................3

3a VHW with a solid postmedian line of white. Fig. 398...........
.....................................*Callophrys sheridani* Edwards.

Range: Moderate elevations (6-10,000 ft.) in the Rockies from southern New Mexico to southern Alberta and southern British Columbia. Food plant: *Eriogonum umbellatum*. One brood (late iii-v, Colorado). Northward this tends to strong reduction of the postmedian line VHW, and may then possibly be confused with the sympatric *affinis*.

Fig. 398. *Callophrys sheridani* ♂ V. Silver Lake, Utah.

3b VHW postmedian line a row of prominent white spots...........
...................................*Callophrys viridis* Edwards
Range: From San Francisco north to southern Oregon. Food plant: probably *Erigonum latifolium*. Apparently single brooded (iii-v).
4a VHW nearly immaculate, or postmedian line a row of white spots of varying number..5
4b VHW with a crooked white postmedian line....................6
5a FW termen evenly convex...............*apama* (see couplet 6a)
5b This margin angled convexly at M₂ or thereabouts, and straight or slightly concave thence to tornus. Fig. 399...................
...................................*Callophrys dumetorum* Boisduval.

Range: Vicinity of San Francisco, California, south into northern Mexico; also in the central and southern Sierra Nevada of California. Food plant: *Eriogonum;* also *Syrmatium, Hosackia, Lotus scoparius.*

Fig. 399. *Callophrys dumetorum* ♂ V. San Francisco, California.

6a VHW postmedian line basally edged with black, then fulvous. Fig. 400...................................*Callophrys apama* Edwards.

Range: Northern Sonora (Mexico) through eastern Arizona, New Mexico north to Colorado and southeastern Wyoming at moderate elevations (6500-10,000 ft.). Food plant: not known, but adults fly in association with *Eriogonum*. Probably double brooded (v-vi; viii: Colorado).

Fig. 400. *Callophrys apama* ♂ V. White Mountains, Arizona.

6b This line without fulvous. Fig. 401.....*Callophrys comstocki* Henne

Range: Known only from the Providence Mts., San Bernardino Co., California. Food plant: *Eriogonum* sp. Possibly double brooded (late iii-iv; viii- the latter reared). Related to, and possibly replacing, *apama*, but distinct enough to be held a full species.

Fig. 401. *Callophrys comstocki* ♂ V. Providence Mountains, California.

Subgenus CYANOPHRYS Clench, new subgenus
Type species: *Strymon agricolor* Butler and Druce 1872.

Hind wing tailed or not; male scent pad present but very small; androconial scales with entire rounded tips; wings below green, above nearly always blue (except *fusius*), usually brilliant and extensive in the male, duller and more basally restricted in the female. Palpi about 1.5 times as long as vertical eye diameter. Tips of valvae not "capped"; cornuti slender.

A rather large group occurring chiefly in the uplands of South and Central America. Only one species is known to occur in our fauna, *Callophrys miserabilis* Clench (Fig. 402).

Range: Central America as far north as southern Texas, where it is resident and not uncommon. Previous records of *"pastor"* apparently are misidentifications of this species. The name *pastor* Butler and Druce is a synonym of *longula* Hewitson, a species which apparently does not extend as far north as the United States. Life history unknown. Apparently multiple brooded (v, vii, viii, xi, xii, Texas).

Fig. 402. *Callophrys miserabilis* ♂ V. Brownsville, Texas.

Genus ATLIDES Hübner

Hind wing tailed; male with compound scent pad. Male genitalia: aedeagus with two terminal cornuti, short, blunt, both with prominent teeth; tip of aedeagus flared, slightly upcurved, without ventral keel; anterior border of vinculum with a marked process opposite shoulder process of posterior border; saccus regularly tapering, extremely long; valvae divergent.

One species in our fauna, *Atlides halesus* Cramer (Fig. 403).

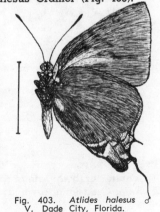

Range: Southern United States northward (except in mountains) to about lat. 37°, from coast to coast, and apparently southward an indeterminate extent into Mexico. Strays have been taken as far north as Brooklyn, New York, northern Indiana and Oregon. Food plant: *Phoradendron* (mistletoe) on Live Oak. Two broods (iv; ix-x in Florida, the second brood slightly earlier northward), the first brood much less common. Rather local but not uncommon in the south; rare northward. A frequent flower visitor.

Fig. 403. *Atlides halesus* ♂ V. Dade City, Florida.

211

Genus DOLYMORPHA Holland

Hind wing tailed or not; scent pad of male present. Male genitalia: aedeagus with two terminal cornuti, one of which has an abrupt, larger disc-like terminal expansion with peripheral teeth; tip of aedeagus slightly flared, upcurved, without ventral keel; saccus about twice

as long as width at middle; valvae distally divergent, each with a ventro-lateral conical, acuminate process at middle.

One species, *Dolymorpha jada* Hewitson (Fig. 404).

A common Central American species, rarely straying north into the United States (southern Arizona?). Life history and other data unknown.

Fig. 404. *Dolymorpha jada* ♂ V. Victoria, Mexico.

Genus EURISTRYMON Clench, new genus
Type species: *Thecla favonius* J. E. Smith 1797.

Hind wing tailed; male with well marked scent pad. Male genitalia: aedeagus slightly flared apically, with two terminal cornuti; no ventral keel; saccus very short (about as long as width at middle, or shorter); valvae with no lateral process, distally divergent.

The palearctic species *pruni* also belongs to this genus.

KEY TO THE SPECIES OF *EURISTRYMON*.

1a D fuscous, without fulvous discal shading or (HW) subterminal orange lunules; wings very rounded. Fig. 405..................
........................*Euristrymon polingi* Barnes and Benjamin

Range: Western Texas, from Alpine to Davis Mts. Life history unknown. Single brooded (v-vi). Apparently quite local, but not uncommon where found, on leaves (especially of oak) and flowers.

Fig. 405. *Euristrymon polingi* ♂ V. Paratype. Alpine, Texas.

1b D with fulvous or orange discal patches or (HW) subterminal orange lunules, or both; wings rather angular..........................2

2 *Note:* Occasional *favonius* may give trouble here. Check locality.

2a VHW subterminal red heavy, continuous, inner edges between veins straight; normally no red capping the bluish patch in cell Cu₂; postbasal dash prominent. Fig. 406.......................
................................*Euristrymon favonius* J. E. Smith.

Range: Southern Florida north through Georgia, rarely (probably strays) as far north as New Jersey; chiefly rather near the coast. Food plant: Oaks. Apparently single brooded (iv-v, Florida). Possibly an extreme subspecies of *ontario*, as intermediates are occasionally taken in Georgia.

Fig. 406. *Euristrymon favonius* ♀ V. Northern Florida.

2b VHW subterminal "red" more orange than red, a series of strongly lunular marks deeply convex basad (which may, however, be limited to one or two in cells M₃ and Cu₁; often a thin orange band caps the bluish patch in cell Cu₂; postbasal dash faint to absent. Fig. 407.............................*Euristrymon ontario* Edwards.

Range: Southern Ontario and Massachusetts south and west through Ohio, Georgia to Texas, New Mexico and Arizona. Food plants: *Quercus* (oaks), also *Crataegus* (hawthorn). One brood (v, vi). Extremely rare in the northeast, slightly commoner in southeast, and rather frequent from Texas westward. *E. autolycus* Edwards is a subspecies of *ontario*.

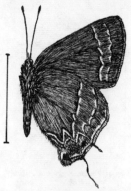

Fig. 407. *Euristrymon ontario* ♂ V. Eureka, Kansas.

Genus HYPOSTRYMON Clench, new genus
Type species: *Thecla critola* Hewitson 1874.

Hind wings tailed; male with a large discal androconial patch, but no scent pad. Male genitalia: aedeagus distally cylindrical, simple, with no cornutus visible; saccus about twice as long as breadth at middle; valvae appearing curiously twisted and excurved distally.

A peculiar and isolated genus, probably nearest *Panthiades*, strikingly recalling certain Indo-Australian *Hypolycaena*. There is a single species, *Hypostrymon critola* Hewitson (Fig. 408), which rarely strays from its native Sonora to southern Arizona. "*Hypolycaena*" *festata* Weeks from Baja California is a close relative.

Fig. 408. *Hypostrymon critola* ♂ V. Patagonia Mountains, Arizona.

Genus PANTHIADES Hübner

Hind wings tailed; male with scent pad. Male genitalia: aedeagus cylindrical or slightly flared at tip, with a single flattened truncated cornutus, subterminal, usually difficult to discern; saccus extremely short or absent entirely; valvae variously developed, often (as in our species) with a ventral tooth at middle.

A probably rather large tropical genus, including these two synonyms: *Eupsyche* Scudder (type, *m-album* Bdv. & Lec.) and *Parrhasius* Hübner (type *polibetes* Cramer). There is enough variation among these that they may one day be reinstated as subgenera when the genus in its full extent is better known.

Our species is *Panthiades m-album* Boisduval & Leconte (Fig. 409).

Range: Southeastern United States, resident as far north as Connecticut, southern Pennsylvania and the Ohio River region, westward to Texas. Strays have been taken as far north as southern Wisconsin and northern Indiana. Supposed to range into Central and South America but this is doubtful. Food plants: Oak and, doubtfully *Astragalus* (milk vetch). Double brooded in the north (late v-vi; late vii-viii), perhaps more southward. Not uncommon in the southeast, but very local and much rarer elsewhere. In western Pennsylvania it has been found mostly in cool ravines in sunlit clearings in deciduous woods, but elsewhere it occurs in other situations.

Fig. 409. *Panthiades m-album* ♂ V. Nashville, Tennessee.

Genus STRYMON Hübner

Hind wing with or without tails; male scent pad absent or more or less diffused. Male genitalia: cornutus single, acuminate, far within shaft of aedeagus; tip of aedeagus cylindrical, not flared or noticeably upturned; tips of valvae with small basally directed teeth covering the surface; saccus well developed, but not unusually so.

As here restricted this genus is wholly American and chiefly tropical, composed of a rather large number of species, a few of which reach the United States, only one of them extensively. The genus seems to have acquired a modest propensity for crossing water barriers, many members occurring in the West Indies and a few on islands off the continental west coast. The species are keyed out in the pattern key above.

Fig. 410.........................*Strymon martialis* **Herrich-Schäffer.**

Range: Purely Antillean, reaching southern Florida. Food plant: *Trema floridana*. Multiple brooded (i, ii, vi, vii, viii, x). Rather local but not uncommon.

Fig. 410. *Strymon martialis* ♂ V. Royal Palm Park, Florida.

Fig. 411.......................................*Strymon acis* **Drury.**

Range: Likewise purely Antillean, reaching southern Florida. Food plant: wild croton. Apparently multiple brooded (i, ii, vii, viii). Locally not uncommon and a frequent flower visitor.

Fig. 411. *Strymon acis* ♂ V. Matheson Hammock, Florida.

Fig. 412...................................*Strymon melinus* Hübner.

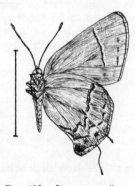

Range: The most widely distributed hairstreak in North America, occurring from Nova Scotia to southern British Columbia, southward over the whole United States and on into Mexico and south to Venezuela. Food plants: *Humulus* (hops), *Phaseolus* (cultivated beans), *Malva* (mallow), *Polygonum* (knotweed), *Hypericum* (St. John's wort), and many others. The larva bores into fruit or seed. Three broods northward (v; vi-vii; ix: Boston, Mass.), perhaps more in the south. In most areas the spring brood is quite scarce (partial?), usually smaller, darker. More addicted to open country than most hairstreaks, in most parts of its range it is common and generally distributed (it is the only North American lycaenid which has been considered an economic pest, on hops and beans), but in certain localities unaccountably scarce.

Fig. 412. *Strymon melinus* ♂ V. Salt Lake, Utah.

Fig. 413...................................*Strymon avalona* Wright.

Range: Found only on Santa Catalina Island, off the coast of southern California. Food plant: *Lotus*, especially *argophyllus* var. *ornithopus*; also L. *scaparius*.

Fig. 413. *Strymon avalona* ♂ V. Catalina Island, California.

Fig. 414...................................*Strymon rufofusca* Hewitson.

A widely distributed tropical continental species occurring in southern Texas (xi, xii). Life history unknown.

Fig. 414. *Strymon rufofusca* ♂ V. Victoria, Mexico.

216

Fig. 415....................................*Strymon cestri* **Reakirt.**

Range: A rather common Central American species taken twice, many years apart, in southern Texas (iii, x). Life history unknown.

Fig. 415. *Strymon cestri* ♂ V. Valles, Mexico.

Fig. 416....................................*Strymon yojoa* **Reakirt.**

A common Central American species, taken once (iii) in southern Texas.

Fig. 416. *Strymon yojoa* ♂ V. Barro Colorado, Canal Zone.

Fig. 417...............................*Strymon columella* **Fabricius.**

Range: Southern Florida, the West Indies, Central America, southern Texas and southern California. Food plant (California): *Sida hederacea*. In Florida apparently two brooded (vi; ix-xi); in Texas apparently common all year.

Fig. 417. *Strymon columella* ♂ V. Pharr, Texas.

Fig. 418....................................*Strymon bazochii* **Godart.**

Range: Tropical America (including Antilles), extending as far north as southern Texas, where it is apparently resident. Life history unknown. Possibly double brooded (v; x-xii; Texas).

Fig. 418. *Strymon bazochii* ♂ V. Victoria, Mexico.

Genus ERORA Scudder

Tail-less; males without scent pad. Male genitalia: cornutus single, long acuminate, far within shaft of aedeagus; tip of aedeagus with an acuminate, distally pointed tooth on external wall; tip of valva without surficial teeth; excurved in a blunt hook; saccus moderate (about twice as long as width at middle). Two species in our fauna.

KEY TO THE SPECIES OF *ERORA*.

1a DHW, male, with definite small tornal patch of blue; fringe of both wings in female with little or no orange; eastern North America. Fig. 419.....................................*Erora laeta* Edwards.

Range: Southern Nova Scotia and southern Quebec, south in Appalachians to Tennessee, west to northern Michigan, south-central Kentucky. Food plants: beech (*Fagus*), beaked hazelnut (*Corylus rostrata*). Perhaps three broods southward (approx. late iv-v; vi; viii). Extremely rare, chiefly in beech-maple forest, possibly living mostly in tops of large beeches.

Fig. 419. *Erora laeta* ♂ D. Bear Mountain, Vermont.

1b DHW, male, without blue, or at most with a terminal dull blue line, at tornus; female with fringe distinctly orange; southwestern United States and Mexico. Fig. 420.....*Erora quaderna* Hewitson.

Range: Guatemala and southern Mexico, north into Arizona, western New Mexico and southern Utah, everywhere only in the mountains. Food plant: unknown. At least two broods (iv; vi--vii).

Fig. 420. *Erora quaderna* ♂ V. Huachuca Mountains, Arizona.

Genus ELECTROSTRYMON Clench, new genus
Type species: *Papilio endymion* Fabricius 1775.

Hind wing tailed; male without scent pad. Male genitalia: tip of aedeagus cylindrical, slightly upturned, with a single slightly blunted cornutus well within the shaft; valvae simple, apically divergent, the tips without surficial teeth and not excurved; saccus moderate, about twice as long as its breadth at middle.

218

Only the one species is at present known to belong, but other tropical Theclas are similar and may also be members.

Our species is *Electrostrymon endymion* Fabricius (Fig. 421).

Range: Widely distributed in tropical continental America, ranging as far north as southern Texas where it may be resident. Life history unknown. Probably multiple brooded (v, viii, xi, xii: Texas).

Fig. 421. *Electrostrymon endymion* ♀ V. Victoria, Mexico.

UNPLACED SPECIES (STRYMONITI)

Examples of the following species have not been available for study (especially genitalic dissection) and hence cannot be placed in the foregoing sequence.

Fig 422.....................*"Strymon" laceyi* **Barnes & McDunnough.**

Still known from only a few specimens, this rare species occurs in southern Texas. Life history unknown. Apparently multiple brooded (v, vii, x, xii).

Fig. 422. *"Strymon" laceyi* ♀ V. Holotype. Del Rio, Texas.

Fig. 423.............................*"Strymon" buchholzi* Freeman.

An apparently rare species found in southern Texas (x, xi) and northern Mexico. Life history unknown. According to its description falling close to *melinus, rufofusca* and *avalona* and hence probably a true *Strymon*.

Fig. 423. *"Strymon" buchholzi* ♂ V. Barretal, Mexico.

"Strymon" facuna Hewitson.

A few specimens identified as this rare species have been taken in southern Texas (vii, viii). The identification is perhaps doubtful, for several complications exist.

Tribe GERYDINI

Genus FENISECA Grote

The single member of this genus, *Feniseca tarquinius* Fabricius (Fig. 424) is our only representative of an Old World group of butterflies with carnivorous larvae.

Fig. 424. *Feniseca tarquinius* ♂ D. Illinois.

Range: Nova Scotia to southeastern Ontario, southward to northern Florida, with three arms extending westward: one across northern Michigan to southeastern Manitoba; one from West Virginia to eastern Kansas and southeastern Nebraska; one from Florida to New Orleans and northwest to central Oklahoma. There is a record from Decorah, Iowa, midway between the first two of these. Food: woolly aphids (*Schizoneura, Pemphigus*), particularly on *Alnus* (alder), but also on *Ribes* (currants), *Crataegus* (hawthorn), *Fagus* (beech), *Fraxinus* (ash), *Hamamelis* (witch hazel) and other plants. Often common along streams where alder grows. Not attracted to flowers.

Tribe LYCAENINI

Coppers

by Harry K. Clench

Venation essentially as in most Plebejini; androconia usually absent; fore tarsus of male fused, distally produced to a long curved point, spined well below the level of origin of the macrotrichia (two long setae on anterior face near tip); tarsal claws always without endodont (inner tooth). Male genitalia with the uncus lobes (labides) very characteristically long and digitate; anellus present; aedeagus long, acuminately pointed.

Only two genera are known to belong to this tribe, *Lycaena* (below) and the Indomalayan *Heliophorus* Geyer, so closely related that separation is possible almost only by pattern characters.

Genus LYCAENA Fabricius

A curious and possibly quite ancient genus, strongly developed in both the Palaearctic and the Nearctic regions, with a small handful of outliers—one in Guatemala, one in South Africa and several, most perplexingly, in New Zealand. Two subgenera are recognized.

KEY TO THE SPECIES OF *LYCAENA*.

1a VFW with spot (occasionally small) in cell Cu$_2$, just below origin of Cu$_2$ (subgenus *Tharsalea*)....................................**4**

1b VFW without this spot (subgenus *Lycaena, exc. dione*).........**2**

2a VFW orange in disk...**3**

2b VFW gray or white, no orange in disk (occasional specimens of *dione*) **4**

3a DHW fuscous, with fulvous only subterminally as a sharp dentate band. Fig. 425.......................*Lycaena phleas* Linnaeus.

Range: (a) Nova Scotia and the Gaspe west to Minnesota, south to Virginia, northern Georgia (mountains), Missouri and Kansas; (b) northern Ellesmere Id. and adjacent Greenland south to southern Baffin Id. and Southampton Id., west to the mouth of the Mackenzie R.; (c) Upper Yukon R., southeast along the Canadian Rockies to southern Alberta; (d) an isolated colony at 12,000 ft. on Mt. Maclure in Yosemite National Park, California; (e) an old record of a colony at Miles City in eastern Montana. Food plant: *Rumex*, especially *acetosella* (sheep sorrel). Broods vary according

Fig. 425. *Lycaena phleas* ♀ D. No data. This is an aberrant specimen with the FW dark markings "smeared."

to temperature of the locality; probably single brooded for (b) and (d) above (vii-early viii); double brooded in the north of (a) (vi-vii; viii-ix) to four broods in southern Pennsylvania (v-vi; vi-vii; vii-viii; ix-x), perhaps more southward; (a) above is the best known, and may represent an introduction by human agency from Europe, for it differs little if at all from north European *phleas*; it is generally common in open fields, often even in vacant lots in cities. The remaining populations are native and uncommon to very rare in collections. Of (c) and (d), as well as the somewhat dubious (e), very little is known.

3b VHW with at least some fulvous discally, and usually most of wing fulvous. Fig. 426 . . . .*Lycaena cupreus* Edwards.

Range: Rocky Mts. above timber line from northern British Columbia south into New Mexico; southern Oregon, south through the Californian Sierras, at high elevations but below timber line. Life history unknown. One brood (vii-viii). Not uncommon but its choice of habitat, especially in the Rockies, makes it very difficult to capture. The Rocky Mts. subspecies (*snowi* Edwards) has heretofore been treated as a separate species.

Fig. 426. *Lycaena cupreus* ♂ V. Oregon.

4a HW with a definite tail at Cu_2, at least as long as width between Cu_1 and Cu_2 terminally 5

4b No such tail; at most (*xanthoides*) a tooth about half as long as terminal width of Cu_1-Cu_2 6

5a VHW yellow, almost unmarked. Fig. 427 . .*Lycaena hermes* Edwards.

Range: Extremely localized, in the canyons around San Diego, California, southward into northern Baja California. Food plant: *Rhamnus*. One brood (vi-vii). Not uncommon.

Fig. 427. *Lycaena hermes* ♂ D. San Diego, California.

5b VHW chiefly gray, with pattern of dark dots and line segments. Fig. 428 . . . .*Lycaena arota* Boisduval.

Range: Mostly below 8000 ft., from Colorado and northern New Mexico west to the Pacific, from southern Oregon to southern California. Food plant: *Ribes*. One brood (chiefly vii, viii). Locally common and partial to flowers. The subspecies *virginiensis* Edwards was formerly considered a separate species.

Fig. 428. *Lycaena arota* ♀ V. Sulphur Springs, Colorado.

6a VFW (and usually DFW also) with distal edge of postmedian double spot in cell Cu_2 distinctly distad of corresponding spot in cell Cu_1; VFW whitish, almost or completely without a contrasting orange or yellowish flush in disk.....................................7

6b This spot directly beneath (*mariposa*) or definitely basad (all others) of cell Cu_1 spot; VFW disk often flushed with yellow or orange...11

7a VFW subterminal row of spots heavy, bar-like below M_3, abruptly absent or much fainter costad; no markings at all distad of them...8

7b VFW subterminal row of spots more crescentic, continued costad of M_3 not much fainter than below that vein, with a crenulate band, or other spots, distad of it.....................................9

8a Males D bright metallic coppery; females with yellow or orange in disk or both wings above, FW with subterminal orange stripe, heaviest at tornus. Fig. 429................*Lycaena rubidus* Behr.

Range: Rocky Mts. (up to about 11,000 ft.) and adjacent prairie areas from Alberta to Colorado and western Nebraska, west across Great Basin to eastern Washington, eastern Oregon and the California Sierras. Food plant: *Rumex*. One brood (chiefly viii). Occurs in open fields and is fond of flowers.

Fig. 429. *Lycaena rubidus* ♂ V. Utah.

8b Males D bright blue; females gray (rarely blue-flushed) without yellowish or orange in disk and FW without orange stripe subterminally. Fig. 430................*Lycaena heteronea* Boisduval.

Range: Moderate elevations (6-10,000 ft.) in the Rocky Mts. from southern British Columbia and Alberta south to northern New Mexico; westward to the Sierras of California. Food plant: *Eriogonum*. One brood (vii-viii). Common and an avid flower visitor. Found in open dry fields and flats (except in the Tehachapi and Tejon Mts. where it is described as favoring small woods clearings and protected mountain meadows). The remarkable sky blue color of the males of this species led early authors to place it among the blues—and may still mislead the unwary beginner.

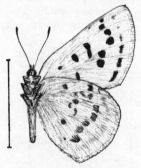

Fig. 430. *Lycaena heteronea* ♀ V. Jefferson County, Colorado.

9a D males bright coppery purple; both sexes **VHW** subterminal orange bright, a series of crescents between the veins broadly separated from each other, extending costad to M₁. Fig. 431..............
......................................*Lycaena gorgon* Boisduval.

Range: Southern Oregon to southern California, at moderate to low elevations. Food plant: *Eriogonum elongatum*. One brood (late v, vi). Often rather common, and partial to flowers.

Fig. 431. *Lycaena gorgon* ♂ V. Marin County, California.

9b D males gray; both sexes below with subterminal orange not as above: either dull (even absent), or broadly continuous, or not reaching costad much beyond Cu₁...........................10

10a VHW spots in discal area enlarged to occupy nearly all their interspace width; ground grayish with prominent subterminal row of white crescents. Fig. 432..............*Lycaena editha* Mead.

Range: Montane, from northern Colorado to central Montana, west to the Sierras of California. Food plants: *Potentilla tenuiloba, Horkelia fusca*. One brood (vii-viii). Common in open meadows on flowers. It is possible that this is only an unusually well differentiated subspecies of *xanthoides*.

Fig. 432. *Lycaena editha* ♀ V. Wasatch Mountains, Utah.

10b VHW spots small, punctiform, or if slightly enlarged, never more than half their interspace in width; subterminal white crescents present occasionally, but not prominent. Fig. 433.............
.................................Lycaena xanthoides Boisduval.

Range: The two principal subspecies are widely disjunct and formerly considered distinct species: *dione* Scudder, from southern Alberta east to southern Manitoba, south to eastern Colorado, central Oklahoma and northern Illinois; *xanthoides* Boisduval, vic. San Francisco, California south to northern Baja California, supposedly (but doubtfully) extending eastward into the Great Basin. Food plant: *Rumex obtusifolia* for *dione; Rumex hymenosepalus* for *xanthoides*. One brood (late v-vi in Calif., Okla.; late vi-vii, northern *dione*). Often rather common and fond of flowers.

Fig. 433. *Lycaena xanthoides* ♀
V. Alameda County, California.

11a VHW gray, with black marks bordered with white shading; no trace of pinkish color or reddish marks; VFW postmedian double spot in cell Cu_2 directly below corresponding spot in cell Cu_1. Fig. 434..............................Lycaena mariposa Reakirt.

Range: Chiefly montane, from central Alberta west to the coast (Queen Charlotte Ids.), south to Colorado and the California Sierras. Food plant: *Polygonum douglassii, Rumex*. Single brooded (chiefly vii-early viii). Occurs in forest clearings and along roads through forests; fond of flowers.

Fig. 434. *Lycaena mariposa* ♂
V. Paratype. California.

11b VHW not so; either reddish (to orange or lavender) or yellowish (to white), usually with at least a trace of subterminal orange or reddish lunules; VFW double spot in cell Cu_2 definitely basad of corresponding spot in cell Cu_1..............................12

12a VHW light gray to white, with broad, sharply contrasting sub-terminal orange-red band; LFW nearly always > 16 mm. Fig. 435..*Lycaena thoe* Guérin.

Range: Central Maine, southern Ontario northwestward to Ft. Simpson, N.W.T.; southward to northern New Jersey, Maryland, the Ohio R., Kansas and Colorado; an isolated record from Mississippi. Food plant: *Rumex crispus* (curly dock), perhaps also *Polygonum* and *Zanthoxylum*. Two broods (vi, viii). Local, not uncommon in moist meadows.

Fig. 435. *Lycaena thoe* ♀ V. Illinois.

12b VHW variously colored, but when white lacking the broad red subterminal band (at most a thin crenulate line) and much smaller (LFW 13 mm. or less, usually much less)......................13

13a VHW bicolored: basally yellow, distally lavender. Fig. 436......
....*Lycaena nivalis* Boisduval.

Range: Montane, from southern British Columbia south to Colorado, Utah and the middle Sierras of California. Life history unknown. One brood (late vi-early vii). In the Rockies flies chiefly out on sagebrush flats, mostly along the benches above streams.

Fig. 436. *Lycaena nivalis* ♂ V. Colorado.

13b VHW never bicolored..14

14a VHW yellow to white; females DFW without orange shading. Fig. 437................................*Lycaena epixanthe* Boisduval.

Range: Newfoundland to New Jersey, westward to southeastern Manitoba, Wisconsin and northwestern Indiana. Possibly also occurring in west central Saskatchewan (vic. Lloydminster). Food plant: *Vaccinium macrocarpon* (wild cranberry). One brood (late vi-mid vii, Mass.). Flies low, only in boggy areas where its food plant occurs.

Fig. 437. *Lycaena epixanthe* ♂ V. Maine.

14b VHW ocher, orange or brick red; females DFW usually with at least a trace of orange or ocher scaling.....................15

15 *Note:* The two species, *dorcas* and *helloides* are in some areas impossible or very difficult to separate, especially in the Rocky Mts. region, where this couplet should be used with caution and as a guide only.

15a DHW males with a crenulate orange subterminal line; females with much bright orange above, including basad of postmedian spots on FW and in disk of HW; multiple brooded. Fig. 438......
...................................*Lycaena helloides* Boisduval.

Range: Southern British Columbia eastward to Michigan and southern Ontario, south to northern Baja California, northern New Mexico, western Nebraska and northern Iowa. Food plants: *Polygonum* (*aviculare*, probably others), *Rumex*; also recorded from *Oxytheca* and *Gayophytum*. Multiple brooded, the exact number variable: three in Michigan (early vi; vii, late viii), up to six or seven in California. See remarks under *dorcas* below.

Fig. 438. *Lycaena helloides* ♀ V. California.

227

15b DHW males without orange subterminally (except dot at tornus): females with orange above usually duller, nearly confined to band just beyond postmedian spots of FW: single brooded, usually bog-associated. Fig. 439........................*Lycaena dorcas* Kirby.

Fig. 439. *Lycaena dorcas* ♂ V. Grand Rapids, Michigan.

Range: Labrador and Newfoundland southwest to southern Michigan and northwestern Ohio, thence northwest to Alaska and the mouth of the Mackenzie River; isolated outlying colonies near Bathurst, New Brunswick and Springfield, Maine. Food plants: various species of *Potentilla*. Single brooded (late vii-early viii, Michigan). The identity of the montane form (*florus* Edwards) inhabiting the Rocky Mountains from Colorado and Utah north to southern Alberta and British Columbia is uncertain. It occurs within the region occupied by *helloides*, and outside of the presumed range of *dorcas*; and at lower elevations seems to intergrade with true *helloides*. Yet it favors the cool environment of *dorcas* and is very similar to *dorcas* in appearance. Thus it could be (a) a montane subspecies of *helloides* which has extended itself into the *dorcas* environment and become modified to superficially resemble *dorcas*; or (b) an outlying subspecies of *dorcas* which freely hybridizes with *helloides* (there is no hybridization where both occur in the Michigan-Manitoba region). Careful field studies in the Rockies are needed.

Tribe PLEBEJINI
The Blues
by John C. Downey

KEY TO THE GENERA OF PLEBEJINI.

1a FW with vein R_1 touching vein Sc..............................**2**

1b FW with vein R_1 not touching Sc..................................**4**

2a FW with R_1 touching Sc only briefly: HW with delicate tail at tip of Cu_2; tarsal claws with inner tooth................*Everes* p. 240

2b FW with R_1 joining Sc and running united with it to costal margin; HW without a tail; tarsal claws without inner tooth.............**3**

3a VHW with four black metallic spots in cells M_1-Cu_1 (other metallic spots may be present).........................*Brephidium* p. 242

3b VHW without black metallic spots...................*Zizula* p. 241

4a VHW with one or two submarginal metallic, or partly metallic spots **5**

4b VHW lacking metallic scaling...................................**7**

5a VFW with median transverse light and dark bands; spots limited to marginal area; scaling thin (D showing markings of V) . . . .
. . . . *Leptotes* p. 240

5b VFW with median and postmedian spots in addition to marginal series (sometimes reduced); D not showing markings of V 6

6a DHW usually with at least one prominent black spot near anal angle; VHW with some wavy transverse white lines in addition to black spots . . . . *Hemiargus* p. 234

6b DHW usually without prominent black spot near anal angle; V without white lines, black spots usually prominent and surrounded by white . . . . *Plebejus* p. 230

7a VHW with broad, transverse, postmedian white stripe between median ocelli and submarginal chevron-shaped spots; fringes of wings with marked stripes at ends of wing veins; orange spots or markings absent or obsolete . . . . *Phaedrotes* p. 236

7b VHW without noticeable transverse white stripe; fringes of wings uniformly colored, or, if striped, with prominent orange bars or spots present (except *Philotes speciosa*) 8

8a Orange spots often present; V with marginal and submarginal spots or chevrons in addition to a median-postmedian row 9

8b Orange spots absent; V without marginal or submarginal spots or chevrons; transverse median-postmedian row of rounded black spots sharply ringed with white . . . . *Glaucopsyche* p. 236

9a Orange spots often present; V with spots noticeably black against ground color (not faded), particularly the marginal and submarginal series; VHW never with darkened discal and marginal ground color 10

9b Orange spots absent; V with spots vague or faded against gray to whitish background, particularly the marginal and submarginal series; VHW occasionally with brownish tint to ground color in discal and marginal areas . . . . *Celastrina* p. 241

10a Fringes of wings without marked stripes at ends of veins; DFW usually with distinct bar or spot at end of cell; D marginal black line narrow 11

10b Fringes of wings with distinct black stripes at ends of veins (particularly on V); DFW usually without bar or spot at end of cell (except where orange spots present on DFW); D marginal line usually prominent and wide . . . . *Philotes* p. 237

11a V ground color not uniform; VHW with white or cream-colored halos around spots distal to postmedian region expanded and touching so that distal region of wing appears lighter; DFW with very prominent discal bar (often on DHW also) sometimes surrounded by white scales; D blue of males with grayish or silver cast; V spots variable, but without prominent orange bars or spots . . . . *Agriades* p. 235

11b V ground color appearing uniform (except for basal infusion of greenish or dark scales); VHW halos around spots not markedly enlarged; DFW discal bar present or absent; D or V usually with prominent orange bars or spots (if absent, ground color is uniform) ....*Plebejus* p. 230

Genus PLEBEJUS Kluk
by John C. Downey

This genus is found throughout the temperate parts of the Holarctic region.

KEY TO THE SPECIES OF *PLEBEJUS*.

1a VHW with submarginal row of metallic scales (may be reduced in worn specimens); VHW usually with transverse submarginal yellow or orange band or series of crescent-shaped orange spots..2

1b VHW lacking submarginal metallic scales (or these extremely reduced); VHW with orange spots limited to cells Cu$_1$ or Cu$_2$ only, or orange absent..7

2a DFW with orange scaling on veins and in irregular spot near inner angle; DHW with submarginal orange bar surrounding marginal brown spots; D ground color dark brown in both sexes. Fig. 440... ....*Plebejus neurona* Skinner.

Range: Southern California in the Sierra Nevada, Tehachapis and San Bernardino ranges. Early vi. Food plant: *Eriogonum wrightii*.

Fig. 440. *Plebejus neurona* ♂ D. Kern County California.

2b DFW without orange scaling on veins; D ground color of males blue, of females usually brown................................3

3a DHW (as well as DFW) with discal bar; VHW with transverse median row of light brown ocelli which are paler than postmedian row of black spots on VFW. Fig. 441.....*Plebejus shasta* Edwards.

Range: Alberta south to western Nebraska and Colorado, west to the California Sierras: chiefly high montane (vii).

Fig. 441. *Plebejus shasta* ♂ V. No data.

3b DHW with discal bar absent; VHW with transverse median row of black spots of the same shade as those of VFW (but usually smaller) **4**

4a VFW with double row of black marginal spots; DHW with faint marginal series of spots, often surrounded with light orange suffusion (more marked in female); VFW without spot in discal cell (basal to bar); D of males with large marginal border of brown scales gradually merging with proximal blue in limbal area. Fig. 442.................................*Plebejus emigdionis* Grinnell.

Range: Southern California on the lower Mohave plateau and southern edge of the San Joaquin Valley (v). Food plant: *Atriplex* (saltbush).

Fig. 442. *Plebejus emigdionis* ♂ V. San Bernardino County, California.

4b VFW without a double row of black marginal spots, or with outermost row only faintly visible; DHW with or without marked orange band near margin; VFW with or without spot in discal cell; D without marginal border except a rather narrow terminal line.........**5**

5a VFW without marginal orange spots; VFW with a black spot in discal cell basal to discal bar; DHW with a solid or broken orange submarginal band and marginal black spots. Fig. 443...........
........................*Plebejus acmon* Westwood and Hewitson.

Range: Western United States east to Great Plains and in scattered colonies to Minnesota, Nebraska and Kansas. Multiple brooded, flying from early spring to late fall. Food plants: *Astragalus* (loco weed), *Hosackia*, *Eriogonum* (umbrella plant), *Lotus* (birds-foot trefoil) and others. Included here are *Plebejus lupini* Boisduval, *P. monticola* Clemence, and *P. chlorina* Skinner, all of which have, at one time or another, been considered distinct species.

Fig. 443. *Plebejus acmon* ♀ V. No data.

5b VFW with marginal orange bar or spots; VFW with no spot in discal cell basal to discal bar; D of males without orange; D of females with submarginal orange bar or series of crescent shaped spots **6**

6a V with terminal black line boldly outlining distal margin, particularly on VFW; V with maculation pronounced; male genitalia with forearm of falx (gnathos) projecting nearly half its length beyond the caudal margin of the shoulder of the falx, arms of furca (juxta) equal to or shorter than width of valva at broadest point. Fig. 444......................................*Plebejus melissa* Edwards.

Range: New Hampshire and Massachusetts west through the Great Lakes states to Kansas, Colorado and California (entire western United States), south to North Carolina and north to mid-Canada. Two broods (late v-mid vi; late vii). Food plants: *Lupinus* (lupine), *Astragalus* (loco weed), *Medicago* (alfalfa) and other legumes.

Fig. 444. *Plebejus melissa*
♂ V. No data.

6b V with terminal line reduced or absent, but enlarging abruptly at veins giving appearance of outer row of small spots; V maculation may be reduced (in western specimens); male genitalia with forearm of falx (gnathos) projecting much less than half its length beyond the caudal margin of the shoulder of the falx; arms of furca (juxta) longer than width of valva at broadest point. Fig. 445......
..............................*Plebejus argyrognomon* Bergstraesser

Range: Holarctic, northern United States and Canada, montane regions of western United States. Food plants: *Empetrum nigrum* (black crowberry), perhaps *Lupinus* (lupine) and/or *Kalmia polifolia* (pale laurel).

Fig. 445. *Plebejus argyrognomen*
♂ V. El Dorado County, California.

7a VHW with prominent orange spot in cell Cu$_1$; V ground color dark gray; VHW with marginal white scales surrounding spots giving the impression of a white line just inside the black terminal line; D of male uniformly colored, with blue distinctly tinged with purple; D of female brown, with purplish infusion in basal areas particularly on FW; D terminal line narrow. Fig. 446.................
....*Plebejus optilete* Knoch.

Range: Palaearctic Region; the Yukon River valley from the southern Yukon to central Alaska, and eastward to the region of the Great Slave Lake and Manitoba. Food plant: probably *Vaccinium*.

Fig. 446. *Plebejus optilete* ♂ V. Eagle, Alaska.

7b VHW with or without orange spots; V ground color light gray or brownish-gray; D usually not uniformly colored but variable (i.e., discal bar of FW pronounced or absent; submarginal infusion of orange scales or none; terminal line variable in size and distinction) 8

8a DFW with discal bar usually prominent; VHW with transverse median row of spots surrounded by gray or brownish tinted scales which are not in sharp contrast with the ground color; VHW with discal bar usually with more black scales than surrounding gray scales; VHW with black spots of nearly equal size as those on VFW. Fig. 447.....................*Plebejus saepiolus* Boisduval.

Range: Central and southern Canada south to Maine, northern Michigan, Minnesota, Iowa, and in the mountains to New Mexico. One brood, vi-vii. Food plant: *Trifolium hybridum* (alsike clover).

Fig. 447. *Plebejus saepiolus* ♀ V. Riverside County, California.

233

8b DFW with discal bar present or absent; VHW with transverse median row of spots surrounded by ring of white scales which stand out in sharp contrast to ground color (often the black pupils of the spots are obsolete); VHW discal bar usually with more white scales than black; VFW often with larger black spots than VHW. Fig. 448.............................*Plebejus icarioides* Boisduval.

Range: Western United States and Canada. Food plants: *Lupinus* (lupine) and *Trifolium* (clover). *P. icarioides* includes the forms *P. pheres* Boisduval and *P. pardalis* Behr, previously considered to be good species.

Fig. 448. *Plebejus icarioides* ♂
V. Fort Klamath, Oregon.

Genus HEMIARGUS Hübner

Three species of *Hemiargus* belong to our fauna.

KEY TO THE SPECIES OF *HEMIARGUS*.

1a VFW with prominent postmedian band of large, black, roughly circular spots ringed with white, these as large as any spots on VHW. Fig. 449.................................*Hemiargus isola* Reakirt.

Range: Minnesota, southern Michigan, western Ohio, Louisiana and Mississippi, westward to British Columbia and California, and southward to Costa Rica. In the north and east of its range rare, local, and sporadic, probably not overwintering. Elsewhere common. Food plant: *Prosopis* (mesquite).

Fig. 449. *Hemiargus isola*
♂ V. El Dorado County, California.

1b VFW not so marked.......................................2

2a V with ground color in space between postmedian and submarginal markings contrastingly white; DHW usually with marginal ocelli in cells Cu$_2$ and 2V. Fig. 450.....Hemiargus thomasi Clench.

Range: Southern Florida, Bahamas, and Antilles. Food plants: *Pithecolobium guadaloupensis* (catsclaw) and *Guilandina crista*. Muliple brooded (iv, v, ix, xi). Locally common.

Fig. 450. *Hemiargus thomasi* ♂ V. Hope Town, Bahamas.

2b V with ground color in space between postmedian and submarginal markings not contrastingly white. DHW usually with marginal ocellus in cell Cu$_2$ only. Fig. 451.........................
...................................Hemiargus ceraunus Fabricius.

Range: Florida, Georgia, Alabama to southern Texas. Food plants: *Chamaecrista* (partridge peas), *Abrus precatorius* (crabs eye vine). Multiple (3?) brooded (i, ii, v, ix, x, xi). Common and widespread.

Fig. 451. *Hemiargus ceraunus* ♂ V. La Moriniere, Haiti.

Genus AGRIADES Hübner

One species of this circumpolar genus, *Agriades glandon* Prunner (Fig. 452) occurs in our area.

Range: Circumpolar; in our area found from eastern Alaska and the mouth of the Mackenzie River east to Labrador and Newfoundland, south to southern Manitoba, the Black Hills (South Dakota) and in the mountains to New Mexico, Arizona, and southern California. Food plants: perhaps *Diapensia lapponica* or *Vaccinium*. Single brooded (mostly vi, vii). Common in open wet meadows. This species was formerly known as *Plebejus aquilo* Boisduval.

Fig. 452. *Agriades glandon* ♂ V. Long's Peak, Colorado.

Genus GLAUCOPSYCHE Scudder

There are only two species in our area—one widespread, the other possibly extinct.

KEY TO THE SPECIES OF *GLAUCOPSYCHE*.

1a From San Francisco Peninsula of California.....................2

1b Not from San Francisco Peninsula of California. Fig. 453.........
.................................*Glaucopsyche lygdamus* Doubleday

Range: Eastern Alaska and the lower Mackenzie River southeastward to Nova Scotia, and south (in mountains) to Georgia, Alabama and Arkansas; south in the Rockies to Colorado and northern New Mexico; western Kansas; south on the West Coast to the tip of Baja California. Food plants: *Lathyrus* (everlasting peas), *Lotus, Lupinus* (lupine), *Astragalus, Vicia* (vetch), *Hedysarum boreale, Adenostoma fasciculatum* (greasewood).

Fig. 453. *Glaucopsyche lygdamus* ♂ V. Golden, Colorado.

2a D male rather light blue; V spots with black pupils often reduced or absent. Fig. 454...............*Glaucopsyche xerces* Boisduval.

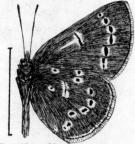

Range: Previously San Francisco Peninsula of California. Now reported to be extinct. Food plants: *Lotus, Lupinus* (lupine). This species is (or was!) very closely related to *G. lygdamus.*

Fig. 454. *Glaucopsyche xerces* ♂ V. San Francisco, California.

2b D male darker blue; V spots very rarely reduced or absent......
.......*Glaucopsyche lygdamus* Doubleday (see couplet 1b above).

Genus *PHAEDROTES* Scudder

There is but one species in this genus, *Phaedrotes piasus* Boisduval (Fig. 455).

Range: Western, chiefly montane, from southern Alberta and British Columbia south through western Nebraska to Colorado, west to eastern Washington, the California Sierras, and the coast of southern California. Probably one brood (late v-early vii). Food plant: *Lupinus* (lupine). Local and generally uncommon.

Fig. 455. *Phaedrotes piasus* ♀ V. No data.

Genus PHILOTES Scudder
by John C. Downey

Several species of the small butterflies in this genus are superficially extremely similar. They can be separated with assurance only by reference to the male genitalia.

KEY TO THE SPECIES OF *PHILOTES*.

1a VHW without orange spots.................................2

1b VHW with submarginal orange bar or series of spots (may be reduced in a few forms)..3

2a DFW and VFW with prominent orange spots (also on DHW of female); DFW with a dark bar at end of discal cell. Fig. 456.....
.............................*Philotes sonorensis* Felder and Felder.

Range: Central (rare) and southern California. ii-iv. Food plant: *Sedum* (stonecrop).

Fig. 456. *Philotes sonorensis* ♀ V. Azusa, California.

2b **Orange spots absent from all wings; DFW without dark bar at end of discal cell. Fig. 457**......*Philotes speciosa* Henry Edwards.

Range: Central Mohave Desert of California (iv). Food plant: *Oxytheca perfoliata.*

Fig. 457. *Philotes speciosa* ♂ V. Southern California.

3a **VFW with submarginal orange band which diminishes in size but is nevertheless prominent toward the apex. Fig. 458**..............
......................*Philotes spaldingi* Barnes and McDunnough

Range: Great Basin, central and eastern Rocky Mountains (Utah and Colorado). Food plant: perhaps *Eriogonum.*

Fig. 458. *Philotes spaldingi* ♂ V. No data.

3b VFW usually without orange band, when present much diminished compared to that of **VHW** and never extending apically more than ½ the wing breadth...**4**

Fig. 459. Valva of *Philotes bat-toides.*

4a Male genitalia with bifurcate valvae (Fig. 459). Fig. 460....
.........*Philotes battoides* Behr.

Range: Western United States. Food plant: *Eriogonum. Philotes glaucon* Edwards is a race of *battoides.*

Fig. 460. *Philotes bat-toides* ♂ V. Fair-view, California.

4b Male genitalia with valvae not bifurcate........................**5**

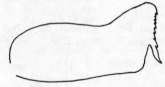

Fig. 461. Valva of *Philotes enoptes.*

5a Male genitalia with valvae (when flattened) with terminal one-fourth widened laterally; terminal tooth margin not markedly separated from the rest of the valva and at about a 90° angle to the main axis of the valva (Fig. 461)............**6**

5b Male genitalia with valvae roughly J-shaped (terminal one-third widened laterally); terminal tooth margin on finger-like disto-lateral projection of valva and at less than a 90° angle to main axis of valva (See Fig. 464)...**7**

6a VHW with submarginal orange band conspicuous (either continuous or broken into separate spots); variable in size; where sympatric with *mohave,* flying in September and October. Fig. 462.........
....*Philotes enoptes* Boisduval.

Range: Western United States. Food plant: *Eriogonum.*

Fig. 462. *Philotes enoptes* ♂ V. Brighton, Utah.

6b **VHW with orange spots often reduced or obsolete; a small species (LFW about 10 mm.) from Colorado and central Mohave deserts of California, flying from March to mid-May. Fig. 463** ....
Philotes mohave Watson and W. P. Comstock.

Range: Colorado and central Mohave deserts of California.

Fig. 463. *Philotes mohave* ♂ V. Paratype, Mohave Desert, California.

7a **Male genitalia with lateral margin of valva describing a 90° angle just proximal to spines; length of longest spines on distal edge valva greater than half the width of the valva at its narrowest part. (Fig. 464). Fig. 465** ....*Philotes pallescens* Tilden and Downey.

Fig. 464. Valva of *Philotes pallescens*.

Fig. 465. *Philotes pallescens* ♀ V. Dugway Proving Ground, Utah.

Range: Tooele County, Utah (possibly more widespread).

7b **Male genitalia with lateral margin of valva angled gradually outward (about 45°) proximal to spines; length of longest spines on distal edge of valva much less than half the width of the valva at its narrowest point (Fig. 466). Fig. 467** ....
.........................*Philotes rita* Barnes and McDunnough.

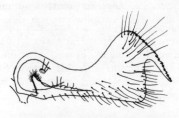

Fig. 466. Valva of *Philotes rita*.

Fig. 467. *Philotes rita* ♀ V. Cherry, Arizona.

Range: Arizona.

Genus EVERES Hübner

Our species, *Everes comyntas* Godart (Figs. 468, 469), is the only Nearctic member of the Plebejini which has tailed hind wings.

Fig. 468. *Everes comyntas* ♂ V. Tuscaloosa, Alabama.

Fig. 469. *Everes comyntas* ♂ V. Salt Lake City, Utah.

Range: Eastern Alaska, the mouth of the Mackenzie River, and southern Yukon Territory, south to northern Florida, California, and the Gulf of Mexico, on through Mexico to Costa Rica. Apparently absent from Nova Scotia, New Brunswick and a small wedge of territory immediately to the west. Food plants: many Leguminosae, including *Desmodium* (tick trefoils, beggar's ticks), *Lespedeza* (bush clovers), *Phaseolus* (bean), *Galactia* (milk pea), *Trifolium* (clover), *Vicia* (vetch), *Astragalus crotalariae*. Multiple brooded, with an early spring brood marked everywhere (ii-v or vi, depending on locality); later broods tend to be few and discrete in the west, in the east fusing into a continuous flight until frost. The paler western populations (Fig. 469) have long been considered a separate species, *E. amyntula* Boisduval, but H. K. Clench assures me that there is no basis for this other than tradition.

Genus LEPTOTES Scudder

Two species of this genus are found in the United States.

KEY TO THE SPECIES OF *LEPTOTES*.

1a VFW covered with brown bars and spots except for a broad white area (at least 2 mm. wide) basad of the inner angle. Fig. 470.....
....*Leptotes cassius* Cramer.

Fig. 470. *Leptotes cassius* ♂ V. Florida.

Range: Southern Florida and southern Texas, southward throughout tropical America, rarely straying northward (Kansas). Food plants: *Plumbago* (leadwort), *Galactia volubilis* (hairy milk pea), *Phaseolus* (beans), and others. Widely known as *Leptotes theonus* Lucas.

1b VFW covered with brown bars and spots, without a broad white area basad of inner angle. Fig. 471......*Leptotes marinus* Reakirt.

Range: Western Illinois, Nebraska, west to central California and south to Texas and Central America. Food plants: *Wisteria, Medicago* (alfalfa), *Plumbago* (leadwort), *Astragalus* (locoweed), *Dolichos,* and other Leguminosae.

Fig. 471. *Leptotes marinus* ♂ V. Los Angeles, California.

Genus CELASTRINA Tutt

One Holarctic species, *Celastrina argiolus* Linnaeus (Fig. 472), occurs in our area.

Range: Throughout the United States and Canada from the subarctic south well into Central America; apparently absent from most of Florida. Food plants: a wide variety including *Cornus* (dogwood), *Ceanothus* (New Jersey tea), *Vaccinium* (blueberry), *Spiraea* (meadowsweet), *Actinomeris, Lotus,* and *Verbesina* (crownbeard). This species is one of the first to fly in the spring. It is one of our most variable butterflies, with a number of geographic and seasonal forms as well as sexual dimorphism. There is a possibility that *argiolus* as used here contains more than one genetic species.

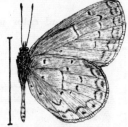

Fig. 472. *Celastrina argiolus* ♂ V. No data.

Genus ZIZULA Chapman

Our species of this genus, *Zizula cyna* Edwards (Fig. 473), has been erroneously considered to be an imported African species, *Z. gaika* Trimen. Genitalia and pattern show it to be abundantly distinct.

Range: Arizona, New Mexico and southern Texas, south far into Central America.

Fig. 473. *Zizula cyna* ♂ V. Alpine, Texas.

241

Genus BREPHIDIUM Scudder
Pigmy Blues

This genus contains two of the smallest known species of butter-flies, the LFW of some specimens being only 8 mm.

KEY TO THE SPECIES OF *BREPHIDIUM.*

1a V with ground color grayish-white basally, brown distally. Fig. 474.................................*Brephidium exilis* Boisduval.

Range: Texas and Colorado to southern California, south to Venezuela, rarely straying north to Kansas, Nebraska, Oregon. Food plants: *Atriplex bracteosa* (lamb's tongue), *Chenopodium* (pigweed), *Petunia parviflora.* Often common, especially in California. Flight weak and low.

Fig. 474. *Brephidium exilis* ♂ V. No data.

1b V with ground color uniformly brown. Fig. 475.................
..................................*Brephidium pseudofea* Morrison.

Range: Coastal Georgia, Florida and Alabama, straying slightly northward (Atlanta, Georgia). One probable stray from Galveston, Texas. Food plant: Dr. George W. Rawson, who has recently worked out the life history, writes that the larva feeds on *Salicornia* (glasswort). Multiple brooded (ii, iv, ix). Locally common in coastal salt marshes. Low flying and easily caught.

Fig. 475. *Brephidium pseudofea* ♂ V. No data.

Subfamily RIODININAE
Metal-marks

The members of this subfamily are readily identified by the extension of the male prothoracic coxa below the articulation of the trochanter (Fig. 475A). Riodinines hold their wings spread after landing.

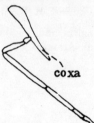

coxa

Fig. 475A. Prothoracic leg of ♂ *Apodemia nais.*

Genus EUSELASIA Hübner

A single member of this large tropical genus, *Euselasia abreas* Edwards (Fig. 476), has been described from our area ("Arizona"). It occurs widely southward.

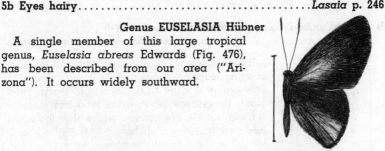

Fig. 476. *Euselasia abreas* ♂ D. (After Seitz.)

Genus APODEMIA Felder and Felder

One one species of this primarily Mexican genus, *Apodemia mormo*, has an extensive distribution in our area.

KEY TO THE SPECIES OF *APODEMIA*.

1a D coppery with gray-brown dusting and a pattern of short brown dashes; DFW with a small precostal white spot at end of cell; VHW with a coppery submarginal band, outwardly edged with black spots between the veins. Fig. 477....*Apodemia nais* Edwards.

Range: Central Colorado (both slopes of Rockies) south to Mexico. Food plant: *Prunus* (wild plum).

Fig. 477. *Apodemia nais* ♂ D. Jefferson County, Colorado.

1b Not so marked...2

2a FW with apex sharply pointed; HW with anal angle pointed; D dull brown with numerous white spots. Fig. 478........
..........*Apodemia multiplaga* Schaus.

Range: Extreme southern Texas; Mexico.

Fig. 478. *Apodemia mul-tiplaga* ♂ D. Iguala, Mexico.

2b Without this combination of characters.........................3

3a D not marked with numerous white spots.....................4

3b D marked with numerous white spots.........................5

4a Ground color bright yellow-brown. Figs. 479, 480..............
...................*Apodemia phyciodoides* Barnes and Benjamin.

Range: Cochise County, Arizona.

Fig. 479. *Apodemia phyciodoides* ♂ D. Holotype. Chirica-hua Mountains, Co-chise County, Ari-zona.

Fig. 480. *Apodemia phyciodoides* ♀ V. Allotype. Paradise, Cochise County, Arizona.

4b Ground color dark brown. Fig. 481........
....*Apodemia walkeri* Godman and Salvin.

Range: Extreme southern Texas, southward.

Fig. 481. *Apodemia walkeri* ♂ D. Pharr, Texas.

244

5a Small (LFW usually < 13 mm.); DFW ground color gray, without broad flush of reddish-brown. Fig. 482.. *Apodemia palmeri* **Edwards.**

Range: Imperial Valley and adjacent deserts in California; Arizona; Utah; Mexico. Food plant: *Beloperone californica*.

Fig. 482. *Apodemia palmeri* ♂ D. Riverside County, California.

5b Large (LFW usually > 13 mm.); DFW with broad flush of reddish-brown across the inner two-thirds. Fig. 483.....................
.... *Apodemia mormo* **Felder and Felder.**

Range: Southern western United States, from the Rocky Mountains to California, southward through much of Mexico. Exact northern limits in Great Basin area need clarification. Food plants: *Atriplex* (saltbush), *Eriogonum* (false buckwheat).

Fig. 483. *Apodemia mormo* ♂ D. No data.

Genus EMESIS Fabricius

Two species of this genus have been recorded from the United States.

KEY TO THE SPECIES OF *EMESIS*.

1a FW with costa strongly concave in the middle; FW with prominent yellowish-white mark near the costa. Fig. 484.................
.... *Emesis emesia* **Hewitson.**

Range: Extreme southern Texas, south into Mexico. There is a record from Mesa Verde, Colorado, which may be referable to this species.

Fig. 484. *Emesis emesia* ♂ V. Victoria, Mexico.

245

1b FW with costa only slightly concave in the middle; FW without a prominent mark near the costa. Fig. 485...............
......................*Emesis zela* Butler.

Range: Arizona, southward into Mexico.

Fig. 485. *Emesis zela* ♂
D. Mexico.

Genus LASAIA Bates

Both of our species are a faintly metallic greenish-blue.

KEY TO THE SPECIES OF *LASAIA*.

1a DFW with a distinct dark patch near middle of costa. Fig. 486................
...............*Lasaia narses* Staudinger.

Range: Recorded from southern Texas.

Fig. 486. *Lasaia narses*
♂ D. No data.

1b DFW without a distinct dark patch near middle of costa. Fig. 487..............
..................*Lasaia sessilis* Schaus.

Range: Extreme southern Texas, southward.

Fig. 487. *Lasaia sessilis*
♂ V. Pharr, Texas.

246

Genus CARIA Hubner

One species, *Caria domitianus* Fabricius (Fig. 488), is found in our area. It ranges from extreme southern Texas to South America.

Fig. 488. *Caria domitianus* ♂ V. Pharr, Texas.

Genus CALEPHELIS Grote and Robinson
The Little Metal Marks
by Wilbur S. McAlpine

This is a genus of small, weak flying butterflies, which frequently alight with the wings spread (often on the underside of a leaf). In most cases one must examine the genitalia in order to make positive identification. The genitalic illustrations all show the ventral aspect of the valvae and transtilla; some also have the aedeagus in place.

KEY TO THE SPECIES OF *CALEPHELIS*.

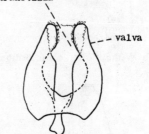

1a Male genitalia with transtilla (transverse plate connecting dorsal basal corners of valvae and projecting posteriorly above them) truncated, the end forming a nearly straight line (Fig. 489); D a rather uniform rich reddish brown, overlaid with a whitish misty film, metallic lines very prominent; fringes checkered. Fig. 490.....
......*Calephelis wrighti* Holland.

Fig. 489. Male genitalia of *Calephelis wrighti* (ventral view).

Range: Southern California, western Arizona, and adjacent Mexico. Food plant: *Bebbia juncea*.

Fig. 490. *Calephelis wrighti* ♂ D. Riverside, California.

1b Without this combination of characters.........................2
2a Male genitalia with tip of transtilla projecting to or beyond the ends of the valvae (See Fig. 493).............................3

2b Male genitalia with tip of transtilla not projecting to the ends of the valvae (See Fig. 500)..6

3a Male genitalia with tip of transtilla blunt, ends of valvae very blunt (Fig. 491); fringes not checkered; D rather uniform light brown, approaching orange. Fig. 492............ *Calephelis virginiensis* Guerin-Meneville.

Fig. 491. Male genitalia of *Calephelis virginiensis* (ventral view).

Range: Florida and Gulf Coast west to Louisiana and perhaps Texas, north to Virginia. Probably three broods.

Fig. 492. *Calephelis virginiensis* ♂ D. Leland, North Carolina.

3b Without this combination of characters........................4

4a Male genitalia with transtilla slender, projecting well beyond tips of valvae, valvae short, broad, heavily spined terminally with spines extending far basad on inner surface (Fig. 493); fringes usually quite noticeably checkered; D dull, dark reddish brown. Fig. 494..............
......*Calephelis rawsoni* McAlpine.

Fig. 493. Male genitalia of *Calephelis rawsoni* (ventral view).

Range: Known from the following Texas localities near San Antonio: Leon Springs, New Braunfels, and Kerrville. Apparently three brooded.

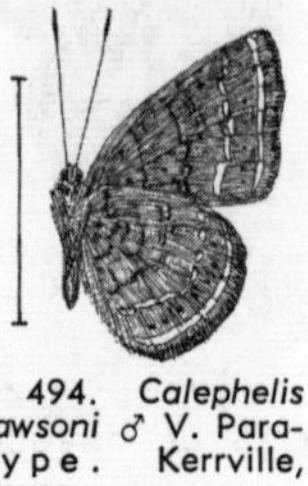

Fig. 494. *Calephelis rawsoni* ♂ V. Paratype. Kerrville, Texas.

4b Without this combination of characters.........................**5**

5a Male genitalia with point of transtilla projecting beyond tips of valvae, transtilla with short lateral processes (Fig. 495); D uniform light, dull chocolate brown; FW outer margin slightly undulate, not rounded.................................*Calephelis argyrodines* Bates.
Range: Davis Mountains of Texas, south to northern South America.

Fig. 495. Male genitalia of *Calephelis argyrodines* (ventral view).

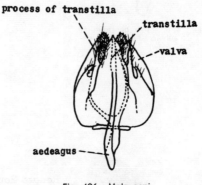

process of transtilla

transtilla

valva

aedeagus

Fig. 496. Male genitalia of *Calephelis muticum* (ventral view).

5b Male genitalia with point of transtilla not projecting beyond points of valvae, merely reaching ends of valvae, transtilla with long lateral processes (Fig. 496); D (when fresh) a rich, bright mahogany color; FW with outer margin rounded. Fig. 497...................
......................................*Calephelis muticum* McAlpine.

Range: Ohio (near Cincinnati), southern Michigan, Illinois (near Chicago), and Missouri (Willard area). Food plant: *Cirsium muticum* (swamp thistle).

Fig. 497. *Calephelis muticum* ♂ D. Willis, Washtenaw County, Michigan.

6a Male genitalia with tip of transtilla truncate or slightly indented, not pointed or rounded (do not confuse with *wrighti* [See Fig. 489]—in which entire end of transtilla is truncate) (Fig. 498); LFW > 12 mm. Fig. 499.. .... *Calephelis borealis* Grote and Robinson.

Fig. 498. Male genitalia of *Calephelis borealis* (ventral view).

Range: Southern New England south to Virginia and west to Indiana. Food plant: *Senecio obovatus* (ragwort). This species occurs in open woods on high ground, usually near streams where its food plant grows.

Fig. 499. *Calephelis borealis* ♂ D. Sussex County, New Jersey.

6b Male genitalia with tip of transtilla rounded or pointed; LFW < 12 mm. 7

7a Male genitalia with tip of transtilla broadly rounded (Fig. 500); FW of male sharply pointed. Fig. 501.....*Calephelis nemesis* Edwards.

Range: Southern California and Arizona (in desert areas), New Mexico (?), and Texas. Food plants: *Clematis drummondii* (virgin's bower) in Texas, *Baccharis glutinosa* in California. The eastern form has been called *C. australis* Edwards. *C. guadeloupe* Strecker is a synonym.

Fig. 500. Male genitalia of *Calephelis nemesis* (ventral view).

Fig. 501. *Calephelis nemesis* ♂ D. San Diego, California.

7b Male genitalia with tip of transtilla pointed (Fig. 502); FW of male not sharply pointed. Fig. 503.............*Calephelis nilus* Felder.

Range: Southern Texas to Arizona, south to Venezuela. Probably three broods. *C. perditalis* Barnes and McDunnough is a subspecies of *nilus*.

Fig. 502. Male genitalia of *Calephelis nilus* (ventral view).

Fig. 503. *Calephelis nilus* ♂ V. Victoria, Mexico.

251

INDEX AND PICTURED-GLOSSARY

It should be noted that all generic names begin with a capital while the species names begin with a small letter. Both are italicized. Generic names of larval food plants are followed by an asterisk (*), specific names of larval food plants are not indexed.

A

ABERRATION: an individual strikingly different from the average of the population from which it was taken.

ABDOMEN: the last of the three major body divisions of a butterfly, containing the digestive and reproductive organs; in adult, does not bear legs. Fig. 503A.

Figure 503A

Abies 81
abreas 243
Abrus* 235
acadica 186, 196
acastus 136
Acerates* 85
acheronta 170
acis 183, 215
acmon 231
Acraeinae 83
Actinomeris* 241
ACUMINATE: tapering to a long point.
Adelpha 163
Adenostoma* 236
adenostomatis 187, 193
Admirals 163
AEDEAGUS: penis; the male intromittent organ. (See Fig. 12)
affinis 209
agarithe 69
Agriades 235
agricolor 211
aidea 174
alberta (Boloria) 123
alberta (Oeneis) 102
alcestis 191
alder 40, 41, 149, 220
alexandra 55
alfalfa 55, 56, 60, 232, 241
alma 139
Alnus* 40, 41, 149, 220
alope 94
Alpine 25
Alpines 96
Althaea* 154

Amelanchier* 40, 194
Amorpha* 62
amymone 161
amyntula 240
Amyris* 47
Anacardium* 168
Anaea 172
ANAL MARGIN (see Fig. 11)
ANAL SPOT: spot at the anal angle of HW. Fig. 504.

Figure 504

Anartia 156
anchisiades 42
andraemon 47
andria 173
ANDROCONIA: scent scales; scales of unusual form found in male butterflies.
ANELLUS: juxta; a sclerotized structure supporting the aedeagus. Fig. 505.

Figure 505

ANEPISTERNUM (see Fig. 5)
Angle Wings 149
ANGULATE: forming an angle.
anicia 130
ANTENNA, -AE: jointed appendage found on each side of the head between the eyes. Commonly called "feelers." (see Fig. 4)

Antennaria* 153
Anteos 67
Anthocaris 71
antiopa 147
Antirrhinum* 154
apama 210
Apatura 171
Apaturini 170
APEX (see Fig. 11)
aphids 220
aphirape 120
Aphrissa 69
aphrodite 114
APICAL: at or near the apex.
Apocynum* 85
APODEME: an infolding or internal process of the exoskeleton serving for muscle attachment.
Apodemia 243
Appias 80
apple 164, 194
aquilo 235
Arabis* 73, 74, 75
Arbutus* 203
arcas 38
Arceuthobium* 207, 208
archippus 85, 164
Arctic 25
Arctics 100
Arctostaphylos* 124, 201, 203
areolata 90
argante 69
argiolus 241
Argynnini 112
Argynnis 113
argyrodines 249
argyrognomon 232
ariane 94
aristodemus 47
Aristolochia* 36, 115
AROLIUM: membranous lobe or pad between the tarsal claws. Fig. 506.

Figure 506

253

INDEX

Figure 507

CLASP: a process of the valva. Fig. 508.

Figure 508

claudia 112
*Clematis** 251
clodius 33
clorinde 67
Clouded Sulphur 56
clover 56, 62, 65, 233, 234, 240
clymena 159
clytie 182, 197
clyton 170
*Coelopleurum** 43
coenia 154
Coenonympha 93
Coliadinae 52
Colias 53
colon 129
columella 183, 184, 217
comma 151
Compositae 133, 135, 140, 153
Compton Tortoise Shell 148
comstocki 210
comyntas 240
CONCOLOROUS: of the same color.
CONNATE: united at the base.
CONSPECIFIC: members of the same species.
CONTIGUOUS: adjacent and touching.
Coppers 220
coresia 169
*Corethrogyne** 136
*Cornus** 241
CORNUTI: sclerotized spines or teeth in the vesica of the male genitalia. Fig. 509.

Figure 509

coronis 118
*Corydalis** 33
*Corylus** 218
Cosmopolite 153

COSTA (C): the thickened anterior margin of wing; the dorsal margin of the valva of the male genitalia.
COSTAL MARGIN (see Fig. 11)
cottonwood 41, 164, 165
COXA: basal segment of a leg. (see Fig. 6)
crabs eye vine 235
cranberry 121, 227
Crassulaceae 34
*Crataegus** 40, 164, 165, 194, 195, 213, 220
CRENULATE: with small scallops.
creola 88
Crescents 127
cresphontes 49
creusa 75
critola 214
CROCHETS: hooks on the prolegs of caterpillars.
croton 173, 174, 215
*Croton** 173, 174, 199
crowberry 124, 232
crownbeard 241
crucifers 70, 73-79
crysalus 178
CUBITUS (Cu): fifth vein of wing, 2 branched. (see Fig. 10)
cudweed 153
cupreus 222
currant 40, 149, 151, 152, 220
*Cuscuta** 203
cyananthe 158
Cyanophrys 211
cybele 115
Cyllopsis 89
cymela 90
*Cymopterus** 44
cyna 241
cyneas 139
*Cynodon** 90

D

Dagger Wings 167
daira 65
damei 94
dammersi 74
damoetas 135
Danainae 84
Danaus 85
*Daucus** 42
deerberry 164
definita 137
*Dentaria** 77
DENTATE: with toothlike projections.
*Desmodium** 66, 240
devilliers 36
Diaethria 159
diana 115
*Diapensia** 235
*Dictamnus** 49
DIGITATE: fingerlike.
DIMORPHIC: occuring in two forms.
dina 66
dione 225
disa 99
DISCAL AREA (see Fig. 11)
DISCAL CELL (see Fig. 10)

DISCOCELLULAR VEINS (udc, mdc, ldc): the veins closing the outer end of the discal cell.
discoidalis 97
DISCRIMEN: midventral suture of a thoracic segment.
DISJUNCT: distinctly separated.
Dismorphiinae 52
DISTAL: toward the free end of an appendage; farthest from the main body.
distincta 126
dock 226
Dog Faces 53
dogbane 85
dogwood 241
*Dolichos** 241
Dolymorpha 212
domitianus 247
dorcas 228
doudoroffi 203
drusilla 80
Dryadula 112
Dryas 111
dryope 186, 196
dumetorum 210
dymas 132
Dynamine 167
dyonis 167
*Dyssodia** 53

E

echion 182, 184, 200
editha (Euphydryas) 128
editha (Lycaena) 224
edwardsii (Satyrium) 186, 195
edwardsii (Speyeria) 117
egleis 118
elada 133
Electrostrymon 218
eleuchia 168
elm 147, 150-152
elva 131
EMARGINATE: with the margin notched.
Embauba 170
emesia 245
Emesis 245
emigdionis 231
*Empetrum** 124, 232
Enantia 52
endeis 138
ENDODONT: inner tooth of the tarsal claw. Fig. 510.

Figure 510

Figure 512

Figure 513

INDEX

Figure 514

Figure 515

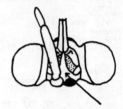

Figure 516

INDEX

INDEX

PULVILLI: membranous lobes lateral to the tarsal claws. Fig. 518.

Figure 518

PUNCTIFORM: shaped like a point or dot.
Purple Wings 160
*Purshia** 192
purslane 112, 157
pyracmon 92

Q

quaderna 218
Queen 85
*Quercus** 164, 167, 178, 191, 194-196, 213
Question Mark 149

R

RADIUS (R): third vein of wing, usually 3-5 branched in forewing. (see Fig. 10)
ragwort 250
rapae 76
rattleweed 58
rawsoni 248
Red Admiral 152
red bay 41, 50
Red-spotted Purple 164
Regal Fritillary 116
Rhamnaceae 195
*Rhamnus** 40, 222
*Rhododendron** 124, 152
*Rhus** 199
*Ribes** 40, 149, 151, 152, 220, 222
ridingsii 94
Ringlets 93
Riodininae 242
rita 239
rock cress 73, 74, 75
Rosaceae 164
rossii 99
rubidus 223
rubricata 90
*Rubus** 33, 120, 194
rudkini 45
rufofusca 185, 216
*Ruellia** 146
*Rumex** 221, 223, 225, 226, 227
*Ruta** 47
rutulus 41

S

SACCUS: anterior projection from the base of the vinculum of the male genitalia. (see Fig. 12)
saepiolus 233
saepium 184, 193
sage 153
St. John's wort 216
Salicornia* 242
*Salix** 41, 54, 57, 58, 61, 122, 123, 125, 126, 147-149, 164-166, 194-196
sallow 126
salmonberry 126
salome 64
saltbush 231, 245
Sandia 205
sara 73
*Sassafras** 50
Satyrinae 86
Satyrium 192
Satyrs 86
satyrus 150
*Saxifraga** 34
SCALES: highly modified flattened hairs which form a shingle-like covering for the wings. Fig. 519.

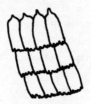

Figure 519

SCALLOPED: edge marked with rounded hollows, without intervening angles. Fig. 520.

Figure 520

SCENT PAD: a compact patch of androconia.
schryveri 203

SCLERITE: any piece of the exoskeleton delimited by sutures; a piece of hardened exoskeleton surrounded by membrane. Fig. 521.

Figure 521

SCLEROTIZED: referring to the exoskeleton, hardened into strong plates (see membranous).
Scotch lovage 43
Scrophulariaceae 128, 129
scudderii 57
sedges 86, 100
*Sedum** 33, 34, 112, 154, 203, 237
SEGMENT: a ringlike or tubular division of the body or of an appendage, bounded by sutures.
selene 120
semidea 105
Semnopsyche 114
*Senecio** 250
senna 64, 65, 68, 70
sennae 70
sensitive plant 66
SERRATE: sawlike; with notched edges.
SERRULATE: finely serrate.
sessilis 246
SEX PATCH: a patch of androconia. Fig. 522.

Figure 522

SEXUAL DIMORPHISM: males and females strikingly different in color or form.
shadberry 40
shadbush 194
shasta 230
sheridani 209

INDEX

Figure 523

Figure 524

INDEX

TRUNCATED: cut off square-
ly at tip.
tulip-tree 41
tullia 93
turnip 79
turpentine broom 45
turtlehead 127

U

uhleri 101
*Ulmus** 147, 150-152
Umbelliferae 42, 43, 46
umbrella plant 231
UNCUS: the dorsal distal
structure of the male geni-
talia. (see Fig. 12)
*Urtica** 147, 149-152
Urticaceae 152

V

*Vaccinium** 33, 54, 55, 57,
59, 120, 121, 164, 194,
202, 203, 227, 233, 235,
241
VALVA, -AE: paired append-
ages of the male genitalia.
(see Fig. 12)
Vanessa 152
VANNAL VEINS (1V, 2V,
3V): sixth, seventh, and
eighth veins of wing, 1V
usually absent, 3V often
reduced or absent. (see
Fig. 10)
vau-album 148
VEIN: a supporting strut of
the wing. (see Fig. 10)
*Velaea** 44
*Verbena** 138, 154
*Verbesina** 241

VESICA: a membranous eversible tube lying in the end
of the aedaeagus. Fig. 525.

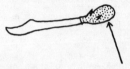

Figure 525

vesta 142
vetch 236, 240
Viceroy 164
*Vicia** 236, 240
vidleri 98
*Vincetoxicum** 85
VINCULUM: the U-shaped
sclerite to which the valvae of the male genitalia
are attached. (see Fig. 12)
*Viola** 33, 112, 113, 120,
121, 123, 127
violets 112, 113, 120, 121,
123, 127
virginiensis (Calephelis) 248
virginiensis (Lycaena) 222
virginiensis (Pieris) 77
virginiensis (Vanessa) 153
virgin's bower 251
viridis 210

W

walkeri 244
weidemeyerii 166

West Coast Lady 154
White Admiral 166
wild buckwheat 192
wild cherry 41, 191
willow 41, 54, 57, 58, 61,
122, 123, 125, 147-149,
164-166, 194-196
windi 203
winter cress 73
*Wisteria** 241
witch hazel 220
wolfberry 175
Wood Nymphs 86, 94
wooly-aster 136
wrighti 247

X

xami 205, 207
Xamia 205
xanthoides 225
xerces 236
xicaque 92

Y

yojoa 184, 217
youngi 100

Z

*Zamea** 188
*Zanthoxylum** 49, 50, 160,
226
zebina 198
Zebra Butterfly 110
zela 246
zelicaon 42
zephyrus 152
zerene 118
Zerene 54
Zizula 241